DEREK INTRODUCES

100 ICONIC INDIANS

Derek O'Brien was born in Kolkata. He began his career as a journalist for *Sportsworld* magazine but soon shifted to advertising. After working for a number of very successful years as Creative Head of Ogilvy, Derek decided to focus all his energy and talent in his passion—quizzing.

Today, Derek O'Brien is Asia's best-known quizmaster and the CEO of Derek O'Brien & Associates. He is the host of the longest-running game show on Indian television, the Cadbury Bournvita Quiz Contest, for which he was voted the Best Anchor of a Game Show at the Indian Television Academy Awards for three years in a row. He also hosts the longest-running corporate quiz show, the Economic Times Brand Equity Quiz. Always innovating and keeping abreast with the times, Derek is also credited with having conducted the first quiz on Twitter in 2010.

Derek O'Brien has written several bestselling reference and quiz books. In 2011, he was voted to the Rajya Sabha as a Member of Parliament (MP) and is the Chief Whip of the Trinamool Congress in the Rajya Sabha.

Keep in touch with Derek on Twitter, where his handle is @quizderek.

Other books by Derek O'Brien
(from Rupa Publications)

Bournvita Quiz Contest Quiz Book 2012

The Ultimate BQC Book of Knowledge (Volumes 1 and 2)

The Best of Bournvita Quiz Contest

Speak Up, Speak Out: My Favourite Elocution Pieces and How to Deliver Them

My Way: Success Mantras of 12 Achievers

DERECK INTRODUCES

Published in Red Turtle by
Rupa Publications India Pvt. Ltd. 2014
7/16, Ansari Road, Daryaganj
New Delhi 110002

Sales Centres:

Allahabad Bengaluru Chennai
Hyderabad Jaipur Kathmandu
Kolkata Mumbai

ISBN: 978-81-291-2938-3

10 9 8 7 6 5 4 3 2 1

First impression 2014

Printed at Thomson Press India Ltd, Faridabad

CONTENTS

ART AND CULTURE

LANGUAGE AND LITERATURE

FILMS

GENERAL

INTRODUCTION

When I was in school, and as the history test loomed near, one thought would often cross my mind while I tried hard to remember all those dates and events: Why do we need to study history? Surely, how Akbar governed Mughal India and when Ashoka fought the Kalinga War had absolutely no relevance to our lives? But like every other student, I had to quell these disruptive thoughts and get on with my work. In school, we often have very little say in what we are being told to learn and have to stick to the syllabus.

So why am I now writing a book on 100 Iconic Indians for young readers of today? Why do you need to know about Sardar Patel, or Chanakya, or Aryabhata? Did I finally get an answer to this question? Or have I become a boring adult, ready to tell you what to read and how to think? I certainly hope this is not true. I would like to believe that the answer lies somewhere in the process of my growing up. I realized that history—and the stories of people who came before us—*does* have a strong relevance in our lives today.

Understanding the past and being aware of the present is the best way to deal with the challenges of tomorrow. Let me give you a simple example. Suppose there is an empty stretch of land near your house, which has been turned into a garbage dumping ground. It stinks and is unhealthy for everyone in the area. A group of residents decide to tackle the issue by involving the city authorities. The place is cleared and residents are told not to dump their garbage there. However, this works only for a few days and soon things revert to the way they were. Then, everyone gets together and examines what has been going wrong in the past. They learn that trash bins placed on the road earlier broke because they were not of good quality. They discover that there is no public toilet within a two-kilometre radius. They observe that the garbage collection agency has not collected garbage regularly from each house as they are supposed to, so people have thrown their garbage there.

When all the factors are analysed and understood, the people and civic authorities are able to come together to tackle the problem in its entirety. Soon you have a cleaner, healthier neighbourhood. (This is, incidentally, a true story that happened in a Bangalore locality, where the dump eventually became a green park.)

Now, extend this example from your neighbourhood to the country, or even the world, and you will see how we as a society need to continually learn from our past. When India gained independence, we knew the old systems of governance through kings and queens would not work in a country as diverse as ours, so we became a democracy where every citizen has rights. When one learns about Ashoka's edicts where he talked about non-violence and an equitable society, we understand how that made him the greatest emperor of his time, and that following his ideals would work in the modern era too.

Perhaps the best part about reading history is that you read some very odd stuff and yet know that it all actually happened. Strange facts, strange people, strange places—all of these abound in the pages of a history book, only if you are willing to look.

So all this brings us back to the question: Why am I writing about 100 Indians and why did I choose these men and women? To know the history of India, we need to know the stories of the people who have helped shape it. Chosen from every major walk of life, these personalities have achieved greatness by doing something extraordinary and changed our society and thinking in different ways. The people whose biographies appear in the pages of this book have been among those who have impacted in different ways the way we live, think and perceive the world around us. From the fields of politics to arts, from business to sports, they have brought about change by leading, inventing, creating and excelling in their fields. These 100 people are only some of the many who have done this. From a country as vast as ours, and which has such a long history, it is very difficult to choose only 100. But the ones written about in this book are incomparable for their incredible dedication, learning and nation-building capabilities.

In order to make each piece more interesting, I have added a box where you can read the highlights at a glance, and a short quiz which you can use to know some more interesting facts about the person.

Writing and researching this book has been a tremendously rewarding experience for me and my dedicated research team. We have pored over books and encyclopedias and online resources to put together these profiles in a relevant and interesting manner. I do hope you will find this book appealing and useful. And for some of you, I also hope it is useful when you are working on your history homework and asking yourself what I asked myself many years ago as a schoolboy: Why study history?

Keep reading. Keep learning.

With every good wish,
Derek O'Brien

P.S. Feel free to interact with me on Twitter (my handle is @quizderek) or on Facebook at https://www.facebook.com/DOBnA.

HISTORY

AKBAR

Akbar is often regarded as one of the greatest Mughal emperors of India. During his reign from 1556 to 1605, he followed the policy of expansion establishing his supremacy over most of the Indian subcontinent. His reign was also marked by many reforms that strengthened his central administration and financial system. He abolished 'Jiziya', a poll tax that non-Muslims had to pay to Islamic rulers. Akbar was tolerant towards all religions; he organized sessions for which people from different religions were invited to participate in. He developed a new religion or a way of life called 'Din-i-Ilahi'. Though he was illiterate himself, he took great care of the scholars, poets, painters and musicians in his kingdom.

Akbar was born as Abu al-Fath Jalal al-Din Muhammad in 1542 in Umarkot (in modern-day Pakistan). He was born to Humayun, who was living in Sind after he had been defeated and driven out from his capital of Delhi by Sher Shah Suri. Though Humayun recovered a part of what he had lost, he did not live long enough to consolidate his position. After Humayun died in an accident in 1556, Akbar, who was then in Punjab, was proclaimed as his successor, at the age of thirteen. His inheritance, at the time, consisted of an unstable dominion that extended a little over the Punjab and the area around Delhi.

Soon after Akbar became king, Himu, the Afghan general of Adil Shah Suri attacked the Mughals. He fought Akbar at the battlefield of Panipat, but was defeated. The battle proved to be of great significance as it brought an end to the Afghan-Mughal contest for supremacy in the country, with the Mughals emerging as the victors.

The Second Battle of Panipat turned out to be even more decisive than the first battle as it marked the actual beginning of the Mughal Empire in India.

In the first few years of his reign, Akbar was mentored by his chief minister, Bairam Khan, who guided, supported and helped him in exercising his authority and expanding his empire. After Bairam Khan retired, Akbar began to govern his kingdom on his own.

Akbar's first conquest was of Malwa in 1561, and then Garah Katanga in Central India. He knew that he needed the support of the Rajputs in his task of consolidating his empire and so he adopted a policy of conciliation and conquest towards them and won their loyalty. According to the terms, if the Rajputs wanted to be in control of their ancestral property, they had to acknowledge Akbar as the emperor, pay him tribute, and supply troops when required. Matrimonial alliance was another policy that he followed seriously. In addition to this, he offered service to the people of the community, which were translated into financial reward and honour for the people who joined the service.

However, Akbar did not spare those who refused to acknowledge his supremacy. This led him to capture the historic fortress of Chitor in 1568. After conquering Gujarat in 1573, Akbar shifted his focus to Bengal, which he annexed in 1576. He defeated Maharana Pratap at the Battle of Haldighati in 1576. In 1592, Orissa (modern-day Odisha) was also made a part of his empire.

The last part of his reign was marked by numerous successful conquests. These include his victory over Kashmir in 1586, Sind in 1591 and Qandahar (now Afghanistan) in 1595. By 1601, Khandesh, Berar and a part of Ahmadnagar were also annexed.

There were several untoward incidents towards the end of his life; the death of his close friend Faizi, the murder of Abul Fazl by Jahangir and Jahangir's proclamation as an independent king of Allahabad, are said to have caused him grief. He passed away in 1605, after suffering from severe diarrhoea.

GOOD TO KNOW

- In AD 1575, Emperor Akbar founded the city of Allahabad by the name of Illahabas, which meant 'The City of Allaha'.
- Akbar is said to have owned 9,000 cheetahs, of which he maintained a detailed record.
- Todar Mal was one of the navratnas or nine gems of Akbar's court.

QUIZ

1. Akbar planted 1,00,000 trees of which fruit in Darbhanga, in a place now known as Lakhi Bag?
   a) Mango
   b) Apple
   c) Coconut

Answer: Mango

2. Which of the Nine Jewels in Akbar's court was actually named Mahesh Das?
   a) Tansen
   b) Birbal
   c) Mullah Do Piaza

Answer: Birbal

3. What was the name of Akbar's mother?
   a) Noor jahan
   b) Mumtaz mahal

c) Hamida Bano Begam

Answer: Hamida Bano Begam

4. Who wrote *Ain-i-Akbari*?
   a) Abul Fazl
   b) Raja Todar Mal
   c) Birbal

Answer: Abul Fazl

GLOSSARY

- Panipat: is a city in the Indian state of Haryana.
- Navratans: are a group of mine people with extraordinary skills in an emperor's court.

ASHOKA

Ashoka, also known as 'Devanampiya Piyadasi', or Beloved of the Gods, was the last major king of the Mauryan dynasty. He is mainly remembered for his role in spreading Buddhism across India and abroad during his reign.

Till the mid 1830s, when James Princep was able to decipher an inscription in the Brahmi script, he was considered only one of the many rulers on the list of Mauryan kings. The final confirmation that the name appearing as Devanampiya Piyadasi in the inscriptions was that of Ashoka, came in 1915.

Ashoka was the son of the Mauryan king, Bindusara. While some historians believe that he ascended the throne immediately after his father's death, many argue that there was a gap of around four years involving a struggle for succession among his many brothers.

His career as an administrator took off when he started serving as the governor at Taxila. It involved suppressing a revolt and handling commercial activities. Of the various events during Ashoka's rule, the Kalinga War is considered to be the most significant as it marked a turning point in his life. In around 260 BC, Ashoka attacked the Kalingans for their resources and also to safeguard the profitable Mauryan trade-route. In spite of his victory, the young king was filled with great remorse and guilt when he realized the magnitude of destruction caused by the battle. This changed him completely. He started practising Dharma, changed his foreign policy, and refrained from military conquest that led to merciless killings. He gradually developed a policy of 'Dharma Vijaya', or conquest by piety, instead of conquest by weapons.

As an ardent follower of Buddhism, Ashoka studied scriptures and undertook Dharma-Yatra. In the course of these tours, he visited the people of his empire spreading the concept of dharma and sangha. He appointed new officials called Dharma Mahamatras to promote religion. He also set up Dhrama Stambhas, or pillars of morality, in various places in his empire. He is credited with the construction of a splendid palace besides many stupas, monasteries and temples. The first temple built at the site of the Mahabodhi Temple Complex at Bodh Gaya was built by him. The Ashokan inscriptions were generally in the local script, Prakrit. However, some were also composed in Brahmi and Kharoshthi scripts. It was during his reign that the Buddhist Sanghas were reorganized, with the meeting of the Third Buddhist Council at Pataliputra at around 250 BC.

Ashoka was tolerant of other religions and sects. He never imposed his religious beliefs on others. He practiced what he preached, the virtues of compassion and tolerance. In his bid to spread the religion to other countries, he sent missionaries abroad. It is believed that he sent his son, Mahindra, and daughter, Sanghamitra, to Sri Lanka to spread Buddhism.

GOOD TO KNOW:

- After his birth, his mother Subhadrangi named her son Ashoka signifying that now her life was 'a-shoka', or 'without sorrow'.
- The state emblem of India has been adapted from the Sarnath Lion Capital of Ashoka. The Sarnath Lion Capital of Ashoka is also the inspiration behind the chakra on the national flag of India.

- Ashoka is said to have thrown the bodies of ninety-nine of his half-brothers into 'Agam Kuan', or the unfathomable well, in Patna. It has now become a historic site.

QUIZ

1. In which state is the famous Sanchi Stupa located?
   a) Madhya Pradesh
   b) Bihar
   c) Odisha

Answer: Madhya Pradesh

2. Who was Ashoka's spiritual teacher?
   a) Mahavira
   b) Moggaliputta Tissa
   c) Bindusara

Answer: Moggaliputta Tissa

3. Who was Ashoka's grandfather?
   a) Chandragupta Maurya
   b) Bimbisara
   c) Bindusara

Answer: Chandragupta Maurya

GLOSSARY

- Devanampiya Piyadasi: means 'Beloved of the Gods'.
- Dharma Vijaya: means conquest by piety and righteousness, and not through violent blood shedding.
- Dharma yatra: were tours of morality undertaken by Ashoka in order to instruct his people in Dhamma.
- Vihara yatras: were pleasure tours undertaken with the purpose of enjoyment.
- Sangha: is a Buddhist order of monks
- Dharma stambhas: means the pillars of morality

BABUR

Babur is regarded as the founder of the Mughal dynasty in India. He was a multifaceted personality with interests in diverse fields. He was not only a good soldier and military strategist, but also had great interest in art and literature. He claimed lineal descent from Tamerlane on his father's side and from Chingiz Khan on his mother's side.

Born in 1483 in Fergana, present-day Uzbekistan, Babur inherited the principality in 1494, at the age of eleven when his father unexpectedly passed away. His early life was full of difficulties but that did not deter him from taking life head-on. Like his father, he attempted, many times, to recover Timur's old capital of Samarkand but failed miserably. He made his last unsuccessful attempt on Samarkand in 1511–12, and then gave up the idea, as he realized that the quest would not yield any results. He decided to focus on expansion, and led many expeditions to the Southeast and in some other direction.

Finally, he got the opportunity to advance to the epicentre of India after twelve years, when he was invited to India by Daulat Khan (a noble of the Punjab who was discontented with Ibrahim Lodi) and Alam Khan (an uncle of Ibrahim Lodi and aspirant to the throne of Delhi) to invade India. He, at once, responded to the invitation, entered Punjab and occupied Lahore in 1524. But soon, the Indian confederates there realized that they had committed a grave mistake, changed their stance, and turned against him. Though Babur retired to Kabul for a while, he returned with full-force and met Ibrahim Lodi at the historic battlefield of Panipat on 21 April 1526. He won the battle by motivating his army, his use of artillery and other innovative Turkish strategies. He occupied Delhi three days later and reached Agra on the 4th of May .

Though the First Battle of Panipat was an important milestone in his political career but it did not give him virtual sovereignty over the country because there were other rulers who aspired for political supremacy. What followed was a series of battles that helped Babur consolidate his position in India. In 1527, he met Rana Sanga, the hero of Rajput national revival, along with the rulers of Marwar, Amber, Gwalior and Ajmer, at the Battle of Khanua and defeated him. He later encountered the allied forces of the Afghans of Bihar and Bengal on the banks of the Ghaghara, and defeated them on 6 May 1529. Thus, he was able to bring a considerable portion of India under his control. His empire extended from Qandahar in the west to Bengal in the east, and the southern border of the empire was marked by the forts of Ranthambhor, Gwalior and Chanderi.

Babur died a premature death, and thus could not cherish his success for long. According to a popular belief, when his son, Humayun, became extremely ill in 1530, he offered his own life to God in exchange for Humayun's. Humayun soon became well, but Babur's health declined and he died the same year.

GOOD TO KNOW

- In world literature, Babur's journal *Babur Nama*, is considered as one of the earliest examples of an autobiography.
- Babur built a famous garden called the Ram Bagh, by the Yamuna River in Agra.

QUIZ

1. Who succeeded Babur as the Mughal emperor?
   a) Humayun
   b) Akbar
   c) Shah Jahan

Answer: Humayun

2. In which present-day state is Panipat located?
   a) Punjab
   b) Haryana
   c) Uttar Pradesh

Answer: Haryana

3. What does the name 'Babur' mean in Arabic?
   a) Tiger
   b) Vulture
   c) Snake

Answer: Tiger

GLOSSARY

- Mughal dynasty: was a Muslim dynasty of Turkic-Mongol origin. This dynasty ruled most of northern India from the early 16th to the mid-18th century.
- Samarkand: is a city in east-central Uzbekistan and is one of the oldest cities of Central Asia.

CHANAKYA

Chanakya, also known as Kautilya or Vishnugupta, was a Hindu statesman, philosopher and strategist, who wrote a classic treatise on the running of the state, military strategy and economy titled *Artha-shastra* (*The Science of Material Gain*). He played a very important part in the downfall of the Nanda dynasty.

Chanakya was born into a Brahman family in Pataliputra, Magadh (present-day Bihar). He later relocated to Taxila where he received his education. During his childhood, he is believed to have studied and memorized the Vedas, which was considered to be one of the most difficult scriptures.

He played an important role in installing Chandragupta Maurya on the throne of Magadh, served as his counsellor and adviser, and helped found the great Mauryan Empire of northern India.

He wrote many books. His book *Arthashastra* is a compilation of his political ideas and is considered as the first systematic book on polity and economics. It has detailed discussions on economic policies, international relations and war policies. In this book, he advocated the development of an effective espionage system reaching into all strata of the society.

Kautilya is also credited with the creation of two other books: *Chanakya Niti* and *Nitishastra*.

Chanakya Niti gives a vivid description of the various nitis or strategies of Chanakya. *Nitishastra* is a written work dealing formally and systematically with the different means on the perfect way of life. Through this book, one can get a glimpse of Chanakya's comprehensive and thorough study of the Indian pattern of life.

He has often been compared to Niccolo Machiavelli, Aristotle and Plato. Though Kautilya is condemned for his ruthlessness and trickery, he is praised for his political wisdom and knowledge of human character.

GOOD TO KNOW

- According to legend, while Chanakya served as the Prime Minister of Chandragupta Maurya, he started adding small amounts of poison in Chandragupta's food so that he would get used to it. The aim of this was to prevent the Emperor from being poisoned by enemies.
- The main philosophy of Chanakya was, 'A debt should be paid off till the last penny; an enemy should be destroyed without a trace'.

QUIZ

1. Which subject was taught by Chanakya as a professor at the Takshashila University?
   a) History
   b) Economics
   c) Political Science

Answer: Political Science

2. In Jawaharlal Nehru's Discovery of India, Chanakya has been called the Indian ___________? Fill in the blank.
   a) Napoleon
   b) Machiavelli
   c) Confucius

Answer: Machiavelli

3. In *Arthashastra* which tax has been referred to as Sita tax?

a) Revenue from merchants
b) Revenue from crown lands
c) Road cess

Answer: Revenue from crown lands

GLOSSARY

- Mauryan dynasty: is a dynasty centred around Pataliputra (later Patna).
- Nities: are policies.

CHANDRAGUPTA MAURYA

Chandragupta Maurya, referred to as Sandrokuptos, Sandrokottos or Androcottus in many Latin and Greek accounts, was the founder of the Mauryan dynasty. He reigned between 321 and 297 BC after overthrowing the Nanda dynasty. He is considered to be the first emperor to unify most of India under one administration. There is a debate regarding the origin and caste status of the Maurya family. In Buddhist texts, the Mauryas are described as people belonging to a Kshatriya clan called the Moriyas. The origin of the designation is sometimes ascribed to Mura, the mother or grandmother of Chandragupta. They have also been recognized as the members of the ruling clan of the Republic of Pipphalivahana.

When Chandragupta was young, he is said to have met and offended Alexander the Great in Punjab. Though Alexander ordered his death, Chandragupta escaped and sought refuge in a place where he met his mentor, Chanakya. On Chanakya's advice, Chandragupta gathered a troop, garnered support from the people, got rid of his adversaries through carefully chalked-out plans and ended the rule of the Nanda dynasty. After his great victory, he focussed his attention on the Northwest in order to take advantage of the vacuum created by Alexander's departure. He won most of the battles and reached the Indus, but decided not to go further as Alexander's successor Seleucus Nicator had already established control in the region. Later, around 305 BC, he returned and defeated the Greek king, acquiring a large part of his territory, including Herat, Kabul, Qandahar, and Baluchistan.

The campaign did not affect the strong relationship between the Mauryas and Seleucids. Seleucus Nicator sent the famous historian, Megasthenes, to Chandragupta Maurya's court. While he was in India, he collected notes on the country which were compiled in the book *Indica*.

Chandragupta Maurya's empire, that stretched from the Himalayas and the Kabul valley to the southern tip of the country, is considered as one of the most extensive empires in the history of India.

The continuation of the Mauryan dynasty for more than two generations was partly due to the efforts of Chanakya's strategies.

The Jaina tradition claims that Chandragupta converted to Jainism. Towards the end of his life, he is said to have appointed his son, Bindusara, as the king, and gone to Shravanabelagola in Karnataka. There, he is said to have ended his life by 'Sallekhana', or death by starvation, in the orthodox Jaina manner.

GOOD TO KNOW

- According to legend, while Chandragupta Maurya was sleeping after his meeting with Alexander the Great, a lion woke him up by licking his body, kindling in him the hope of becoming a king.
- Chandragupta Maurya gave Seleucus Nicator five hundred elephants in exchange of his territories in Asia.
- It is believed that the fund for carrying out Chanakya and Chandragupta Maurya's plan to overthrow the Nanda dynasty came from a treasure chest that was discovered in the Vindhyas.
- In order to overthrow the Nanda dynasty, Chandragupta

Maurya used the strategy that he had learned from a mother who was scolding his son for eating from the centre of a dish, as the centre is supposed to be the hottest part of the plate. He used the same strategy in his military conquests.

QUIZ

1. Who among these was Chandragupta Maurya's grandson?
   a) Bindusara
   b) Ashoka
   c) Chandragupta Vikramaditya

   Answer: Ashoka

2. Who wrote *Mudrarakshasa,* a work revolving around the manoeuvres of Chanakya to win over Rakshasa, a minister of the Nandas, to Chandragupta's side?
   a) Kalhana
   b) Kalidasa
   c) Vishakhadatta

   Answer: Vishakhadatta

3. Which of these was another name of Chanakya?
   a) Kautilya
   b) Kabir
   c) Tenali Raman

   Answer: Kautilya

GLOSSARY

- Sallekhana: is a ritual or process in Jainsism in which a person starves himself to death.
- *Arthshastra*: is a treatise on Economics and Polity, written by Chanakya.

GAUTAMA BUDDHA

Gautama Buddha was the founder of Buddhism. He was born as Siddhartha in Lumbini near Kapilavastu, around 563 BC, to Mayadevi and Suddhodana, who was the head of the Sakya clan of Kapilavastu.

Born into a well-to-do family and raised in great comfort, he realized the harsh realities of the world at the age of twenty-nine, when he came across an elderly person, a weak man who was suffering from illness, a corpse and an ascetic. He understood that old age, sickness and death are an inextricable part of life. He stayed away from the world of materialistic pleasure, and eventually left his home in search of the truth of life which, he believed, would lead to freedom from suffering, pain and misery.

In his pursuit of truth, he visited many places like Rajagriha and Uruvila. After having realized that austerities were of no use to him in achieving his goal, he decided to meditate. He took a bath in the holy Nairanjana River, and sat under a pipal tree in Bodh-Gaya to seek the ultimate truth. It was here that he ultimately attained enlightenment and became the 'Buddha', or the enlightened one.

At a deer park near Benares, he gave his first sermon on deliverance from suffering to five ascetic companions. The sermon is referred to as Dharmachakrapravartan Sutta.

Buddha wandered about preaching his doctrine for more than forty years. He established an order of monks and nuns known as 'Sangha'. Buddha taught his followers the four 'Noble

Truths', known as Arya Sattya, which referred to suffering, the origin or cause of suffering, the end of suffering and the way leading to the destruction of sorrow.

In his views, nirvana could be attained by following the 'Middle Path' called the 'Eightfold Path' (Ashtangika marg) which are right views, right speech, right conduct, right livelihood, right effort, right mindfulness, right aspirations and right contemplation.

He died in 483 BC at the age of eighty in Kushinagar, thought to be Kasi in the Gorakhpur district of Uttar Pradesh. In his history, his decease is referred to as as Parinirvana.

GOOD TO KNOW

- *Pali Tipitaka* is the earliest, systematic, and most complete collection of Buddhist sacred literature.
- Lumbini, the birth place of Buddha, is presently located in the Southwestern Terai of Nepal.
- The *Buddhacarita* or *The Acts of the Buddha*, believed to be one of the oldest full-length biographies of Buddha was written by Ashvaghosha, an Indian poet.

QUIZ

1. In which country is the Temple of the Tooth located?
   a) Sri Lanka
   b) Pakistan
   c) Bhutan

Answer: Sri Lanka

2. If Hinayana is one, which is the other type of Buddhism?
   a) Mahayana
   b) Suryayana
   c) Satyayana

Answer: Mahayana

3. What was the original name of Buddha?
    a) Gautama
    b) Siddharta
    c) Satyavrata

Answer: Siddharta

GLOSSARY

- Nirvana: refers to the release from the cycle of rebirth.
- Ahimsa: is a term for non-violence.

GURU NANAK

Guru Nanak was the founder of Sikhism. He was born on 15 April 1469 to Mehta Kalyan Das and Mata Tripta in Rai-Bhoi-di, Talwandi (in present-day Pakistan). He learnt Hindi and Sanskrit at the age of seven. By the time he was sixteen years old, he was well versed in both Persian and Sanskrit, and was considered the most learned young man in the area. He married Mata Sulakhni ji, who bore their two sons: Sri Chand and Lakhmi Das. In the early 1500s, he was known to have been a storekeeper in a 'Modikhana' in Sultanpur Lodhi.

Guru Nanak decided to dedicate himself to the service of mankind on receiving 'God's call' at the age of thirty-eight. He founded Sikhism, a religion based on the belief that God was supreme, universal, all-powerful, truthful, formless (Nirankar), omnipotent and the creator of all things (Karta Purakh).

Guru Nanak advocated a middle path between renunciation (Tyaga) and enjoyment, and advised his followers to value truth and selflessness. He did not believe in the authority of the Vedas and the caste-system. Sewa, Kirtan, Satsang and faith in 'One' omnipotent God formed the basic tenets of Sikhism. He and his disciples encouraged Punjabi and Gurumukhi literature.

Guru Nanak travelled extensively to preach his unique and divine doctrine, based on all that was good in Hinduism and Islam. Apart from travelling in Punjab, he undertook four long tours called Char Udasis, covering different religious places in India and abroad to spread Sikhism.

Guru Nanak was also a great poet and musician. He wrote 974 hymns which were included in the holy book of the Sikh, the *Guru Granth Sahib*. He composed many tunes in Indian classical ragas along with Bhai Mardana, his follower.

From 1522 to1539, Guru Nanak lived in Kartarpur city (now in Pakistan). He introduced daily Kirtan and the institution of Langar.

When he realized that the end was near, he selected one of his disciples, Guru Angad, as his spiritual successor. He passed away in Sachkhand on 22nd September 1539 in Sachkhand.

GOOD TO KNOW:

- According to Puratan Janam Sakhi, a treatise based on the life of Guru Nanak, strange things happened on the day Guru Nanak was born; the trees dripped juice, the poor suddenly became rich and the diseased were healed.
- According to Sikh history, when Guru Nanak was twenty-two years of age, he refused to eat and speak for many days, but was declared physically fit by the physician. When asked, Guru Nanak said, 'I have no physical ailment. Thou, the simple physician, knows not the pangs arising from the heart.'

QUIZ

1. Who succeeded Guru Nanak after he passed away?
   a) Guru Angad
   b) Guru Tegh Bahadur
   c) Guru Gobind Singh

Answer: Guru Angad

2. In which country is Nankana Sahib, the birthplace of Guru Nanak?
   a) Pakistan

b) Bangladesh
c) Sri Lanka

Answer: Pakistan

3. What name did Guru Nanak give to Bhai Lehna?
   a) Guru Angad Sahib
   b) Guru Gobind Singh
   c) Guru Ram Das

Answer: Guru Angad Sahib

GLOSSARY

- Kirtan: is a religious prayer or hymn sung with the accompaniment of musical instruments.
- Langar: a free kitchen in Gurudwaras where food is served to all visitors for free, irrespective of caste, creed or religion.

ISHWAR CHANDRA VIDYASAGAR

Ishwar Chandra Vidyasagar was a social reformer, philosopher and scholar.

Ishwar was born on 26 September 1820 in the village of Birsingha, in Midnapore district of West Bengal.

His father, Thakurdas Bandyopadhyaya, was a poor Brahmin and his mother, Bhagabati Devi, was a pious follower of Hinduism. His father worked as a clerk in a firm in Calcutta. Ishwar Chandra was sent to the village pathshala when he was five years old.

According to the customs of the time, he was married at an early age of fourteen to Dinamani Devi. They had only one son. He was greatly influenced by his parents, whom he respected immensely and remained devoted to all through his life.

Ishwar's father wanted him to be well-versed in Sanskrit. So, he went to the Sanskrit College in Calcutta in 1829.

Ishwar showed a remarkable proficiency in his studies, and even though he was a Sanskrit Pandit, he had no qualms about learning English. Even when he worked as the first Pandit in Fort William College, he took private tuitions to understand the language better. He also learned Hindi in 1841.

Ishwar finished his education and worked as the assistant secretary of the Sanskrit College. There, he made certain proposals that were rejected, and he resigned as a mark of protest. In 1850, he was appointed Head Pandit of Fort William College and the very next year, he was made a Professor in the

Sanskrit College, where he also served as the Principal later. He introduced various measures of reform in the institution. He improved the scope of studying English and made it possible for the people of lower castes to attend the conservative college.

In 1855, Ishwar became Special Inspector of Schools for the districts of Hooghly, Midnapore, Burdwan and Nadia. He took this opportunity to establish a number of model vernacular and girls' schools in these areas.

He started several schools for the spread of education and brought changes in the functioning of the Sanskrit College. He improved the scope of studying English and made it possible for the people of lower castes to attend the conservative Sanskrit College.

He was also a part of the Government Wards Institution and was actively involved in the functioning of the Indian Association for the Cultivation of Science.

Ishwar fought against the social evils such as polygamy and sati, and favoured widow remarriage and female education.

Ishwar's books *Betal Panchabingshati* (*Twenty-five Tales of a Goblin*) and *Sitar Banabas* (*The Exile of Sita*), among others, are considered works of great importance even today.

Ishwar passed away on 29 July 1891 in Calcutta.

GOOD TO KNOW

- Ishwar Chandra Vidyasagar was so poor that he could not afford a light and had to study under a street lamp.
- In 1880, Queen Victoria conferred on Ishwar the title of C.I.E. (Companion of the Order of the Indian Empire), in recognition of his outstanding social reforms. He was made an honorary member of the Royal Asiatic Society of England in 1864.
- Ishwar studied Sanskrit for twelve years and five months.

He studied all its various branches: Literature, Vedanta, Smriti, Nyaya, Alankar and Jyotish.

QUIZ

1. Which honorary title was given to Ishwar by the authorities of the Sanskrit College for his high attainments in learning?
   a) Deshbandhu
   b) Vidyasagar
   c) Lokmanya

Answer: Vidyasagar

2. Which book by Ishwar Chandra Vidyasagar is based on a famous play by Kalidasa?
   a) *Hitopadesha*
   b) *Panchatantra*
   c) *Shakuntala*

Answer: *Shakuntala*

3. In which Indian city would you find Vidyasagar College, known earlier as Metropolitan College?
   a) Kolkata
   b) Lucknow
   c) Chennai

Answer: Kolkata

GLOSSARY

- *Betal Panchabingshati*: is a collection of stories involving riddles presented to the legendary king Vikramaditya by a betal or a spirit.
- Pandit: is a Hindu scholar who is learned in Sanskrit and also in Hindu philosophy and religion.

MAHAVIRA

Lord Mahavira was the twenty-fourth and last Tirthankar of Jainism. He was born around 599 BC at Kundagrama, near Vaishali (now in modern-day Bihar) into a Kshatriya family. His father, Siddhartha, was a chief of Kundapura and Trisala, and belonged to the royal family of the tribe, Licchavis. He belonged to the Jnatra clan.

Though Mahavira was born into a well-to-do family, he renounced the world when he was thirty years old and spent about twelve years of his life as an ascetic.

In order to gain knowledge, or Gnan, that led to complete freedom from different bonds, he lived a very simple life; in fact, he practised severe austerity, meditated day and night, and spent a lot of time in burial grounds and under trees.

He avoided acts that were considered morally wrong, especially the ones that caused harm to human life. In the thirteenth year of his penance, he attained omniscience, or Kevaljnan, outside the town of Jrimbhikagrama, on the banks of the Rijupalika River. He had now become a Kevalin (omniscient), a Jina (conqueror) and 'Mahavira' (the great hero).

In the next thirty years, he travelled to different parts of the country to preach and spread the eternal truth that he had realized. In addition to the four basic vows of non-injury to living beings (Ahimsa), speaking the truth (Satya), not stealing (Asteya) and limiting one's possessions (Aparigraha), he preached a fifth vow, the chastity (Brahmacharya).

The doctrine of non-injury occupies a very important place in Jainism, as it attributes souls not only to birds and animals but also to plants, metals and water, among others.

The ultimate aim of Mahavira's teachings was liberation from the cycle of birth, life, pain, misery and death, and the achievement of the permanent state of bliss, or Moksha.

In his sermons, he explained the concept of 'Karma' to his followers. He preached that the threefold path of 'Samyak Darshana', 'Samyak Jnana' and 'Samyak Charitra', together were the actual path that led to the freedom of the soul from the bondage of karma. He felt that it was necessary to discard all external things, including garments, if one had to attain complete freedom from bonds.

He died at the age of sventy-two, traditionally around 527 BC, in Pavapuri, Bihar. After his death, hundreds of disciples and devotees took away his ashes from his cremation site. It is said that the demand for his ashes was so great that a large amount of soil was removed from around the funeral pyre, creating the water tank. Many years later, a temple of white marble called Jalmandir was built there, to commemorate his nirvana.

GOOD TO KNOW

- Tirthankara is another word for jina meaning 'ford builder', i.e., one who builds fords and helps others to cross the ocean of suffering.
- Lord Mahavira delivered his first sermon on the Vipula Peak in Rajgir, now considered as an important Jain pilgrimage site.
- Vimal Vasahi, the oldest of the Dilwara temples at Mount Abu in Rajasthan, is dedicated to Adinath, the first of the Jain tirthankaras.

QUIZ

1. Who was the twenty-third Tirthankara of Jainism?
   a) Rishabhdev
   b) Arishtanemi
   c) Parshvanatha

Answer: Parshvanatha

2. In which state is the famous statue of Gomateshwara located?
   a) Karnataka
   b) Madhya Pradesh
   c) Uttar Pradesh

Answer: Karnataka

3. Which festival is celebrated by the Jains as Nirvana Din, or the day of emancipation of Lord Mahavira?
   a) Holi
   b) Diwali
   c) Makar Sankranti

Answer: Diwali

GLOSSARY

- Kevaljnan: The perfect enlightenment. It is the highest spiritual knowledge that can be attained in Jainism.
- Samyak darshana: Right faith.
- Samyak jnana: Right knowledge.
- Samyak charitra: Right conduct.
- Karma: refers to a person's actions or deeds in the present life that will decide his fate in future births.
- Kshatriya: In the varna hierarchy, the kshatriyas occupied the second position and included the warrior aristocracy, landowners and royalty.

RAJA RAM MOHAN ROY

Raja Ram Mohan Roy is considered as one of the pioneers of renaissance in India. He fought to reform the society because he believed that social and religious reform was the very foundation of political advancement. He founded the Brahmo Samaj, advocated the freedom of Press and championed women's causes. Gopal Krishna Gokhale called him the 'Father of modern India'.

Ram Mohan Roy was born on 22 May 1772 in Radhanagar, West Bengal. His family belonged to the Vaishnava sect of Hindus.

His father sent him to Patna to learn Persian and Arabic. The knowledge he gathered there later helped him to relate Sufi writings with the Vedantic philosophy. It made him tolerant towards other religions. He also studied Hinduism, Islam, Christianity and Judaism.

Roy worked with the East India Company at various places in Bengal, before settling down in Calcutta in 1815. He formed the Atmiya Sabha or friendship association, to discuss topics on theology and also to translate the Upanishads. The discussions soon led to the establishment of the Brahmo Samaj, a reformist sect. The Brahmo Samaj preached the worship of one god and focussed on prayers, meditation and readings from the Vedas and the Upanishads. It attacked many rituals and rites, superstitious beliefs, idol worship, priesthood and any kind of religious sacrifice. It also discussed issues related to widow remarriage, casteism and untouchability.

In 1816, Roy opened an English-medium school for boys. In 1821, he started a weekly newspaper in Bengali, one of the few of its kind in any Indian language.

Roy fought against the evil practice of sati. His brother's wife was forced to commit sati after his death, and that had left a deep impact in his mind. He drew the attention of the government towards it and persuaded William Bentinck to abolish it. In 1829, the practice was declared as illegal and punishable as a criminal offence.

After the abolition of sati, Roy turned his attention towards other issues related to women in India. He fought for women's rights to property and protested against child marriage, purdah system, the dowry system and polygamy.

Roy was also the torchbearer of Indian journalism and worked towards educating the masses on issues beseeching the country, so that they could form an opinion of their own in regard with the British government.

In 1830, Roy sailed to England to petition on behalf of the Mughal emperor Akbar Shah II, in order to increase the emperor's allowance. He visited Manchester, Bentham and Liverpool, besides London. He passed away in Bristol on 27 September 1833.

GOOD TO KNOW

- The epitaph for Ram Mohan Roys' tomb in Bristol mentions his full name as Raja Rammohun Roy Bahadoor.
- In 1822, the journal *Mirat-ul-Akbar* was published by Ram Mohan in Persian.

QUIZ

1. Which title was given to Ram Mohan Roy by Mughal emperor Akbar II?

a) Guru
b) Nawab
c) Raja

Answer: Raja

2. Which of these newspapers was founded by Ram Mohan Roy?
   a) *Bengal Gazette*
   b) *Sambad Koumudi*
   c) *Basundhara*

Answer: *Sambad Koumudi*

3. In 1820 he published the ethical teaching of Christ under the title *Percepts of ___, the Guide to Peace and Happiness.*
   a) *Ram Krishna*
   b) *Jesus*
   c) *Joan of Arc*

Answer: *Jesus*

GLOSSARY

- Rennaissance: literally meaning 'rebirth', was the period characterized by a surge of interest in Classical learning and rapid development in Europe. It was marked by the discovery and exploration of new continents, the growth of commerce, innovations in the field of printing and many other fields.
- Sati: refers to the immolation of a widow on her husband's funeral pyre.
- Polygamy: is the practice or custom of having more than one wife or husband at the same time.

RANI LAKSHMIBAI

Rani Lakshmibai, also known as the Rani of Jhansi, was one of the greatest nationalist leaders of the First War of Independence in 1857.

Lakshmibai was born as Mannikarnika on 19 November 1835 in Varanasi, to Moropanth, a Brahmin. She lost her mother at the age of four and was raised by her father. She spent a lot of time in the court of Peshwa Baji Rao II, and was trained in martial arts. She was also proficient in sword-fighting and horse riding.

The young Mannikarnika became Lakshmibai when she married Raja Gangadhar Rao, the Maharaja of Jhansi in 1842. After their child died, when he was only four months old, they adopted a baby boy and named him Damodar Rao. Maharaja Gangadhar Rao passed away on 21 November 1853, when she was only eighteen years old.

Lord Dalhousie, the then Governor General of India, used this opportunity to annex Jhansi. After Maharaja Gangadhar Rao's death, the British refused to recognize the legitimacy of the adopted son, Damodar Rao, under the Doctrine of Lapse. They proposed an annual pension of sixty thousand for the queen and asked her to vacate the Jhansi Fort. She refused the offer and strengthened the defense system of Jhansi. When the Sepoy Mutiny broke out at Meerut in 1857, Lakshmibai was declared the regent of Jhansi, and she ruled on behalf of the minor heir Damodar Rao. In order to consolidate her position, she organized her army and trained women in the art of warfare. In all of this, her trusted warriors provided her with all the help she needed. Some of these people were: Gulam Gaus Khan, Dost Khan, Khuda Baksh, Lala Bhau Bakshi, Moti Bai, Sunder-Mundar, Kashi Bai, Deewan Raghunath Singh and Deewan Jawahar Singh. She was also supported in her cause by the people of Jhansi, irrespective of their religion or caste, who were ready to lay down their lives for their motherland.

In 1858, when the British attacked Jhansi, Lakshmibai fought bravely for almost two weeks. but could not save the city. It fell to the British forces after this Great War.

On the day of the battle, Lakshmibai, dressed as a man, with her son tied to her back, fought fiercely. When the situation went out of hand, she left Jhansi and went to Kalpi where many other rebels, including Tantia Tope joined her. From there, they went to Gwalior where a battle took place.

Rani Lakshmibai died on 18 June 1858 at the age of twenty-three.

GOOD TO KNOW

- The tale of the brave queen Rani of Jhansi has been told by Subhadra Kumari Chauhan in the poem 'Jhansi ki Rani'.
- Sir Hugh Rose, the General of the British forces, called her 'the best and the bravest of them all'.

QUIZ

1. Rani Lakshmibai was raised in the household of...
   a) Peshwa Baji Rao II
   b) Shivaji
   c) Ranjit Singh

Answer: Peshwa Baji Rao II

2. Which of these was another name of Rani Lakshmibai?

a) Chhabili
b) Pyari
c) Sharmilee

Answer: Chhabili

3. In which of these cities is Lakshmibai's cremation site located?
   a) Gwalior
   b) Jhansi
   c) Varanasi

Answer: Gwalior

GLOSSARY

- First War of Independence: is another phrase used to refer to the Sepoy Mutiny of 1857 or Revolt of 1857
- Doctrine of Lapse: was a policy formulated by Lord Dalhousie, governor-general of India (1848–56), to address questions related to succession to Hindu Indian states. According to Hindu law, an individual or a ruler without natural heirs could adopt a person who would then have all the personal and political rights of a son. But Dalhousie stated that any princely state or territory under the direct influence (paramountcy) of the British East India Company as a vassal state under the British Subsidiary System, would automatically be annexed if the ruler was either 'manifestly incompetent or died without a direct heir'.

RAZIA SULTAN

Razia Sultan was the empress of the Slave dynasty, who reigned from 1236 to 1240. In the history of India, she has been the only woman to occupy the throne of Delhi.

As Razia was born after many sons, Iltutmish celebrated her birth with great pomp and grandeur. From an early age, Razia showed remarkable expertise in archery and horse riding. She often accompanied her father in various military expeditions. The Sultan nominated Razia as his heir apparent and declared that she would become the ruler of Delhi after his death.

However, after the death of Iltumish, the Chahalgani (or the forty nobles) rejected the terms of his will and instead declared Ruknuddin Firuz Shah as the Sultan of Delhi. The new king abdicated his responsibility and immersed himself in the pursuit of worldly pleasures, leaving the affairs of state to his mother, Shah Turkan. He was soon deposed and Razia became the ruler as her father had desired.

When Razia came into power, she had great difficulty in establishing her position as some of the nobles found it difficult to accept a woman for their Sultan. She used tact and diplomacy to win over her enemies. She made certain changes in the manner in which the affairs of the court were carried out. She discarded the veil and preferred to conduct the affairs of her court in the open darbar, in male attire. She is credited with having raised the laws and reformed the abuses of the government.

But the nobles refused to be dominated by a woman.

To add to that, they were offended by her association with a slave named Jalal-ud-din Yakut, whom she had made 'Amir-i-Akhoor'; a strategic post that signified the holder's proximity with the king. The Turkish nobles who wanted to take advantage of the important offices in the state did not approve of this.

One of the main reasons for the dissatisfaction of the Turkish nobles was Razia's desire to exercise power directly. The first rebellion was at Lahore by its governor Kabir Khan. Razia marched to Lahore and forced Kabir Khan to surrender. Next, Ikhtiyar-ud-din Altuniya, the governor of Sirhind, revolted against her. She tried to subdue the revolt but was eventually defeated and imprisoned. While she was away, her brother Muiz-ud-din Bahram was proclaimed Sultan.

To find a solution to this problem, she married Malik Altuniya, the governor of Bhatinda and returned to Delhi with him. On the way, she was deserted by Altuniya's followers, defeated by Muiz-ud-din Bahram and put to death along with her husband.

The brief rule of Razia was greatly appreciated by historians like Minhaj, Barani and Ferishta. Describing her, they admit that, 'the men of discernment could find no defect in her except that she was created in the form of a woman.'

GOOD TO KNOW

- According to chronicler *Minhas-us-Siraj*, Razia Sultan was a 'great sovereign, a just and beneficent ruler, and endowed with all the admirable attributes necessary for kings'.
- Razia Sultan refused to be addressed as Sultana since it meant 'wife or consort of a sultan', and preferred to be called Sultan.

QUIZ

1. Who played the role of Razia in the film *Razia Sultan* released in 1983?
    a) Waheeda Rehman
    b) Hema Malini
    c) Parveen Babi

Answer: Hema Malini

2. Who was Razia Sultan's maternal grandfather?
    a) Firoz Shah Tughluq
    b) Qutubuddin Aibak
    c) Balban

Answer: Qutubuddin Aibak

3. Who succeeded Razia Sultan as the king of the Mamluk dynasty?
    a) Nasir-ud-din Mahmud
    b) Muiz-ud-din Bahram
    c) Prince Muhammad

Answer: Muiz-ud-din Bahram

GLOSSARY

- Amir-i- Akhoor: is a term for the superintendent of the stable.
- Mamluk dynasty: is another name for the Slave dynasty, the first dynasty of the Delhi Sultanate period.
- Darbar: refers to a Court.
- Chahalgani: is a term for the forty nobles of the Mamluk dynasty.

SHAH JAHAN

Shah Jahan was the fifth ruler of the Mughal dynasty. He is most famous as the builder of the monument, the Taj Mahal. His reign, from 1628 to 1658, is regarded as the Golden Age of the Mughals.

Shah Jahan was born on 5 January 1592 to the Mughal emperor Jahangir and the Rajput princess Manmati. In his early years, he excelled in the martial arts and impressed everyone with the skill with which he won territories for his father as commander of his armies in several campaigns. He proved his expertise in art and architecture, when he built his own quarters within Babur's Kabul Fort when he was only sixteen years old.

After Jahangir's death, there was a struggle for succession between Shah Jahan and Prince Shahriyar, but with the help of Jahangir's wife Nur Jahan's brother, Asaf Khan, he emerged victorious.

He was proclaimed emperor in 1628, under the title Shah Jahan Padsha Ghazi. The name Shah Jahan comes from the Persian language, and it means 'King of the World'.

As king, Shah Jahan brought two major rebellions, initiated by Jujhar Singh (a Bundela chief) and Khan Jahan Lodi (a powerful Afghan noble) under control. He also overthrew the Portuguese in the Hooghli and Bengal regions, where they had become extremely powerful and had started the practice of slave-trading. He tried to capture Qandahar from the Persians thrice, to strengthen their position in the Northwest Frontier, but failed each time.

In keeping with the dream of reconquering the territories of his ancestors in Central Asia, he occupied Balkh and Badakhshan when a civil war broke out in the ruling house of the Oxus region in 1646.

Shah Jahan found it difficult to annex these regions. He sent his son Aurangzeb with a large army, but the Uzbegs showed a strong united front which ultimately led to his failure.

He expanded his empire in the south by capturing Daulatabad, Asigarh and Golconda. His position in the Deccan was consolidated further when the Sultan of Bijapur acknowledged him as emperor.

Under the patronage of this great builder, Mughal art and architecture reached its zenith. He built the Moti Masjid, the Jama Masjid, the Shalimar Gardens and the Red Fort. 'Takht-i-Taus', or The Peacock Throne, considered as one of the most expensive thrones ever made, was kept in the Red Fort during his reign until Nadir Shah's invasion in 1739. One of the New Seven Wonders of the World, the Taj Mahal, was also built by him.

In 1657, Shah Jahan fell ill. Like in many other cases in history, this triggered a struggle for succession among his four sons. Aurangzeb, after defeating the other contenders, declared himself emperor in 1658. He imprisoned Shah Jahan in the Agra Fort until his death in 1666.

GOOD TO KNOW

- Shah Jahan's full imperial title was Al-Sultan al'Azam wal Khagan al-Mukarram, Abu'l-Muzaffar Shahab ud-din Muhammad, Sahib-i-Qiran-i-Sani, Shah Jahan I Padshah Ghazi Zillu'llah (Firdaus-Ashiyani).
- In 2009, the Archeological Society of India used a mud

pack of multani–mitti to remove the yellowish tinge on Taj Mahal.

- It is believed that after Shah Jahan had built the Taj Mahal, he intended to build a black marble mausoleum for himself but his dream could not come true as he died before fulfilling it.

QUIZ

1. What was Shah Jahan's name before he was proclaimed Emperor and given his title?
   a) Khurram
   b) Alamgir
   c) Khausrau

   Answer: Khurram

2. Where was Shah Jahan imprisoned during the last years of his life?
   a) Red Fort
   b) Agra Fort
   c) Jaisalmer Fort

   Answer: Agra Fort

3. What was the name of Shah Jahan's daughter?
   a) Nur Jahan
   b) Hamida Begum
   c) Jahanara

   Answer: Jahanara

SHIVAJI

Shivaji, popularly known as Chhatrapati Shri Shivaji Maharaj, was the founder of the Maratha kingdom in India. He was a great ruler and occupies a prominent place in the history of India. A born leader and a great strategist, he started as a jaigirdar and became a king. The Maratha nation that he built stood up to the Mughal Empire, both during and after Aurangazeb's reign, and continued to remain a dominant power in India during the eighteenth century.

Born to Shahji, a jagirdar in the hill fort of Shivner, Shivaji descended from a line of prominent nobles when India was under strict Muslim dominance. He grew up as a brave and adventurous soldier. In his early years, he spent a lot of time with the hill-men of the Maval community.

In 1646, Shivaji captured the fortress of Torna, five miles east of which he built the fort of Raigarh. After the death of his guardian tutor, Dadaji Khonddev, in 1647, Shivaji acquired many forts from their hereditary owners, or the local officers of Bijapur. In the mid-1650s, he captured the small Maratha principality of Javli. In 1657, he came into direct conflict with Aurangzeb, when his troops raided and looted the Mughal districts of Ahmednagar and Junnar. Aurangazeb was prompt in sending his force, and Shivaji was defeated. In 1659, aiming to destroy the power of Shivaji once and for all, the Sultan of Bijapur sent an army under Afzal Khan to attack him. But Shivaji killed Afzal Khan with tiger claws made of steel. He was hailed as a hero and a formidable warlord. Shivaji deliberately harassed the Mughals further by looting the rich coastal town of Surat.

In order to find a solution to the problems posed by Shivaji and worried about his rising strength, Aurangzeb sent Jay Singh, the Raja of Amber and Dilir Khan to punish Shivaji. Shivaji concluded the treaty of Purandhar with Jay Singh in 1665 where Jay Singh also convinced him to visit the imperial court at Agra. On his visit to Agra, Aurangzeb deliberately humiliated him. When Shivaji protested, he was imprisoned by the Mughal guards.

To escape confinement, Shivaji pretended to be ill and as a show of penance, sent baskets filled with sweets to be dispensed among the poor.

On August 17, 1666, he and his son were able to escape from Aurangzeb's clutches in two baskets. His followers gave him a warm welcome as their leader. In the following years he successfully recaptured all the lost territories and expanded his dominion. He collected tribute from Mughal regions and looted their rich cities. He reorganized his army and worked towards the well-being of his subjects.

In 1674, he formally crowned himself king at Raigarh and assumed the title of Chhatrapati. He understood the importance of naval power for trade as well as defence. He ruled for six years, through a cabinet of eight ministers known as the 'Ashtapradhan'. These ministers held the posts of Amatya, Sachiva, Peshwa, Mantri, Sumant, Senapati, Danadhyaksa and Nyayadhisa. Shivaji divided his kingdom into a number of provinces and appointed a viceroy as the head of each province. To simplify the process of revenue collection and administration, he further divided his kingdom into a number of prants, parganas and tarfs.

Shivaji died on 3 April 1680.

GOOD TO KNOW

- Shivaji initiated an era called Rajyabhishekha Shaka from the date of his coronation. This era continued till the end of the Maratha rule in 1818.
- Shivaji had to be publicly purified and 'made a Kshatriya' before his coronation.

QUIZ

1. Who granted Shivaji the title of Raja and gave him a jagir in Berar?
   a) Shah Jahan
   b) Aurangzeb
   c) Sultan of Bijapur

   Answer: Aurangzeb

2. What was the name given to Shivaji's sword?
   a) Zulfiqar
   b) Bhawani
   c) Tizona

   Answer: Bhawani

3. In which modern city of India is the Chhatrapati Shivaji Terminus located?
   a) New Delhi
   b) Chennai
   c) Mumbai

   Answer: Mumbai

GLOSSARY

- Ashtapradhan: was a council of eight ministers set up by Shivaji to advise him.
- Amatya: is a finance minister.
- Mantri: is a minister.
- Sachiva: is a superintendent.

- Sumant: is a foreign secretary.
- Danadhyaksha: is a royal chaplain.
- Nyayadhisa: is a chief justice.
- Peshwa: is a prime minister.
- Senapati: is a commander-in-chief.
- Jagir: is a large plot of land given by a king or a ruler to a person against regular receipt of revenue. The owner of such a jagir is a jagirdar.

SWAMI VIVEKANANDA

Swami Vivekananda was a Hindu spiritual leader, philosopher and reformer. He is widely regarded as the first Indian philosopher to have introduced Vedic philosophy to the western world. In 1893, he participated at the World's Parliament of Religions in Chicago as a spokesperson for Hinduism. In 1897, he founded the philanthropic, volunteer organization called Ramakrishna Mission.

Vivekananda was born as Narendranath Dutta on 12 January 1863 to Bishwanath Dutta, a successful lawyer with numerous interests, and Bhuvaneshwari Devi. As a child he was intelligent and lively. In 1879, he joined Presidency college in Calcutta. While in college, he came across books written on western philosophy which failed to satisfy his inquisitive mind. In 1881, he met Shri Ramakrishna, his guru, who was a priest in a Goddess Kali temple, who influenced him deeply with his teachings and views about the world.

After his father's sudden demise, he found solace in the ashram of his guru. In 1885, Shri Ramakrishna was shifted from Calcutta, first to Shyampukur and then to Cossipore as he was diagnosed with throat cancer. Vivekananda and his friends, accompanied their guru. Sri Ramakrishna infused in them the spirit of renunciation and 'brotherly love' towards each other.

In August 1886, after the death of Shri Ramakrishna, Vivekananda and his friends lived together in a ruined building in Baranagar. In January 1887, they undertook formal vows of

Sanyasa, and also acquired new names.

In 1890, to fulfil a greater mission in life, Vivekananda left the newly established monastic order and started living the life of a wandering monk. During his journey across India, he was moved by the misery, poverty and backwardness of the people in the country. He believed that the people of India needed two kinds of knowledge to improve their position: secular knowledge to improve their economic condition and spiritual knowledge to instill self-confidence. He realized that India needed an organization committed to its people. It was perhaps this need that led him to establish the Ramakrishna Mission.

While he was touring the country, he came to know about the World's Parliament of Religions, to be held in Chicago in 1893. He wanted to spread the message of the great religious leader Ramakrishna Paramhansa. His disciples in Chennai and the Raja of Khetri, collected funds to finance his travel and stay. Hence, he set for America on 31 May 1893.

As he arrived in Chicago, he came to know that he would not be allowed to speak in the Parliament of Religions because of lack of credentials. A professor of the Harvard University came forward and helped him to become a bonafide delegate. On 11 September 1893, the opening day of the Parliament, Swami Vivekananda got a chance to speak and started his speech with the words: 'Sisters and Brothers of America.' With those very words, he became the most popular speaker in the event. He delivered a number of speeches on the theme of universal religious tolerance.

After the Parliament, Swami Vivekananda stayed on in USA for some more time, lecturing in different cities. In 1895, he visited England and the rest of Europe. Here he met Ms Margaret Noble who would later become one of his well-known disciples. He came back to the Indian subcontinent in early

1897. In the same year, he established the Ramakrishna Mission and in December 1898, he and his fellow monks set-up their headquarters in Belur Math.

In 1899, he again travelled around the world, preaching about religion and philosophy. He passed away on July 4, 1902.

GOOD TO KNOW

- John D. Rockefeller, the famous philanthropist, was advised and influenced by Swami Vivekananda to make his first donation for charity. Fifteen years after that incident he set up the Rockefeller Foundation.
- The National Youth Day in India, is celebrated on Swami Vivekananda's birthday, 12 January.

QUIZ

1. What name did Swami Vivekananda give to Margaret Elizabeth Noble when he initiated her into the vow of Brahmacharya?
   a) Madam Cama
   b) Sister Nivedita
   c) Matahari

   Answer: Sister Nivedita
2. In 1893, Swami Vivekananda met him in a ship and influenced him to set up a Research Institute of Science for India (later became known as Indian Institute of Science) who was he?
   a) Lal Bahadur Shastri
   b) C.V. Raman
   c) Jamshetji N. Tata

   Answer: Jamsetji N. Tata
3. In May 1896, Swami Vivekananda met which famous German philosopher in London?

a) Immanuel Kant
b) T.H. Green
c) Max Mueller

Answer: Max Mueller

GLOSSARY

- Math: is the Sanskrit word for monastery.
- Parliament of the World's Religions: was an event held in Chicago in 1893.
- Margaret Noble/Sister Nivedita: was a dedicated disciple of Swami Vivekananda.

TIPU SULTAN

Tipu Sultan, also referred to as the Tiger of Mysore, was the ruler of Mysore from 1782 to 1799. He was known for his military tactics and skill in the art of warfare. Tipu used war rockets in some of the battles with the British. His skill and dexterity in handling them earned him great fame as the 'innovator of the world's first war rocket.'

Tipu was born on 1750 in Devanahalli, to Hyder Ali. He had great interest in the art of warfare and learned military tactics from the French officers employed by his father. He assisted his father in numerous wars and battles, and led his troops to victory against a British contingent led by Colonel John Braithwaite in the Second Anglo-Mysore War. When Haider Ali died in 1782, Tipu was in his early thirties. After ascending the throne, Tipu first made peace with the British in 1784. He declared himself 'Padishah' and he sent out diplomatic missions to ensure alliances with Turkey and France. In his mission, he requested the French king to supply him with 10,000 French troops to fight the English in India. On both fronts he failed, as these missions proved to be unsuccessful and his enmity with the British grew rapidly.

In 1789, when Tipu attacked the Raja of Travancore, he incensed the British who were his ally. Though he held the British at bay for more than two years, he had to cede half his dominions and a sum of thirty million rupees to the British according to the terms of the Treaty of Seringapatam. He also had to handover two of his sons aged five and eight, as hostages to the British. The British soon came to know of his unsuccessful attempt at negotiation with the French. The Governor General, Lord Mornington (later the marquess of Wellesley), used this opportunity to launch the fourth Mysore War. Seringapatam, Tipu's capital, was stormed by British-led forces on 4 May 1799, and Tipu died defending it.

Tipu was an able administrator. For the economic development of the region, he introduced measures to increase the cultivation on waste lands, and the harvest of commercial crops, such as sugarcane. He also encouraged sericulture, and the use of timber for military and commercial use. He established many gun foundries and saltpetre factories, that functioned under the state ownership. During his reign, he encouraged trading of valuable commodities, such as sandalwood, silk, spices, coconut, rice, sulphur and elephants.

GOOD TO KNOW

- The inner walls of Tipu Sultan's mausoleum are covered in the tiger-stripe or babri design that he loved. This design appeared on a number of things and places including his jackets, turbans and handkerchiefs, books in his library and on his currency notes. The tiger motif also appeared on the uniforms and weapons of his soldiers.
- During his war with the British, Tipu Sultan, designed a mechanical tiger, which showed a reflection of his anger and disgust towards the Englishmen. It is a large tiger with bright yellow stripes, pouncing on an English soldier and tearing him to pieces. The soldier's hands are raised in pain, the eyes are wide open with terror and his face showing great fear. Tipu's toy tiger is securely placed in a large glass casket in the Victoria and Albert (V&A) museum in London.

QUIZ

1. In which present-day state is Seringapatam located?
   a) Madhya Pradesh
   b) Karnataka
   c) Maharashtra

Answer: Karnataka

2. Which Bollywood actor played the role of Tipu in the serial *The Sword of Tipu Sultan*?
   a) Dharmendra
   b) Sanjay Khan
   c) Firoz Khan

Answer: Sanjay Khan

3. Which President of India called Tipu Sultan the innovator of the world's first rocket?
   a) Manmohan Singh
   b) Vikram Sarabhai
   c) APJ Abdul Kalam

Answer: APJ Abdul Kalam

GLOSSARY

- Padshah: is a royal title meaning emperor.
- Sericulture: is the rearing of silkworms for the production of silk.

POLITICS

ABUL KALAM AZAD

Abul Kalam Muhiyuddin Ahmed Azad, popularly known as Maulana Azad, was one of the prominent leaders of the Indian independence movement who vehemently opposed the partition of India. A scholar and poet, he was well versed in many languages including Arabic, English, Urdu, Hindi and Persian. He served as the first Education Minister of independent India.

Azad was born on 11 November 1888 in Mecca (now in Saudi Arabia), to Maulana Khairuddin, a Bengali Muslim from Afghanistan. As he belonged to an orthodox family, he pursued traditional Islamic education at home in Kolkata but secretly learned English. He was initially trained to become a clergyman and wrote numerous books reinterpreting the holy Quran. He developed an interest in the doctrines of Jamaluddin Afghani and the Aligarh Movement of Sir Syed Ahmed Khan, and was inspired to visit Afghanistan, Iraq, Egypt, Syria and Turkey. He met many prominent Muslim revolutionary leaders in those countries and was greatly impressed.

On his return, he started his crusade against the British.

In 1912, he started publishing a weekly journal in Urdu called *Al-Hilal* to foster Hindu-Muslim unity. The journal had a huge appeal. It challenged Indian Muslims who showed their loyalty to the British. This angered the British and he was imprisoned several times.

He actively participated in the Khilafat movement held from 1920 to 1924. This movement defended the Ottoman sultan as the Caliph or the head of the worldwide Muslim community.

He formed the Nationalist Muslim Party within the Indian National Congress, and protested against the Muslim League's claim that it represented all Muslims in British India. He was elected president of the Indian National Congress on two occasions, in 1924 and 1940.

In 1992, Azad was posthumously awarded the Bharat Ratna for his indispensable and extremely valuable contribution to India. He is chiefly remembered in history for his integrity and piety. He passed away on 22 February 1958 in New Delhi.

GOOD TO KNOW

- Maulana Abul Kalam's pen name was Azad, which he adopted signifying that he was free from the marginal views of religion and life.
- Abul Kalam, literally means 'lord of dialogue'.
- His weekly *Al-Balagh* aimed at unifying the Hindus and Muslims.

QUIZ

1. What name was given to Azad at his birth?
   a) Feroz Bakht
   b) Saqib Ali
   c) Ammar Hussein

Answer: Feroz Bakht

2. In which city is Maulana Azad National Urdu University located?
   a) Hyderabad
   b) Secundarabad
   c) Bengaluru

Answer: Hyderabad

3. Who played the the role of Azad in the film *Gandhi?*

a) Virendra Razdaan
b) Ben Kingsley
c) Om Puri

Answer: Virendra Razdaan

GLOSSARY

- Aligarh Movement: was the movement led by Sir Syed Ahmed Khan, to educate the Muslims of South Asia.

BAL GANGADHAR TILAK

Bal Gangadhar Tilak, widely regarded as the 'Father of Indian unrest', was a scholar, philosopher and freedom fighter.

Tilak was born on 23 July 1856 in Ratnagiri, in an orthodox Brahmin family and studied mostly in Pune. He graduated in 1876 and obtained a degree in law in 1879. After finishing his education, he plunged into politics. He believed that larger good could only be attained if modern education was taken to the common people by the Indians themselves. He, along with a few of his friends, founded the Deccan Education Society and the Fergusson College in Pune in 1885.

Tilak also worked on two weekly newspapers in order to spread his views; *Kesari* (in Marathi) and *The Mahratta* (in English).

His nationalist views led him into an open conflict with the British and they imprisoned him on the charge of sedition in 1897.

This did not change his views and he declared, 'Swaraj is my birthright and I shall have it.' This historical trial earned him the title of 'Lokmanya'.

Tilak, for a long time, was not a member of the core committee that formulated the policies of the Indian National Congress. His concept of a political party was radically different from those of the other leaders. He wanted to create a militant mass movement to achieve his political aim. He used innovative tactics to help the cause of the Extremists. His difference of opinion with Moderates at the Surat session of the Congress in 1907, eventually led to its split. The opportunist British took the advantage of the situation, and wasted no time in prosecuting him. He was then sent to the Mandalay jail in Burma (Myanmar) in 1908.

After Tilak was released, he helped form the All India Home Rule League in 1916, along with Annie Besant. In the same year he rejoined Congress at the Lucknow session along with the extremists. He put in great effort in carrying out the message of Home Rule across the country.

In April 1920, Tilak started the Congress Democratic Party in order to fight for Swarajya. However, he died on 1 August 1920 in Mumbai.

GOOD TO KNOW

- Tilak was called the 'Maker of Modern India' by Mahatma Gandhi.
- Tilak published a work titled *The Arctic Home in the Vedas*. It is a seminal work on the origin of Aryans presented by Lokmanya Bal Gangadhar Tilak.
- In Maharashtra, Bal Gangadhar Tilak started celebrating Ganesh Chaturthi on a large scale in the 1890s to unite people on a common platform.

QUIZ

1. Which of these books did Bal Gangadhar Tilak write while he was in Mandalay?
   a) *Meri Ekyavan Kavitayen*
   b) *Bharat Ek Khoj*
   c) *Srimad Bhagavadgita Rahasya*

Answer: *Srimad Bhagavadgita Rahasya*

2. In which Indian city would you find the Lokmanya Tilak Terminus?
   a) Ahmedabad
   b) Mumbai
   c) Kolkata

Answer: Mumbai

3. Which Indian prime minister, in his tribute, called Bal Gangadhar Tilak the 'Father of the Indian Revolution'?
   a) Jawaharlal Nehru
   b) Lal Bahadur Shastri
   c) Morarji Desai

Answer: Jawaharlal Nehru

GLOSSARY

- Moderates: were a group of liberal leaders in Indian Nation Congress who refrained from taking violent means to achieve independence for India. Instead they relied more on the policies of 'prayer, petition and plea'.
- Extremists: were the younger group within the congress who believed that freedom can never be achieved through begging. They chose instead the path of agitation, strikes and boycotts to force their demands.

BHIMRAO RAMJI AMBEDKAR

Bhimrao Ramji Ambedkar, often referred to as the architect of the Indian Constitution, was an important nationalist leader. On 29 August 1947, he became the chairman of the Drafting Committee formed by the Constituent Assembly to draft the Constitution of India. He served as the first Law Minister of Independent India.

Ambedkar was born on 14 April 1891 in Mhaow, Madhya Pradesh. His father was a military Subedar, who was a follower of Kabir. He had his early education in Satara. His family shifted to Bombay where he did his matriculation from the Elphinstone High School. He graduated in 1912 from Elphinstone College, Bombay, and went to the USA on a Baroda State Scholarship to join Columbia University. After obtaining a master's degree in economics in 1915 and PhD in 1916, he taught at the Sydenham College of Commerce and Economics, Bombay. In 1920, Ambedkar went to England from where he obtained his M.Sc. in 1921. He was awarded the Doctorate of Science in 1923, and was called to the Bar in the same year. Ambedkar returned to India and started his legal practice at the Bombay High Court in 1924. He became an active social worker, a politician, a writer and an educationist. In politics, he started raising issues associated with the depressed classes and consolidated his position as a leader of the oppressed. In 1926, he was nominated as a member of the Legislative Assembly of Bombay. He held the position till the year 1934. In 1932, the Poona Pact was signed where it was decided that a joint electorate would remain for Hindus, but with higher number of seats for the depressed classes.

In 1927, Ambedkar started a movement at Mahad in Maharastra to provide the untouchables the right to drink water from the Chavdar Tank. In 1930, in order to provide the so called untouchables the right to enter the local temples, he started Satyagraha at Kalram Temple, Nasik. The Independent Labour Party was founded by Ambedkar in 1936, with the aim of spreading education amongst all and establishing social equality.

In 1942, he became the first untouchable to be nominated to the Viceroy's Executive Council.

In October 1956, along with some 2,00,000 Dalits, Ambedkar converted to Buddhism at a ceremony in Nagpur.

In 1945, he founded the People's Education Society which further opened a large number of colleges in the Bombay Presidency for the Scheduled Caste students.

Dr Ambedkar was also a champion of the rights of women. He believed that for social justice and progress of the nation it was important to improve the position of women in society. He stood for the economic equality of women and vehemently pleaded for the spread of women's education. Though it was never passed, the Hindu Code Bill, piloted by him, empowered women to equally inherit property. The Bill abolished the doctrine of rights by birth and provided laws for inter-caste marriage and divorce.

He wrote many books and journals. In 1920, he started a Marathi weekly paper called *Mooknayak* to address issues regarding the depressed classes. He also founded the 'Bahiskrit Hitkarini Sabha' on 20 July 1924 for the upliftment of the depressed classes and aimed to educate, unite and agitate.

The Buddha and His Dhamma is one of his most popular books.

He breathed his last on 6 December 1956.

GOOD TO KNOW

- His surname, Ambavadekar, was changed to Ambedkar by his school teacher in Satara.
- In recognition of his services, Government of India conferred on him Bharat Ratna, posthumously.

QUIZ

1. What is B.R. Ambedkar's autobiography called?
   a) *Waiting for a Visa*
   b) *The Story of My Experiments With Truth*
   c) *The Discovery of India*

   Answer: *Waiting for a Visa*

2. To which religion did Ambedkar convert, in the later part of his life?
   a) Jainism
   b) Buddhism
   c) Christianity

   Answer: Buddhism

3. In 1951, Ambedkar resigned from Nehru's Cabinet protesting against the withdrawal of the _______.
   a) Second Round Table Conference
   b) Hindu Code Bill
   c) Communal Award

   Answer: Hindu Code Bill

GLOSSARY

- *Mooknayak*: was a Marathi weekly magazine meaning 'Dumb Hero'.
- Harijan: is a term used by Gandhi for Dalits, literally meaning 'children of God'.
- Dhamma: is the Buddha's Dharma of enlightment.

DADABHAI NAOROJI

Dadabhai Naoroji, also known as the 'Grand Old Man of India', was an important Indian nationalist leader and well known critic of the British economic policy of India. He is also regarded as one of the founding fathers of Indian Nationalism.

Born in Khadak, near Bombay, Dadabhai Naoroji was the only son of Naoroji Palanji Dordi, a Parsi priest, and his wife, Manekbai. In 1845, he graduated and went to London as a business partner in a firm. In 1850, at the age of twenty-five, he became a leading professor of natural philosophy and mathematics at the Elphinstone Institution in Bombay. He played a key role in reforming societies, and was a founding member of the Bombay Association in 1852.

While in England, Naoroji wished to speak about the responsibilities of the British towards the Indians. He delivered speeches and published articles to highlight his view that the Indians were not being treated fairly under British rule. In the late 1860s, he established the East India Association to keep Britain well-informed of India's needs and requirements, and to ensure fair treatment of the Indians. After his return to India, he succeeded in persuading the princes to fund the Association, which provided a forum for his campaign to allow Indians to enter the Indian Civil Service.

Further, Naoroji expounded the idea of 'Drain Theory' to demonstrate the way in which the wealth and resources of India were being exploited by the British. He published his statements by way of facts and figures in a book titled *Poverty and Un-British Rule in India*. This is believed to be the first economic critique of colonial India. Apart from this, he also founded several magazines and journals such as *Rast Goftar* and *Voice of India.*

In 1892, Naoroji was elected as Member of Parliament for Central Finsbury, London. Being a Parsi and not a Christian by birth, he strictly refused to take the oath of office on the Bible and took an oath in the name of God on his copy of *Khordeh Avesta*, the Zoroastrian sacred text. Apart from this, in 1895 he was appointed a member of the royal commission on Indian expenditure. In 1906, he publicly demanded 'Swaraj' for India from the Congress platform. He was the president of the Indian National Congress in 1886, 1893 and 1906. In the session of 1906, he tactfully postponed the unavoidable split between moderates and extremists in the Congress Party.

Naoroji was also the first Indian to be elected to the British House of Commons.

In his sixties and seventies, Naoroji became interested in English sports; he was the president of the football club in his parliamentary constituency, Central Finsbury.

Naoroji passed away on 1917.

GOOD TO KNOW

- The people of Great Britain found it difficult to pronounce his name correctly. Many newspapers, posters and letters addressed him differently as, Dedabhan Naorji, Devan Novoriji and Dadabhai Nowraggie.
- As Dadabhai Naoroji was the senior-most Indian resident in the United Kingdom, he was often called upon to preside over issues related to Indians residing in the UK.

QUIZ

1. Who did Dadabhai Naoroji succeed as president of the Indian National Congress in 1886?
   a) Badruddin Tyabji
   b) Womesh Chandra Bonnerjee
   c) George Yule

Answer: Womesh Chandra Bonnerjee

2. In which language was the *Rast Gofter* written by Naoroji?
   a) English
   b) Urdu
   c) Gujarati

Answer: Gujarati

3. Who functioned as the secretary to Dadabhai Naoroji when he presided over the 1906 Session in Calcutta?
   a) Subhas Chandra Bose
   b) Bal Gangadhar Tilak
   c) Mohammad Ali Jinnah

Answer: Mohammad Ali Jinnah

GLOSSARY

- Swaraj: means self rule.
- Drain Theory: is a theory stating the drain of wealth from India to Great Britain
- Parsi: is a follower of Zoroastrianism

INDIRA GANDHI

Indira Priyadarshini Gandhi was the second-longest-serving prime minister of India and the only woman to hold the office for so long.

Indira was born on 19 November 1917 in Allahabad, to Pandit Jawaharlal Nehru and Kamala Nehru. She studied at Viswa Bharati University and Oxford University. From the very childhood, she was involved into politics and in spite of being a child, Indira was able to organize the Bal Charkha Sangh, an association where children learnt to spin and weave.

In 1930, she formed Vanar Sena (Monkey Brigade) with 6,000 children at Allahabad to help Congress Party during the non-cooperation movement.

In 1942, Indira was married to Feroze Gandhi and they had two sons, Sanjay and Rajiv Gandhi. In 1955, she became a member of the Congress Working Committee and was later elected as the president in 1959. She also served as Minister for Information and Broadcasting in the Cabinet of Lal Bahadur Shastri. In 1966, on the death of Lal Bahadur Shastri, she became the Prime Minister of India, for the first time.

In the election of 1967 she won by a narrow majority. However, in 1971, she won with a wide majority over a coalition of conservative parties. During this period, one of her major achievements was the role played by the armed forces of India in achieving a hasty and momentous victory over Pakistan. This triumph eventually led to the creation of Bangladesh. In 1972, the new Congress Party achieved a huge victory in the national elections because of her able leadership.

Shortly afterward, she was charged with violating the election laws. In 1975, she declared a state of Emergency in India in response to a verdict of Allahabad High Court, which deprived her of her seat in Parliament and ordered her to stay out of politics for six years.

Early in 1978, those supporting Gandhi broke away from the Congress Party and formed a new party known as the Congress (I) Party. The 'I' here signified Indira. She resumed her power when the new Congress (I) Party got a huge victory in the Lok Sabha election held in 1980.

Among the other important achievements of Indira Gandhi as prime minister was the signing of the Shimla Pact and the Indo-Soviet Treaty of Peace. She played an important role in abolishing privy purses, nationalizing banks and launching the first nuclear tests at Pokhran.

Indira Gandhi also had profound interest in literature, music and fine arts.

She has received many awards in her lifetime. These include Bharat Ratna in 1972; Mexican Academy Award for Liberation of Bangladesh, also in 1972; 2nd Annual Medal, FAO in 1973; Sahitya Vachaspati (Hindi) by Nagari Pracharini Sabha, in 1976.

GOOD TO KNOW

- The pink khadi sari, woven by Jawaharlal Nehru during his stay in jail, was worn in succession by Indira Gandhi, Sonia Gandhi and Priyanka Gandhi on their wedding day.
- After Moraji Desai resigned, Indira Gandhi took over the Finance portfolio. She has been the only woman Finance Minister as of now.

- The Indira Gandhi National Open University, known as IGNOU, named after her, is a distance learning national university.

QUIZ

1. Who succeeded Indira Gandhi as the Prime minister of India?
   a) Rajiv Gandhi
   b) P.V. Narasimha Rao
   c) Shri Chandra Shekhar

Answer: Rajiv Gandhi

2. In which city is Indira Gandhi International airport located?
   a) Mumbai
   b) Kolkata
   c) New Delhi

Answer: New Delhi

3. What was the name of Indira Gandhi's elder son?
   a) Sanjay Gandhi
   b) Rajiv Gandhi
   c) Feroze Gandhi

Answer: Rajiv Gandhi

GLOSSARY

- Vanar sena: was a group of children formed by Indira Gandhi in 1930 to help the Congress party during the Non-Cooperation Movement.
- Bharat Ratna: is the highest civilian Award of the country, instituted in the year 1954.

JAWAHARLAL NEHRU

Pandit Jawaharlal Nehru, also known as Chacha Nehru, was one of the principal leaders of the Indian National Movement. He established the parliamentary form of government, and formulated 'neutralist' policies in foreign affairs. When India became independent in 1947, he also served as its first prime minister.

Pandit Jawaharlal Nehru was born on 14 November 1889 in Allahabad, to Motilal Nehru, a well-known lawyer, and Swarup Rani. After his early education at home, he was sent to Harrow, in England, in 1905. He studied at Trinity College, Cambridge, where he took his Tripos, the final honours examination for a BA degree at Cambridge University, in Natural Sciences. He completed Bar-at-law from the Inner Temple, London, and returned to India in 1912.

In 1916, he married Kamala Kaul and they had a daughter named Indira Priyadarshini.

Nehru was greatly interested in the struggle of nations suffering under foreign domination and actively followed the developments in these countries. He met Mahatma Gandhi for the first time in 1916, at the annual meeting of the Indian National Congress Party in Lucknow. In 1919, he was appointed Secretary of the Home Rule League, Allahabad. The following year, he organized the first Kisan March in Pratapgarh, Uttar Pradesh.

Nehru's interest in politics increased manifolds when he

became General Secretary of the All India Congress Committee in 1923. In 1928, he founded the 'Independence for India League', which aimed to put an end to British control in India. He also served as President of the Lahore Session of the Indian National Congress in 1929, where the goal of 'complete independence' was adopted.

At the A.I.C.C. session in Bombay in 1942, Nehru moved the 'Quit India' resolution. He was arrested along with other leaders on August 8, 1942, and imprisoned at the Ahmadnagar Fort in what is considered his longest and last confinement. He was imprisoned nine times during the freedom movement.

On 15 August 1947, when India became independent, Nehru became its first prime minister.

Nehru served as the prime minister for seventeen years, and is often regarded as the architect of modern India. He played an important part in setting India on the path of development and democracy, by laying the foundation for institutions including, the Parliament, multi-party system, independent judiciary and free press.

In 1950, the year the Constitution of India came into force and India became a Republic, Nehru became the chairman of the Planning Commission, an office he held till his death. In 1952, he also formed a new government after the first General Elections.

His policies on international relations were based on the principles of peaceful coexistence.

Nehru was a prolific writer. He wrote many books, including *The Discovery of India*, *Glimpses of World History* and his autobiography, *Towards Freedom*. He was awarded the Bharat Ratna in 1955.

Nehru is lovingly referred to as Chacha Nehru and his birthday is observed as Children's Day in India. He believed that children are the future of the nation.

Jawaharlal Nehru passed away on 27 May 1964.

GOOD TO KNOW

- The original name of the Nehru family was Kaul. The name Nehru came from the Persian word for canal, nahar, after his ancestor was granted a jagir with a house by a canal.
- The Nehru jacket is similar to the North Indian achkan, which is a closed-neck, coat-like garment.
- During his confinement at the Ahmednagar fort prison, Nehru worked at the rose garden every day.

QUIZ

1. What is the final resting place of Jawaharlal Nehru named?
   a) Shanti Van
   b) Shakti Sthal
   c) Kisan Ghat

   Answer: Shanti Van

2. Which of the following leaders was Jawaharlal Nehru's sister?
   a) Sarojini Naidu
   b) Indira Gandhi
   c) Vijaylakshmi Pandit

   Answer: Vijaylakshmi Pandit

3. Which of these was the official residence of the first prime minister of India?
   a) Samta Sthal
   b) Teen Murti House
   c) Nehru Bhavan

   Answer: Teen Murti House

GLOSSARY

- The Inner Temple: is one of the four Inns of Court in England. The other three are: Lincoln's Inn, Middle Temple and Gray's Inn. They hold exclusive rights of admission to the Bar. In order to practise as a barrister in England, a person must belong to one of these Inns.
- Judiciary: is the judicial authorities of a country.

MAHATMA GANDHI

Mohandas Karamchand Gandhi, also regarded as the 'Father of the Nation', was one of the greatest leaders of the Indian nationalist movement. He is famous for his policy of non-violence, or ahimsa.

Gandhi was born on 2 October 1869 in Porbandar, Gujarat, to Putlibai and Karamchand Gandhi, the dewan (chief minister) of Porbandar. His family belonged to the Vaishnava sect, that encourages non-violence, vegetarianism, fasting for the purpose of self-purification, and fosters mutual tolerance amongst the followers of different creeds and sects.

In 1881, at the age of thirteen, he was married to Kasturbai. He was in school for a period of seven years, from 1881 to 1887 and spent around nine months in a college, before leaving for England in 1888 to pursue law. He returned in 1891 and set up his practice in Rajkot.

In 1893, Gandhi was offered a job by an Indian firm in Natal, South Africa. However, he experienced colonial and racial discrimination at various points and decided to do something about it. He had a firsthand harrowing experience when he was thrown out of a first-class railway compartment at the Pietermaritzburg Station, while travelling to Pretoria. On another occasion, he was asked by the European magistrate to take off his turban. During his stay in South Africa, which lasted more than twenty years, he opposed the discrimination of the Indians. He also protested against the Asiatic (Black) Act and the Transvaal Immigration Act, and started his nonviolent civil disobedience movement.

To take his principles further, he played an important part in establishing Tolstoy Farm near Johannesburg, in 1910, in order to give shelter to the satyagrahis and their families. His efforts bore fruit and in 1914, the South African Government repealed most of the acts against the Indians. The weekly *Indian Opinion* (1903) became Gandhiji's main organ of education and political propaganda.

After returning to India in 1915, Gandhi established the Satyagraha Ashram in Ahmedabad city and shifted it to the banks of the Sabarmati River in 1917. This Ashram became a forum for putting his ideas forward and carrying out his work on social issues like Harijan welfare, rehabilitation of lepers and self-reliance through weaving Khadi.

During the First World War, Gandhi participated in the peasant movements of Champaran (Bihar) and the other in Kaira (Gujarat). He even tried to resolve a labour conflict in Ahmedabad. In 1919, when the First World War was coming to an end, Gandhi raised his voice against the Rowlatt Bills. In the same year he founded the Satyagraha Sabha.

In 1930, through the 'Dandi March' Gandhi called upon the people of India to break the famous Salt-Law. These Salt Acts, levied by the British, prohibited Indians from collecting or selling salt. This forced the Indians to buy this important food item from them, bearing the burden of heavy taxation. Gandhi realized that breaking the Salt Acts was a simple way to break a British law non-violently. He was arrested on 4 May 1930. Though the British Government took stern steps to crush the movement, they failed to suppress it completely. Gandhi was set free on 26 January 1931. This was followed by a pact between Gandhi and the British Viceroy, Lord Irwin, on 5 March

1931. It put an end to a period of Civil disobedience against the British rule that Mahatma Gandhi had started with the Salt March. However, Gandhi was totally disappointed with the British policy of ruthless repression. Hence, he resumed the Civil Disobedience Movement in 1932.

In 1932, while Gandhi was in jail, the Communal Award was announced in order to introduce a separate electorate for the Depressed Classes. To protest against this evil divide and rule policy of the British, amongst the Hindu community, Gandhiji threatened to fast till death if it was not revoked. He started fasting from 20 September 1932. Though this caused a huge furor in the country, the situation cooled down with the signing of the Poona Pact. The Poona Pact, under joint electorate, provided special reservation of seats for the Depressed Classes in legislatures. In 1933, the Harijan issue made Gandhi to go into fast again and, this time, for 21 days.

Gandhi gradually devoted himself exclusively to the cause of the Harijans and eventually published the weekly *Harijan.* After 1934, Gandhi founded a new Centre near Wardha, for propagating various constructive programmes like Basic Education, aiming at universalizing education.

In 1942, Gandhi formulated the 'Quit India' movement which triggered a more intense resistance to the British rule in India. He was terribly shocked by the British plan of partitioning India and Pakistan. He personally claimed, 'Vivisect me before you Vivisect India.' After independence in 1947, Gandhi went to Noakhali in order to improve the conditions of those who were affected by the communal riots that followed the partition. He also fasted to stop a similar riot in Calcutta.

At the age of seventy-eight, Gandhi was assassinated by Nathuram Godse on 30 January 1948.

He was not a recipient of the Nobel Peace Prize though he

was nominated on many occasions. In 1989, when the Dalai Lama was awarded the Peace Prize, the chairman of the committee commented that it was 'in part a tribute to the memory of Mahatma Gandhi.'

GOOD TO KNOW

- Gandhi gave up wearing western clothes at Madurai.
- Gandhi's autobiography *'The Story of My Experiments with Truth'* was translated from Gujarati into English by Mahadev Desai.
- The memorial temple Kirti Mandir in Porbandar, *was* built in memory of Gandhi.

QUIZ

1. *Unto the Last*, a book by John Ruskin, influenced Gandhi so much that he translated it into which language?
   a) Hindi
   b) Gujarati
   c) Sanskrit

   Answer: Gujarati

2. Who was the first person to address Mahatma Gandhi as Mahatma?
   a) Rabindranath Tagore
   b) Nelson Mandela
   c) Mother Teresa

   Answer: Rabindranath Tagore

3. What was called the Sun of the Village Solar System by Gandhi?
   a) Charkha
   b) Khadi
   c) Salt

   Answer: Charkha

4. Mahatma Gandhi's birthday is celebrated as the International day of...
   a) Non-violence
   b) National harmony
   c) Mother Earth

Answer: Non-violence

GLOSSARY

- Civil Disobedience: is the active, professed refusal to obey certain laws, demands and commands of a government, or of an occupying international power.
- Harijan: meaning Child of God, was a term used by Mohandas Gandhi for the Dalits.

SAROJINI NAIDU

Sarojini Naidu was a freedom fighter, political activist, feminist and poet. Often referred to as the 'Nightingale of India', she was the first woman to become the governor of an Indian state and president of the Indian National Congress.

Sarojini Naidu was born on 13 February 1879 in Hyderabad, to Aghornath Chattopadhyay and Barada Sundari Devi. When she was twelve years old, she passed her matriculation and stood first in the Madras Presidency. Later, she studied at King's College in London and Girton College in Cambridge. Though her academic career remained incomplete, she was able to publish her poems in 1905, 1912 and 1917, when she met the English poet Edmund Gosse. In 1898, she married Dr Govindarajulu Naidu, a doctor.

Between 1903 and 1917, Sarojini interacted with Gokhale, Tagore, Jinnah, Annie Besant, C.P. Rama Swami Iyer, Gandhi and Jawaharlal Nehru, and was inspired by them.

In 1915, Sarojini travelled to different parts of the country lecturing on several issues, including nationalism, welfare of youth, dignity of labour and women's emancipation. She met Jawaharlal Nehru for the first time in 1916 and became involved in the issues related to the workers of Champaran.

From 1917 to 1919, Sarojini was actively involved in various campaigns, including the Montagu-Chelmsford Reforms, the Khilafat issue, the Rowlatt Act, the Sabarmati Pact and the Satyagraha Pledge.

She was one of the key members of Gandhiji's team when he launched the Civil Disobedience Movement on 6 April 1919.

In 1919, Sarojini went to England as a part of the all-India Home Rule Deputation. After 1920, as the president of the Bombay Provincial Congress Committee, she travelled extensively across the country and thereby raised opposition against Council entry in Calcutta. She also raised her voice against the anti-Moplah measures in Calicut.

After Gandhiji's trial in 1922, Sarojini gave up wearing silk sarees and wore khadi instead.

Between 1922 and 1926, she was involved in various political activities; she fought for the cause of Indians residing in South Africa, and participated in the Salt Satyagraha and the Round Table Conference in London. She also advocated and campaigned for the participation of women and youth in daily public life.

In 1925, Sarojini was electively chosen as President of Congress. She was imprisoned in 1942, in connection with the Quit India Resolution of the AICC in Bombay.

Sarojini was a prolific writer. Her first volume of poetry, *The Golden Threshold* was published in 1905. It was followed by *The Bird of Time: Songs of Life, Death and the Spring.* Her collected poems, all written in the English language, have been published under the titles *The Sceptred Flute* (1928) and *The Feather of the Dawn* (1961).

Sarojini died on 2 March 1949 in Lucknow, at the age of seventy.

GOOD TO KNOW

- In 1914, Sarojini became a fellow of the Royal Society of Literature.
- Her brother, Harindranath, was a poet, dramatist and an actor.

- She was awarded the Gold 'Kaiser-e-Hind' Medal for organising flood relief work in Hyderabad.

QUIZ

1. All the collected poems of Sarojini Naidu were written in which language?
   a) English
   b) Hindi
   c) Sanskrit

   Answer: English

2. Sarojini Naidu was the first woman president of the…
   a) World Wildlife Fund
   b) Indian National Congress
   c) Theosophical society

   Answer: Indian National Congress

3. Sarojini's Naidu's daughter, Padmaja Naidu, was the governor of which state?
   a) Odisha
   b) Gujarat
   c) West Bengal

   Answer: West Bengal

GLOSSARY

- Moplah: is a class of people in Malabar.

SUBHAS CHANDRA BOSE

Subhas Chandra Bose, popularly known as Netaji, was one of the greatest nationalist leaders during the freedom struggle of India. He, unlike many leaders of the time, strongly felt that that an armed rebellion was necessary to achieve independence from the British.

Subhas Chandra Bose was born on 23 January 1897 in Cuttack, Orissa (present-day Odisha), to Prabhavati Devi and Janaki Nath Bose, a leading lawyer. In 1902, he was admitted to Cuttack Protestant School. He was a good student and graduated in 1919 with a first class in philosophy. He then appeared for the Civil Service examination in 1920 and joined the service. He resigned in 1921 as he was deeply disturbed by the events of the time, especially the Jallianwala Bagh massacre that had taken place in Amritsar. He went to Kolkata to work under Chittaranjan Das, a revolutionary leader, joined the non-cooperation movement, and became a youth educator and journalist.

In 1924, Bose became the chief executive officer of the Calcutta Municipal Corporation. He was deported to Burma (Myanmar) when he was suspected of maintaining contact with secret revolutionary movements but was released in 1927, without trial. Later that year, he was elected President of the Bengal Provincial Congress Committee.

In 1928, when the Motilal Nehru Committee favoured Dominion Status for India, he, along with Jawaharlal Nehru, opposed it. He announced the formation of the Independence

League and moved a resolution demanding 'complete freedom'. In 1932, he met Vithalbhai Patel in Vienna and together they declared that the fight for independence should be from all possible fronts. In 1938 Haripura session, he was elected President of the Indian National Congress. He formed a planning committee, which laid out a broad industrialization policy. However, this idea did not go down well with the Gandhian economic thought and he resigned. In 1939, he founded the Forward Bloc, with the aim of continuing the struggle.

On 26 January 1941, Bose escaped in disguise from his house arrest in Calcutta, and went to Germany via Kabul and Moscow. During his stay in Germany, he tried to spread his ideas through regular broadcasts in English, Hindi, Bengali, Tamil, Gujarati, Telugu and Pashto from the German-sponsored Azad Hind Radio.

After Bose was satisfied with the assurances of support he had garnered in Germany, he left the country in 1943 and headed to Japan. One of the high points of this journey was his voyage in a submarine. From Japan, he went to Singapore where he took over the leadership of the Indian Independence Movement in East Asia from Rash Behari Bose, organized the Azad Hind Fauj (the Indian National Army), became its Supreme Commander and proclaimed the Provisional Government of Azad Hind on 21 October.

The headquarters of the INA was shifted to Rangoon in January 1944. Eventually, Bose along with his troops marched towards India with the war cry 'Chalo Delhi'. Crossing the Burmese border, they entered India on 18 March 1944 but were eventually defeated. This marked the end of Netaji's fortune.

Bose is said to have died in an air crash over Taipei, Taiwan (Formosa) on 18 August 1945.

Netaji Subhas Bose's birth anniversary, 23rd January, is

also observed as Desh Prem Divas, or the National Day of Patriotism, every year.

GOOD TO KNOW

- Bose travelled to Moscow from Afghanistan on the Italian passport of an Italian nobleman 'Count Orlando Mazzotta'.
- Bose gave the name Swaraj and Shaheed Islands to the Andaman and Nicobar Islands.
- In 1997, on the occasion of the birth centenary of Subhas Chandra, the Government of Delhi renamed the Delhi Institute of Technology as Netaji Subhas Institute of Technology.

QUIZ

1. Who succeeded Bose as the president of Congress?
   a) Abul Kalam Azad
   b) Jawaharlal Nehru
   c) M.K. Gandhi

Answer: Abul Kalam Azad

2. Who portrayed Subhas Chandra Bose in Shyam Benegal's biopic *Netaji Subhas Chandra Bose: The Forgotten Hero*?
   a) Sachin Khedekar
   b) Keneth Desai
   c) Irrfan Khan

Answer: Sachin Khedekar

3. Fill in the blank to complete the title of Subhas Chandra Bose's autobiography: *An Indian* ________: *An Unfinished Autobiography*.
   a) *Leader*
   b) *Pilgrim*
   c) *Revolutionary*

Answer: *Pilgrim*

GLOSSARY

- Indian National Army: also known as Azad Hind Fauj, was an armed force formed by Indian nationalists.
- Indian National Congress: is a political party of India, formed in 1885.

VALLABHBHAI PATEL

Vallabhbhai Patel, popularly known as Sardar or the Iron Man of India, was an Indian nationalist leader. He was the first deputy prime minister and home minister of independent India. He played an important role in unifying the country.

Vallabhhbhai Patel was born on 31 October 1875 in Nadiad, Gujarat, into a Leva-Patidar family. He attended primary-school in Karmamasad and high-school at Petlad, but was mainly self-taught. Later, he passed the district pleader's examination and practised as a defence lawyer. In order to improve his skill sets, he sailed to England and joined the Middle Temple in 1910.

Once there, he concentrated on his studies and was called to the Bar at the end of two years instead of the usual period of three years. After passing the final examination, he returned to India in 1913, and became a leading barrister. In 1917, deeply influenced by Mahatma Gandhi's views and opinions, he changed his lifestyle and appearance radically. In 1917, he became the first Indian municipal commissioner of Ahmedabad and remained so till 1924, when he was elected as its president.

In 1918, Patel made his mark by planning the mass campaigns of farmers and landowners of Kaira district, Gujarat, against the decision of the Bombay government to collect full annual revenue taxes inspite of crop failure.

In 1928, he played a major role in leading the landowners of Bardoli in their fight against increased taxes. His success in Bardoli earned him the title sardar (leader), and made him a popular national leader across India.

When India became independent in 1947, as Home Minister, Patel was given the responsibility of integrating the princely states into the Union of India. Like a true statesman, he used powers of persuasion and tact to handle this problematic situation. In a few months, he was successful in reducing the number of princely states from 562 to 26 administrative units.

Patel was equally successful in resolving the problems related to partition, restoring law and order, and dealing with the rehabilitation of innumerable refugees. He reorganized and formed a new Indian Administrative Service, to give administrative stability to the new democracy.

After a prolonged illness, he passed away on 15 December 1950. He was posthumously conferred with a Bharat Ratna in 1991.

GOOD TO KNOW

- There is no official record of Vallabhbhai Patel's date of birth.
- Vallabhai Patel appeared on the cover page of the 24th January issue of *TIME* magazine in 1947.
- India's national police training academy is named after Vallabhbhai Patel and is called Sardar Vallabhbhai Patel National Police Academy.

QUIZ

1. In which of these cities is the Vallabhbhai Patel International Airport?
   a) Secunderabad
   b) Ahmedabad
   c) Hyderabad

Answer: Ahmedabad

2. In which year did Vallabbhai Patel receive the Bharat Ratna?
   a) 1947
   b) 1956
   c) 1991

Answer: 1991

3. In Richard Attenborough's *Gandhi* (1982), which actor played the role of Patel?
   a) Ben Kingsley
   b) Saeed Jaffrey
   c) Amrish Puri

Answer: Saeed Jaffrey

GLOSSARY

- Middle Temple: is one of the four Inns of Court in England. The other three are: Lincoln's Inn, Inner Temple and Gray's Inn. They hold exclusive rights of admission to the Bar. In order to practise as a barrister in England, a person must belong to one of these Inns.
- Leva-Patidar: is a community based in and around the cities of Surat, Navsari and Valsad districts of Gujarat.
- Pleader: is a person working to represent all the legal affairs for and on behalf of the State.

BUSINESS

AZIM HASHAM PREMJI

Azim Hasham Premji is a business entrepreneur who serves as the chairman of Wipro Limited, and is also one of the richest people in the world.

Premji was born on 24 July 1945 in Mumbai. His father M.H. Hasham Premji was the founder of Western Indian Vegetable Products Ltd. The company produced vanaspati, a ghee processed from vegetable oils.

Premji was on the verge of finishing his engineering degree at Stanford University, when his father passed away unexpectedly. Leaving his studies unfinished, he returned to India to take control of the family business. He immediately expanded and diversified the company by venturing into consumer products such as shoes, soaps, light bulbs and hydraulic cylinders.

The company was renamed Wipro in 1977. Two years later, when IBM made its exit due to government policies, Premji used the opportunity to diversify further by moving into the computer business. He established many successful international partnerships to help Wipro build computer hardware for sale in India. However, it was software development that the company found more beneficial.

Azim Premji is married to Yasmeen and they have two children, Tariq and Rishad. Rishad is presently working as Chief Strategy Officer in the IT branch of Wipro. Wipro's value became very high in the late 1990s, and he became one of the richest people in the world, a position he holds to this day.

Premji believes that education is the key to growth and in order to give form to this thought, he established the non-profit Azim Premji Foundation. The mission of the foundation is to improve the quality of elementary education in rural areas. One of the primary functions of the foundation is to provide computer-aided education and child-friendly content in regional languages to thousands of schools across India.

Premji donated US $2 billion to his foundation in 2010, and gave away US $2.3 billion worth of shares of Wipro to his foundation a few days after agreeing to sign Bill Gates and Warren Buffett's Giving Pledge.

Since 2006, Premji has been a director of the Central Board of Reserve Bank of India. He was honoured with the 'Lakshya Business Visionary' award by the National Institute of Industrial Engineering in Mumbai. He received the Padma Vibhushan and the 'Légion of d´honneur' in 2011.

GOOD TO KNOW

- Azim Premji completed his university degree after nearly 33 years through a distance-learning arrangement.
- Premji was the first Indian recipient of the Faraday Medal, awarded by the Institute of Physics.
- By the end of the first decade of the 21st century, the Azim Premji Foundation had provided computer-aided education to more than 16,000 schools.

QUIZ

1. In 1966, Azim Premji dropped out of which university to take over the reins of his family business?
   a) Oxford University
   b) Stanford University
   c) Harvard University

Answer: Stanford University

2. In November 2012, *Forbes* India honoured Azim Premji as 'Outstanding _____ of the Year'.
   a) Businessman
   b) Entrepreneur
   c) Philanthropist

Answer: Philanthropist

3. In 1947, Azim Premji's father was offered the post of Finance Minister by which country?
   a) Pakistan
   b) Bangladesh
   c) Nepal

Answer: Pakistan

GLOSSARY

- Entrepreneur: is a person who sets up a business or businesses, taking on financial risks in the hope of making a profit.
- 'Légion of d'honneur': It is a premier order of the French republic, created by Napoleon Bonaparte on 19 May 1802.

DHIRUBHAI AMBANI

Dhirubhai Ambani was a noted industrialist. He founded the Reliance Industries—the first privately owned Indian company in the *Global Fortune* 500 list.

Dhirubhai Ambani, was born on 6 July 2002 in the village of Chorwad in Saurashtra (Gujarat), to a village schoolteacher. In 1949, he went to the British colony of Aden (in Yemen) at the age of seventeen to join his brother. He started his career as a dispatch clerk at A. Besse & Co. A couple of years later, he was promoted to the level of manager at the company's oil-filling station.

In 1958, Ambani returned to Bombay and after recognizing the potential in yarn trading, he shifted to the business. He purchased land in Naroda, Gujarat, to set up the first Reliance textile mill in 1966, earning the sobriquet 'Prince of Polyester'. He eventually turned Reliance into a petrochemicals giant, despite uncertainty in the economy, strict government regulations and bureaucracy. He approached the banks for finance but they rejected his plea. He took the company public, and more than 58,000 investors from all over India subscribed to Reliance's IPO in 1977. Therefore, he can easily be regarded as one of the pioneers of the equity cult in India.

In the 1980s, the Patalanga plant was commissioned which marked the beginning of its strategic backward integration. In the beginning, the plant manufactured polyester filament yarn and polyester staple fibre. For manufacturing petrochemicals, he next set up the Reliance Hazira plant in 1991. Reliance had become the largest integrated producer of polyester in the world.

Dhirubhai had decided to set up a huge grassroots refinery as his next step towards his great plan for Reliance.

The Jamnagar Refinery was commissioned in 1999 and was believed to be the largest grassroots refinery in the world with an annual capacity of 27 million tons.

Dhirubhai envisioned an India, where every Indian, irrespective of caste, religion, and class, was able to afford a mobile phone. He wanted to lead a communication revolution, where his ultimate aim was to make a phone call which could be cheaper than a post card.

With this end in view, Reliance entered the telecommunications space in the 1990s. The sector was opened for private participation, ushering India into the digital age.

In 2002, Reliance made the largest oil and gas discovery in the KG-D6 block.

On 24 June 2002, Dhirubhai suffered a second major stroke. He passed away on 6 July 2002 in Mumbai.

GOOD TO KNOW

- Dhirubhai Ambani was credited with introducing the stock market to the average investor, and thousands of investors attended the Reliance annual general meetings, which were sometimes held in a football stadium.
- On his return to India, Dhirubhai Ambani started a company called 'Majin' to import polyester yarn and export spices.
- One of his favourite quotes were, 'Pursue your goals even in the face of difficulties, and convert adversities into opportunities.'
- Drirubhai Ambani was born Dhirajlal Hirachand Ambani.

QUIZ

1. Which of these films is based on the life of Dhirubhai Ambani?
   a) *Guru*
   b) *Josh*
   c) *Swades*

Answer: *Guru*

2. In 1998, which institution awarded Dhirubhai Ambani the Dean's Medal for setting an outstanding example of leadership?
   a) Massachusetts Institute of Technology
   b) Wharton Business School
   c) Harvard Business School

Answer: Wharton Business School

3. Fill in the blank to complete the Dhirubhai Ambani quote. 'Think big, think fast, think ahead. ______ are no one's monopoly.'
   a) Thoughts
   b) Actions
   c) Ideas

Answer: Ideas

GLOSSARY

- Petrochemicals: are a large group of chemicals derived from petroleum and natural gas, and used for a variety of chemical purposes.
- IPO: is the process by which a private company can go public by sale of its stocks to the public, to raise capital. It could be a new or an old company which decides to be listed on an exchange and hence, goes public.

GHANSHYAM DAS BIRLA

Ghanshyam Das Birla, also known as G.D. Birla, was a prominent businessman and member of the Birla Family.

Birla was born on 10 April 1894 in the village of Pilani, Jaipur.

Although he did not receive any formal education, G.D. Birla was a voracious reader and by reading books, newspapers, biographies and travelogues, he learnt a lot about history, economics and Sanskrit.

He came to Calcutta in 1910 and started trading in opium, silver and other commodities. After the formation of Birla Brothers in 1918, G.D. set up sugar and paper mills in the 1930s.

He then diversified into various other goods, ranging from textiles, synthetics, engineering, and capital goods. He was vocal about his support of industrialization. He felt that cooperation of labour and capital is essential for rapid industrialization and was strongly against strikes.

Birla felt that Indian labour lacked discipline and was slow to incorporate modern knowledge, which led to reduction in production. He promoted industrialization by advocating coordination of labour and capital, and was strongly against strikes. He funded a large number of public and educational institutions in the country, like the one in Pilani. The Birla Education Trust has been a boon towards the emancipation of women and the betterment of the Harijans.

Birla's political career started with his nomination to the Bengal Legislative Council. With his brothers, he ventured into print media by acquiring two newspapers in Calcutta. He was also influenced by the nationalist leader Madan Mohan Malaviya and later, Mahatma Gandhi.

Birla visited the UK in the 1930s and '40s many times, to interpret Gandhian philosophy. The 1940s and 1960s were difficult years for India because of the partition; yet the Birla Empire flourished and soon became one of the largest industrial groups in the country.

During the 1960s, Birla was considered to be an unofficial ambassador of India to financial institutions such as the IMF and the World Bank. He also contributed heavily in economic planning through the Bombay Plan initiative in the mid 1940s.

(The Bombay Plan was a plan for post-World War II industrialization of India, formulated by JRD Tata, G.D. Birla, Kasturbhai Lalbhai and Shri Ram, among others.)

Birla also took an active part in the affairs of the Indian National Congress. He went against the colonial domination of the Indian economy and was an industrial legend whose activities helped create a surrounding in which Indian enterprise could flourish.

Birla was honoured with the Padma Vibushan in 1957. He received the degree of Honorary Doctor of Laws from Banaras Hindu University in 1967. He died on 11 June 1983.

GOOD TO KNOW

- He rejected being knighted, by the British Crown, in 1932.
- The G.D. Birla Award for Scientific Research was instituted in 1991, with the objective of according recognition to high caliber scientific research undertaken by Indian scientists living and working in India.
- There is a memorial to Ghanshyam Das Birla in Golders Green Crematorium, Hoop Lane, London.

QUIZ

1. In which town would you come across the Birla Institute of Technology and Science?
   a) Aligarh
   b) Pilani
   c) Ajmer

Answer: Pilani

2. Which present-day Indian state is the birthplace of G.D. Birla?
   a) Punjab
   b) Gujarat
   c) Rajasthan

Answer: Rajasthan

3. In which year was the Padma Vibhushan awarded to G.D. Birla?
   a) 1956
   b) 1957
   c) 1958

Answer: 1957

GLOSSARY

- Capital goods: are goods that are used in producing other goods, rather than being bought by consumers.
- IMF: or the International Monetary Fund, is a specialized agency of the United Nations established in 1945. It aims to promote international trade and monetary cooperation and the stabilization of exchange rates.

JEHANGIR RATANJI DADABHOY TATA

Jehangir Ratanji Dadabhoy Tata, also known as J.R.D. Tata, was an industrialist who was the former chairman of Tata Sons. He is also recognized as the founder of civil aviation in India. He was the first Indian to hold a commercial pilot's license. He founded India's first national carrier, Tata Airlines in 1932, which was later renamed as Air India Limited in 1946.

J.R.D. Tata was born on 29 July 1904 in Paris, to Ratanji Dadabhoy Tata and his French wife, Suzzane Briere. His father was Jamshedji Tata's first cousin.

J.R.D. Tata was brought up and educated in France, Japan, England and India. While studying in England, being a French citizen, he was drafted to the French Army when their government passed a law that required all boys who had turned twenty to serve in the army. After his service, though he wished to study further at Cambridge University in London, his father summoned him back to India to join the family business.

In the mid-1920s, he joined the family business as an unpaid apprentice. After his father died, he became a board member of Tata Sons at the young age of 22. He gave up his French citizenship in 1929, and became a citizen of India.

After talks on a proposal that had reached the Tata headquarters about starting an airmail service connecting Karachi, Bombay and Ahmedabad, Tata Aviation Services was established in 1932. The very first flight, in a Puss Moth aircraft, took off from Karachi with J.R.D. as the pilot. In 1953, the airline was nationalized.

In 1938, J.R.D. Tata took over the reins of the company as Chairman from Nowroji Saklatvala even though he was the youngest member on the board of Tata Sons.

In the next five decades he guided the company in its expansion programme. They ventured into numerous fields, including chemicals, automobiles, engineering, hotels, consultancy services, information technology, consumer goods, consumer durables and industrial products.

J.R.D. Tata was vocal about issues of national interest. He had strong views on family planning and population control. His contribution in the field was acknowledged when the UN Population Award was conferred on him in 1992. His interest in the field of science was reflected in the significant part he played in the establishment of the Tata Institute of Fundamental Research of which he was the chairman of the Governing Council. He also served as Member of the Atomic Energy Commission.

J.R.D. Tata took numerous steps to improve the state of education in India, which he felt was one of the many hindrances in the growth of the country. He worked tirelessly as the chairman of J.N. Tata Endowment for the Higher Education of Indians and also the Homi Bhabha Fellowships Council. He also served as the chairman of Sir Dorabji Tata Trust, J.R.D. Tata Trust and Jamsetji Tata Trust.

J.R.D. Tata was the recipient of many national and international awards. Some of them are: the French Legion of Honour (Commander), Padma Vibhushan and the Order of Merit of the Federal Republic of Germany (Knight Commander's Cross). He was awarded the Bharat Ratna in 1992. He passed away on 29 November 1993 in Geneva, Switzerland.

GOOD TO KNOW

- When J.R.D. Tata took over the chairmanship of Tata Sons, the group had fourteen companies, and after fifty years under his leadership, there were nearly ninety-five enterprises which the Tatas had either started or had a controlling interest in.
- In 1982, J.R.D. Tata re-enacted his inaugural flight of 1932, in a fifty-year old De Havilland Leopard Moth to commemorate the 50th anniversary of Indian civil aviation.

QUIZ

1. What is the name of the biography of J.R.D. Tata written by R.M. Lala?
   a) *The Polyester Prince*
   b) *Beyond the Last Blue Mountain*
   c) *Imagining India*

   Answer: *Beyond the Last Blue Mountain*

2. Who succeeded J.R.D. Tata as the chairman of the Tata conglomerate?
   a) Naval Tata
   b) Cyrus Mistry
   c) Ratan Tata

   Answer: Ratan Tata

3. In 1948, J.R.D. Tata was made honourary Group Captain of the...
   a) Indian Army
   b) Indian Navy
   c) Indian Air Force

   Answer: Indian Air Force

GLOSSARY

- Apprentice: is a person who is learning a trade from a

skilled employer, having agreed to work for a fixed period.

- Information technology: is the technology involving the development, maintenance and use of computer systems, software and networks for the processing and distribution of data.

NAGAVARA RAMARAO NARAYANA MURTHY

N.R. Narayana Murthy is a software entrepreneur who co-founded Infosys Technologies Ltd.

Murthy was born on 20 August 1946 in Kolar, Karnataka. He graduated with a bachelor's degree in electrical engineering from the University of Mysore in 1967 and obtained a master's degree in technology from Indian Institute of Technology, Kanpur. Later, he joined the Indian Institute of Management, Ahmedabad, as their Chief Systems Programmer.

During the '70s Murthy helped design an operating system for handling air cargo at Charles de Gaulle Airport, while also working on other projects in Paris. He returned to India in the mid-1970's with the belief that the only way to banish poverty was to create more jobs, which was only possible if there were new companies.

Murthy worked with Patni Computer Systems in Pune for a short while, before launching Infosys in 1981 with six other software professionals.

Infosys grew slowly until the government's decision of economic liberalization and deregulation, in the early '90s, gave the technology and computer sector in India a considerable boost.

Murthy seized the opportunity to expand his business, negotiating deals with many business houses in other countries to provide them with systems integration, software development, consulting and product engineering services.

By 1999 Infosys had joined NASDAQ, becoming the first Indian registered company to be listed on an American stock exchange.

In the following years, Murthy was recognized and listed by several business magazines as an influential entrepreneur. In 2000, the magazine *Asiaweek* included Murthy in its Power 50 list, which consisted of the most powerful people in Asia.

He was named as one of the 'Stars of Asia' by the magazine *BusinessWeek* for three consecutive years, 1998-2000. He was listed as one among the twenty-five most influential global executives by *TIME* magazine and CNN in 2001. *Fortune* magazine named him as the Asian Businessman of the Year in 2003. He was also voted World Entrepreneur of the Year 2003 by Ernst and Young.

In April 2004, Murthy announced that Infosys had posted a total revenue of US $1.06 billion, which was 33 per cent more than the previous year's revenue. This achievement was remarkable as the company had flourished during a time when the information technology sector was facing a crisis globally.

By the time Murthy retired from Infosys in 2006, the company's revenue was US $3 billion. He had served as Chief Executive Officer (CEO) from 1981 to 2002, Chairman and Chief Mentor from 1981 to 2011, and Chairman Emeritus from August 2011 to May 2013.

On 1 June 2013, Narayana Murthy was appointed as an additional director and the executive chairman of the board of Infosys for a period of five years.

He was named one of Asia's Businessmen of the Year (2003) by *Fortune* magazine.

Murthy is a Trustee of the Infosys Science Foundation, a non-profit trust, set up by Infosys and other board members to spread the culture of science mainly through the Infosys Prize, a yearly award given across six scientific categories.

He also serves on the boards of the Ford Foundation, Rhodes Trust, the Indian School of Business and the UN Foundation.

Muthy has around twenty-five honorary doctorates from universities in India and abroad.

He is married to Sudha Murthy and the couple have a son named Rohan Murthy and a daughter named Akshata Murthy.

GOOD TO KNOW

- Narayana Murthy was awarded the 'Legion d'honneur' by the Government of France in 2008.
- *A Better India: A Better World*, is a collection of thirty-eight of Narayana Murthy's speeches made across the world.
- In 1981, Narayana Murthy started Infosys with a small sum of ₹10,000 which he had borrowed from his wife.

QUIZ

1. In 1976, Murthy founded a company that lasted a year and a half. What was its name?
   a) Softronics
   b) Patni
   c) Satyam

Answer: Softronics

2. A type of fund established by Narayana Murthy shares its name with which type of boat?
   a) Kayak
   b) Catamaran
   c) Canoe

Answer: Catamaran

3. In 2003, Narayana Murthy was appointed as Advisor on

Information Technology and Public Administration Policies by the prime minister of which country?

a) Malaysia
b) Japan
c) Thailand

Answer: Thailand

GLOSSARY

- NASDAQ: or the National Association of Securities Dealers Automated Quotations, is an American stock market that handles electronic securities trading around the world.

SCIENCE

ARYABHATA

Aryabhata, or Aryabhata I, was one of the earliest known mathematician-astronomers, whose theories, principles, and ideas contributed immensely to the advancement of science in ancient India.

Though Aryabhata was born around AD 476, there are many theories regarding his place of birth. While one school of thought believes he was born in Pataliputra in Magadha (modern-day Patna in the state of Bihar), others are of the opinion that he was born in Kerala and lived in Magadha during the reign of the Guptas. He is known to have composed at least two important works: *Aryabhatiya* and *Aryabhata Siddhanta* or *Arya Siddhanta*. The latter is not available any more.

Aryabhatiya, which is an elaborate work on mathematics and astronomical studies, is written in verse couplets. It has four distinct sections, namely: *Gitikapada, Ganitapada, Kalakriyapada* and *Golapada.*

Gitikapada dwells upon an alphabetical system of expressing numbers and other related topics. The topics in this section include varga (squares), ghana (cubes), vargamula (square roots), ghanamula (cube roots), area of a triangle and volume of a prism, area of a circle and volume of a sphere, circumference of a circle, bahu (the base of a right-angled triangle), and koti (the upright side of the right-angled triangle), and karna (hypotenuse of the right-angled triangle).

Ganitapada deals mainly with mathematics. Some of the

topics include arithmetic progression, geometrical progression, simple, simultaneous and quadratic equations, and geometrical figures.

Kalakriyapada, with twenty-five stanzas, actually means the estimation of time. It deals with topics like the division of time, definitions of solar year, lunar month, civil day, and sidereal day.

Golapada is the longest section of the work and it is for this section that he is most famous. The word gola means sphere. This section has fifty stanzas and explains the different ways of representing planetary motions.

In *Aryabhata Siddhanta,* he described several astronomical instruments and apparatuses, including gnomon (shanku-yantra), a shadow instrument (chhaya-yantra), a cylindrical stick (yasti-yantra), an umbrella-shaped device (chhatra-yantra), and water clocks of at least two types: bow-shaped and cylindrical.

Aryabhata is also remembered for defining terms like prime vertical, meridian, equator, horizon, hour circle, and parallax.

Aryabhata believed in the geocentric model of the universe. He was the first Indian astronomer to explain that the apparent daily motions of the immovable stars were caused by the rotation of the earth. He explained this theory through the popular example of a person in a moving boat to whom a stationary object appears to move in the opposite direction. He also calculated that the circumference of the earth as being 39968.05 km, which is very close to the modern-day scientific calculation of 40072.66 km. He also argued that the shadows of the moon and the earth are a result of the eclipses and not the mythical Rahu-Ketu.

Aryabhata introduced two systems of estimating time: the audayika system (from sunrise to the next sunrise) and the ardharaatrika system (from midnight to the next midnight).

He also calculated the time for one sidereal rotation of the earth as 23 hours 56 minutes 4.1 seconds.

Aryabhata invented a system of expressing numbers on the decimal place-value model by using the Sanskrit alphabet. Sanskrit alphabet is based on the scientific phonetic principal of 'one sound for one symbol'. He used this phonetic alphabet for representing large numbers with a few letters. This enabled him to give astronomical constants and numerical data in a condensed form to make the process of memorization easy.

The first indigenously built Indian satellite was named Aryabhata in his honour.

GOOD TO KNOW

- One of Aryabhata's most important contributions is his approximation of the value of 'pi', or π.
- The *Aryabhatiya* also reached the Arabs and it was translated under the title *Zij al-arjabhar.* It greatly influenced the development of Arabian mathematics.
- Some of Aryabhata's rules for the calculation of square and cube roots by the arithmetical method are still in use.

QUIZ

1. To distinguish him from another mathematician of the same name, what was Aryabhata referred to as?
   a) The Elder
   b) The Younger
   c) The Wiser

Answer: The Elder

2. In which year was Aryabhata, India's first satellite, launched?
   a) 1951
   b) 1975
   c) 2000

Answer: 1975

3. According to Aryabhata, reflected sunlight was responsible

for the brightness of which of these bodies?

a) Comets
b) Stars
c) Moon

Answer: Moon

GLOSSARY

- Geocentric model: is a model or theory of the structure of the solar system or the universe in which Earth is assumed to be at the centre.
- pi: is the numerical value of the ratio of the circumference of a circle to its diameter (approximately 3.14159), represented by the sixteenth letter of the Greek alphabet (Π, π).
- Gnomon: is the projecting piece on a sundial that shows the time by the position of its shadow.

AVUL PAKIR JAINULABDEEN ABDUL KALAM

Dr Avul Pakir Jainulabdeen Abdul Kalam is a scientist and former president of India who played a pioneering role in the development of the missile and nuclear weapons programmes.

Abdul Kalam was born on 15 October 1931 in Rameswaram, Tamil Nadu. He attended Schwartz High School in Ramanathpuram. He went on to study Physics at St Joseph's College in Tiruchirappalli and aerospace engineering at Madras Institute of Technology (MIT). He, then, worked as a trainee with Hindustan Aeronautics Limited (HAL), Bangalore, and later joined the Indian Committee for Space Research (INCOSPAR).

Before becoming the eleventh president of the country in 2002, Abdul Kalam's career as a scientist can be divided into four distinct phases.

Between 1963 and 1982, Abdul Kalam worked with the Indian Space Research Organisation (ISRO) in various roles. He initiated the Fibre Reinforced Plastics (FRP) activities, working with the aerodynamics and design group. Thereafter, he joined the satellite launching vehicle team at Thumba. Here, he became the Project Director of the Mission for Satellite Launch Vehicle-3 (SLV-3). He played an important role in developing the satellite launch vehicle technology.

In 1982, Abdul Kalam joined the Defence Research and Development Organisation (DRDO). As Director, he focused on the Integrated Guided Missile Development Programme (IGMDP). During this period, the country developed strategic missiles, including Nag (an anti-tank guided missile), Prithvi (a surface-to-surface battlefield missile), Trishul (a quick-reaction surface-to-air missile), and Agni (an intermediate range ballistic missile).

Abdul Kalam became a member of the mission working towards making India a nuclear weapon state, jointly undertaken by DRDO and Department of Atomic Energy (DAE) along with the support of the armed forces. As Chairman of the Technology Information, Forecasting and Assessment Council (TIFAC), he was closely associated with the creation of Technology Vision 2020 and the India Millennium Missions (IMM 2020).

In November 1999, Dr Kalam became Principal Scientific Adviser to the Government of India.

Abdul Kalam joined Anna University in Chennai as Professor of Technology and Societal Transformation. He planned to meet 1,00,000 students in different parts of the country before August 2003 as part of his mission to make India a developed country.

Abdul Kalam has received honorary doctorates from nearly thirty universities and institutions for his contribution to the field of science. He has also been awarded the Padma Bhushan (1981), Padma Vibhushan (1990), and the Bharat Ratna (1997).

Abdul Kalam has authored several books, including *Wings of Fire, Ignited Minds, Mission India, Inspiring Thoughts,* and *India 2020: A Vision for the New Millennium.*

GOOD TO KNOW

- In his new book *My Journey: Transforming Dreams into Actions,* A.P.J. Abdul Kalam mentions that becoming a fighter pilot had been his 'dearest dream'.

- Abdul Kalam is the first scientist to occupy the Rashtrapati Bhavan.
- In 1998, Abdul Kalam, along with cardiologist Dr Soma Raju, developed a low-cost coronary stent known as 'Kalam-Raju Stent'.

QUIZ

1. In the year 2012, what did Dr Abdul Kalam and Dr Soma Raju design for health care in rural areas?
   a) Tablet computer
   b) Mobile phone
   c) ECG machine

   Answer: Tablet computer

2. Who did Dr Abdul Kalam succeed as president of India?
   a) R. Venkataraman
   b) Pratibha Patil
   c) K.R. Narayanan

   Answer: K.R. Narayanan

3. *India* ________*: A Vision for the New Millennium*. Fill in the blank with a number to complete the name of a book by APJ Abdul Kalam.
   a) 2020
   b) 2030
   c) 2045

   Answers: 2020

GLOSSARY

- Bharat Ratna: is the highest civilian award of the country. It was instituted in the year 1954.
- Launch Vehicles: are used to transport and put satellites or spacecrafts into space.

BHASKARA II

Bhaskara II, also known as Bhaskaracharya, was an important mathematician of the twelfth century. He is considered as the first person to write a book on the methodical use of the decimal number system.

Bhaskara II was born in AD 1114 near modern-day Bijapur in Karnataka, into a family of scholars. He learnt mathematics from his father Mahesvara, who was also an astrologer. He also served as the chief of the astronomical observatory in Ujjain, which was an important mathematical centre of ancient India.

Bhaskara II has written many books of which, *Siddhanta Shiromani* written in AD 1150, is the most famous. It has four parts: *Lilavati, Bijaganita, Grahaganita,* and *Goladhaya. Lilavati* deals with arithmetic, elementary algebra, and geometry. *Bijaganita* is an elaborate work on advanced algebra. *Grahaganita* is on astronomy and *Goladhaya* deals with the study of spherical trigonometry.

Bhaskara II is mainly associated with the discovery of the principles of differential calculus and their use in solving astronomical problems and computations. He also spoke about the modern convention of signs (minus by minus makes plus, minus by plus makes minus).

Just as in modern algebra, Bhaskara II used letters to represent unknown quantities, and reduced quadratic equations to a single type and solved them. Working on regular polygons up to those having three hundred and eighty-four sides, he obtained a good approximate value of pi (π) which was 3.141666.

He stated that if a finite number is divided by zero, the result would be infinity.

In his lifetime, he is believed to have defined several astronomical quantities accurately. His calculation of the time taken by the earth to orbit the sun, 365.2588 days, is very close to the modern accepted calculation of 365.2563 days.

His book on astronomy *Karanakuthuhala* is relevant even today, as it is used in maintaining precision in calendars.

Bhaskara II also practised astrology, and he is said to have named his first work after his daughter, Lilavati, who was also a well-known mathematician.

GOOD TO KNOW

- Bhaskara II explained that the square of zero is zero and the square root of zero is also zero.
- Bhaskara II, launched as part of the Satellite-for-Earth-Observations (SEO) program, was also the second experimental remote sensing satellite of India, quite similar to Bhaskara I.

QUIZ

1. In which of his works did Bhaskara II use birds, animals and anecdotes from epics to illustrate mathematical examples and problems?
   a) *Ganitabhyas*
   b) *Aryabhatiya*
   c) *Lilavati*

Answer: ***Lilavati***

2. What was the purpose of the Chakrawal, or the cyclical method introduced by Bhaskara II?
   a) To find the value of pi

   b) To solve algebraic equations
   c) To derive the squares of numbers

Answer: To solve algebraic equations

3. According to a popular saying, whosoever is well-versed with *Lilavati* can tell the exact number of what?
   a) The temperature
   b) Leaves on a tree
   c) Seeds in an orange

Answer: Leaves on a tree

GLOSSARY

- Infinity: is a number which is greater than any assignable quantity or countable number (symbol ∞).
- Observatory: is a place or a building that has a powerful telescope or other scientific equipment that is used for the study and observation of natural phenomena like stars, planets, weather etc.

CHANDRASEKHARA VENKATA RAMAN

Sir Chandrasekhara Venkata Raman, or C.V. Raman, was a physicist who received the Nobel Prize for Physics in 1930 for the discovery of the phenomenon that is now called 'Raman scattering', and is the result of the Raman Effect.

Raman was born on 7 November 1888 in Tiruchirapalli, Tamil Nadu to Parvathi Ammal and R. Chandrasekhara Iyer, who was a lecturer of mathematics and physics. He was known to be excellent in academics. He passed his matriculation examination at the age of eleven and his First Arts (FA) Examination (equivalent to today's Intermediate) at the age of thirteen. In 1903, he joined Madras Presidency College, from where he passed both his BA (1904) and MA (1907) examinations. He topped the Financial Civil Service (FCS) examination, and joined the Indian Finance Department as Assistant Accountant General, Calcutta. In his spare time he carried on his research, which mainly focused on areas of vibration and acoustic, in the laboratory of the Indian Association for the Cultivation of Science. He studied a number of stringed and percussion instruments. Though he was transferred to Rangoon in 1909 and Nagpur in 1910, he continued his research work by converting his home into a laboratory.

In 1917, Raman gave up his high-paying government job and became the Palit Professor of Physics at the University of Calcutta. At the university, Raman was allowed to continue his work in the laboratories of the Indian Association for the

Cultivation of Science. In fact, the Association became the research arm of the University. After the death of Amrit Lal Sircar in 1919, he was elected as Honorary Secretary of the Association and held the post till 1933, when he left Calcutta. He made immense contributions to research in the areas of vibration, sound, musical instruments, ultrasonic, diffraction, photo electricity, colloidal particles, X-ray diffraction, magnetron, dielectrics, among others. During this period, he was recognized for his work on the scattering of light.

In 1924, Raman became Fellow of the Royal Society of London. He announced his discovery of what is now known as the 'Raman Effect', a few years later, at the joint meeting of the South Indian Science Association and the Science Club of Central College, Bangalore.

He received many accolades for his discovery, including his knighthood in 1929 and the Nobel Prize for Physics in 1930. He became the first Asian to receive the Nobel Prize for Physics. In 1934, he became the director of the newly established Indian Institute of Science, Bangalore. He also established the Raman Research Institute in Bangalore and served as its Director. He was awarded the Bharat Ratna in 1954.

Raman passed away on 21 November 1970 in Bangalore.

GOOD TO KNOW

- Raman also gave radio talks, some of which were compiled in a book titled *The New Physics: Talks on Aspects of Sciences*.
- The erstwhile Soviet Union honoured Raman with the International Lenin Prize in 1957.
- In India, 28 February is celebrated as National Science Day to commemorate the discovery of the Raman Effect.

QUIZ

1. Which of these was founded by C.V. Raman?
   a) *Indian Journal of Physics*
   b) *Scientific Indian*
   c) *Science and Us*

Answer: *Indian Journal of Physics*

2. Who along with C.V. Raman and C. Rajagopalachari received the Bharat Ratna in 1954?
   a) Jawaharlal Nehru
   b) S. Radhakrishnan
   c) B.R. Ambedkar

Answer: S. Radhakrishnan

3. C.V. Raman contributed an article on the theory of _______ to the 8th Volume of the *Handbuch der Physik*. Fill in the blank with one of the options.
   a) Magnets
   b) Nuclear fission
   c) Musical instruments

Answer: Musical instruments

GLOSSARY

- Raman Effect: is the change in the wavelength of light that occurs when a light beam is deflected by molecules. It was discovered by C.V. Raman.
- Palit Professor: Taraknath Palit's generosity led to the creation of two professorships (Physics and Chemistry) in the University of Calcutta.
- Acoustic: is a term relating to sound or the sense of hearing.

HOMI JEHANGIR BHABHA

Homi Jehangir Bhabha is a scientist who is often regarded as the chief architect of India's nuclear programme. He contributed immensely to the field of atomic energy. He played an important role in the establishment of two great research institutions: Tata Institute of Fundamental Research (TIFR) and Atomic Energy Establishment, which was renamed as Bhabha Atomic Research Centre (BARC) after his death. He derived a process now known as 'Bhabha scattering'.

Bhabha was born on 30 October 1909 in Mumbai, into a well-to-do Parsee family. He attended Cathedral & John Connon School in Bombay. He went to Elphinstone College and subsequently the Royal Institute of Science, both in Bombay. In 1927, he joined the Gonvile and Caius College in Cambridge with an intention to pursue mechanical engineering. His interaction with mathematics tutor, Paul Dirac ignited his interest in mathematics and theoretical physics. He earned his engineering degree in 1930 and PhD. in 1934.

In 1937, Bhabha and W. Heitler, a German physicist, explained the cosmic ray shower formation. Cosmic rays are fast moving, extremely small particles coming from outer space. When these particles enter the earth's atmosphere, they collide with the atoms of air and create a shower of electrons. His discovery of the presence of nuclear particles (which he called mesons) in these showers was used to establish Einstein's theory of relativity.

Bhabha returned to India in 1939 and stayed on due to

World War II. In 1940, he joined the Indian Institute of Science, Bangalore, as Reader in Physics. In 1941, he was elected Fellow of the Royal Society, London, in recognition of his contributions to the field of cosmic rays, elementary particles, and quantum mechanics.

While working at the Indian Institute of Science, Bhabha recognised the need for an institute devoted to fundamental research and wrote to J.R.D. Tata requesting him for funds. This led to the establishment of Tata Institute of Fundamental Research (TIFR) in Mumbai, in 1945. He remained its Director, until his death in 1966. In 1954, he established Atomic Energy Establishment in Trombay, near Bombay, when he realized that technology development for the atomic energy programme could no longer be carried out within TIFR. The same year Department of Atomic Energy (DAE) was also established.

In 1948, Bhabha was appointed Chairman of the International Atomic Energy Commission. He helped build nuclear reactors such as Apsara, Cirus and Zerlina at Trombay. His great work earned him international acclaim. He served as President of the first United Nations Conference on the Peaceful Uses of Atomic Energy, which was held in Geneva in 1955. He was President of the International Union of Pure and Applied Physics from 1960 to 1963. The Atomic Energy Establishment at Trombay was renamed as Bhabha Atomic Research Centre in 1967.

Bhabha was also a musician,painter, and writer. Some of his paintings have also found a place in the British Art Galleries. He had received many awards, including the Padma Bhushan, an Honorary Fellow of the American Academy of Arts and Sciences, and Foreign Associate of the National Academy of Sciences in the United States.

Bhabha died on 24 January 1966, when his plane crashed near the Mont Blanc peak in the Alps. He was on his way to

Vienna to participate in a meeting of the Scientific Advisory Committee of the International Atomic Energy Agency.

GOOD TO KNOW

- Bhabha's family wanted him to become an engineer, so that he could join the Tata Iron and Steel Company at Jamshedpur.
- Bhabha's grandfather, also named Homi Jehangir Bhabha, was Inspector General of Education in the State of Mysore.
- Bhabha travelled in Europe and worked with Nobel Laureates Wolfgang Pauli (physicist and recipient of the 1945 Nobel Prize for Physics) in Zurich and Enrico Fermi (scientist and one of the chief architects of the nuclear age) in Rome.

QUIZ

1. With which of these physicists did Bhabha work in Copenhagen?
   a) Albert Einstein
   b) Niels Bohr
   c) Marie Curie

Answer: Niels Bohr

2. The name of which of these was suggested by Bhabha?
   a) Proton
   b) Electron
   c) Meson

Answer: Meson

3. When Bhabha joined the Indian Institute of Science at Bangalore, who was its Director?
   a) Vikram Sarabhai
   b) S Ramanujan
   c) C.V. Raman

Answer: C.V. Raman

GLOSSARY

- Meson: is a subatomic particle which has mass in between that of an electron and a proton.
- Paul Dirac: was an English theoretical physicist who described the properties of the electron, including its spin. He was awarded the Nobel Prize for Physics in 1933.
- Atomic Energy: also called nuclear energy, is the energy released during nuclear fission or fusion, especially when used to generate electricity.

JAGADISH CHANDRA BOSE

Jagadish Chandra Bose was a physicist, biologist, botanist, and inventor. He is often regarded as the founder of biophysics as a discipline in India. He is famous for his work in the field of physiology and physics. He made significant contributions to the field of wireless telegraphy and microwave optics technology. He invented several sensitive instruments to demonstrate that plant tissues respond to external stimuli like heat, electric shock, chemicals, and drugs; the most famous one being the Crescograph, which is an instrument for measuring growth in plants. He established the Bose Institute in Calcutta, which focused on the study of plants.

Jagadish Chandra Bose was born on 30 November 1858 in Mymensingh (now in Bangladesh). His father Bhagaban Chandra Bose was a Deputy Magistrate. He attended St Xavier's School and College at Kolkata, and was excellent in academics. After receiving his bachelor's degree from Calcutta University in 1879, he went to the London University to study medicine, but gave it up because he was unwell. The same year, he went to Cambridge to study Natural Science at Christ's College. He returned to India in 1885 and became a lecturer at Presidency College, Kolkata. He was the first Indian to be appointed Professor of Physics in Presidency College.

In the early 1890s, J.C. Bose decided to devote himself to pure research. He devised and developed a new type of radiator for generating radio waves. He also built a highly sensitive

'Coherer', or radio receiver, for receiving radio waves. This coherer was far better than the ones used in Europe.

J.C. Bose was not in favour of patenting any of his inventions. He pursued science for the benefit of mankind and not for money. On one occasion, he filed a patent application for his galena receiver. Though it was granted, he refused to accept his rights and let it lapse.

J.C. Bose was knighted by the British Government in 1916. He was elected Fellow of the Royal Society of London in 1928. He died on 23 November 1937 in Giridih (now in Jharkhand).

His books regarding these research works include *Response in the Living and Non-Living* (1902) and *The Nervous Mechanism of Plants* (1926).

GOOD TO KNOW

- J.C. Bose's appointment to the Presidency College was opposed by Sir Alfred Croft, then Director of Public Instruction of Bengal and Mr Charles R. Tawney, Principal of the Presidency College, but he got the appointment because of the intervention of Lord Ripon, the then Viceroy of India.
- J.C. Bose visited and photographed many historic places in the 1890s. Some of his experiences and literary works were published in a volume called *Abyakta*.
- After his return from Cambridge, J.C. Bose got a lecturer's job at Presidency College, Kolkata on half the salary that his English colleagues received. Though he accepted the job, he refused to draw his salary and compelled the college to give in to his demands. He was paid full salary from the date he joined the college.

QUIZ

1. In which present-day country was J.C. Bose born?
    a) Pakistan
    b) Nepal
    c) Bangladesh

Answer: Bangladesh

2. Near which capital city is the Acharya Jagadish Chandra Bose Indian Botanic Garden located?
    a) Bhubaneshwar
    b) Kolkata
    c) Agartala

Answer: Kolkata

3. Which of these titles is normally associated with J.C. Bose?
    a) Giani
    b) Gurudev
    c) Acharya

Answer: Acharya

GLOSSARY

- Physiology: is a branch of biology dealing with the normal functions of living organisms.
- Radio waves: are waves used for long-distance communication.
- Patent: is a government authority or licence, granting legal right to make or sell an invention for a definite period.

KALPANA CHAWLA

Kalpana Chawla was an Indian-American astronaut, and the first Indian-born woman in space.

Kalpana Chawla was born on 1 July 1961 in Karnal, Haryana. She studied at the Tagore School, and in 1978 became the first girl to attend the aeronautical engineering course at Punjab Engineering College. She successfully graduated in 1982. She then migrated to the United States of America, where she completed her MSc in aerospace engineering from the University of Texas in 1984. This was followed by a PhD in the same field from the University of Colorado in 1988.

After completing her PhD, Kalpana was offered a position as Research Scientist in the Computational Fluid Dynamics Group at NASA Ames Research Centre in Sunnyvale, California. She was granted American citizenship in 1991.

In 1993, she joined Overset Methods Inc. as Vice President and Research Scientist. After she was selected by NASA, Kalpana reported to the Johnson Space Center in March 1995 as an astronaut candidate in the 15th Group of Astronauts.

In 1996, Kalpana became a part of the six member crew of STS-87, which was the twenty-fourth flight of the space shuttle Columbia. She served as the Mission Specialist 1 and backup Flight Engineer for ascent. During the flight, the members of the mission completed most of the tasks that were assigned to them.

Kalpana was assigned the job of deploying the satellite from the payload bay, with the help of the remote manipulator arm.

But because there were numerous problems, the satellite failed to be activated before it was deployed and eventually had to be brought back from the orbit. The STS-87 mission ended with the safe landing of Columbia on 5 December 1997.

In 1998, she became the crew representative for shuttle and station Flight Crew Equipment(FCE), and later served in the Astronaut Offices Crew Systems and Habitability section. She flew on STS-87 (1997) and STS-107 (2003), logging 30 days, 14 hours and 54 minutes in space.

Kalpana died on 1 February 2003, when STS-107 Columbia disintegrated shortly before its scheduled landing.

For her contributions to the field of science, Kalpana Chawla was posthumously awarded the Congressional Space Medal of Honor, the NASA Space Flight Medal, and the NASA Distinguished Service Medal.

The Colorado University-Boulder Alumni Association honoured her through the Kalpana Chawla Outstanding Recent Graduate Award.

GOOD TO KNOW

- Kalpana Chawla once told her only brother, Girish Chawla, that if she had to die, she hoped it would be in a crash.
- Kalpana Chawla often said that she was motivated by the flying feats of the famous industrialist J.R.D. Tata.
- After Kalpana Chawla received her BSc, she was offered a job with the Hindustan Aeronautics Limited in Bangalore. She refused the offer and became a lecturer at Punjab Engineering College.

QUIZ

1. Which of these is a biography of Kalpana Chawla, written by her husband Jean-Pierre Harrison?

a) *The Edge of Time*
b) *Ignited Minds*
c) *Fly Forever*

Answer: *The Edge of Time*

2. In 2004, which of these states instituted a new award, named after Kalpana Chawla, for young women scientists, to recognize their research achievements?
a) Tamil Nadu
b) Karnataka
c) Odisha

Answer: Karnataka

3. In which city is the '74th Street Kalpana Chawla Way' located?
a) Karnal
b) New York City
c) San Francisco

Answer: New York City

GLOSSARY

- NASA: the acronym stands for National Aeronautics and Space Administration.
- STS-87 Columbia: was the fourth U.S. Microgravity Payload flight. STS-87 made 252 orbits of the earth, travelling 6.5 million miles in 376 hours and 34 minutes.
- STS-107 Columbia: was a dedicated science and research mission. The crew aboard this flight successfully conducted nearly eighty experiments.

SATYENDRA NATH BOSE

Satyendra Nath Bose was a prominent physicist, who collaborated with Albert Einstein and developed the Bose-Einstein statistics.

Satyendranath Bose was born on 1 January 1894 in Calcutta. He attended the Hindu High School, and then joined Presidency College. He stood first in both his BSc and MSc examinations in 1913 and 1915 respectively. After completing his MSc, he joined the University of Calcutta in 1916, along with Meghnad Saha, as a lecturer.

Bose worked with Meghnad Saha on a joint research paper titled 'On the influence of the finite volume of molecules on the equation of state'. It was published in the internationally renowned *Philosophical Magazine* in 1918. It is often regarded as his first important contribution to the field of theoretical physics. In 1921, after Dacca University (or Dhaka University, now in Bangladesh) was founded, he joined the department of Physics. While teaching at the university, he developed a satisfactory derivation of Plank's radiation law based on the Albert Einstein's photon concept, as he was not fully satisfied with the existing one. After his paper was rejected by the *Philosophical Magazine*, he sent it to Albert Einstein requesting him to get it published in *Zeitschrift fūr Physic*. Einstein acknowledged the receipt of his letter and translated the work into German. It was published in the August 1924 issue of *Zeitschrift fūr Physic* under the heading 'Plancksgesetz Lichtquantenhypothese' (Planck's Law and Light Quantum Hypothesis). Einstein used Bose's method to formulate the theory of the ideal quantum gas, and predicted the phenomenon of Bose-Einstein condensation.

From 1924 to 1926, Bose stayed in Europe to familiarise himself with the latest developments in his field. He returned to Dhaka in 1926 and was appointed as Professor and Head of the Department of Physics at Dacca University the very next year.

There, he began his research on crystal structures, a field that had not been explored in the country so far. He designed his own experimental equipment and gadgets like X-ray diffraction cameras for rotation and powder photography. Though he was foremost a physicist, he was fascinated by chemistry.

In 1945, Bose returned to the University of Calcutta as the Khaira Professor of Physics. During 1953-54, he published five important papers on the Unified Field Theory. In 1956, he was appointed Vice Chancellor of Visva-Bharati University, Shantiniketan, an institution founded by Rabindranath Tagore.

In 1958 Bose was elected Fellow of the Royal Society of London. In 1959 he was appointed as National Professor, a post he held till his death

Bose strongly felt that science should be presented to the common man in his own simplified language. Therefore, he wrote most of his work in Bengali. He helped establish the Bangiya Bijnan Parishad (Science Association of Bengal), a registered society with the sole objective of promoting and popularizing science through the local language.

Bose loved music and fine arts, and played esraj and flute. He died on 4 February 1974 in Calcutta.

GOOD TO KNOW

- While in school, Bose was given 110 marks out of 100 in mathematics because he had solved a few problems using more than one method.

- Bose wrote an obituary for Albert Einstein, which was published in the journal, *Science and Culture*.
- Bose was associated with various fields of study such as chemistry, mineralogy, philosophy, archaeology, biology, soil science, the fine arts, literature and languages.

QUIZ

1. Which subatomic particle has been named after Satyendra Nath Bose?
   a) Photon
   b) Boson
   c) Electron

Answer: Boson

2. Paul Langevin, a scientist, wanted Bose to pursue the possibility of working in whose laboratory?
   a) Enrico Fermi
   b) Alexander Graham Bell
   c) Marie Curie

Answer: Marie Curie

3. Which of these writers dedicated his book *Visva Parichay* (*Introduction to the World of Science*) to Satyendra Nath Bose?
   a) Amartya Sen
   b) Rabindranath Tagore
   c) Meghnad Saha

Answer: Rabindranath Tagore

GLOSSARY

- Ionosphere: in the Earth's atmosphere, is a layer which contains a high concentration of ions and free electrons.
- Max Planck: was a theoretical physicist who worked on the quantum theory. He received the Nobel Prize for Physics in 1918.

- Khaira professor: is a professorship at Calcutta University, created out of an endowment given by Guru Prasanna Sinha, Raja of Khaira.

SRINIVASA RAMANUJAN

Srinivasa Ramanujan was a mathematician who contributed greatly to the analytical theory of numbers, elliptic functions, continued fractions, and infinite series.

Srinivasa Ramanujan was born on 22 December 1887 in Erode (about 400 kilometres from Chennai, Tamil Nadu), but was raised in Kumbakonam. He passed his primary school examination in 1897 standing first in the district, and then joined the Town Higher Secondary School. At the age of fifteen, he obtained a copy of George Shoobridge Carr's Synopsis of Elementary Results in Pure and Applied Mathematics. This collection of some fifty hundred equations in algebra, calculus, trigonometry, and analytical geometry influenced him greatly. In fact, he kept three notebooks between 1903 and 1914, in which he not only verified the results, but also developed his own theorems and ideas. In 1904, he secured a scholarship to attend the Government College in Kumbakonam but lost it the following year when he failed in his FA examination in his pursuit of mathematics. He attended another college but failed again.

Though Ramanujan lived in poverty, he continued working on his favourite subject. After his marriage in 1909, he was supported by a government official, Ramachandra Rao, who was impressed by his passion for mathematics. He later obtained a clerical post with the Madras Port Trust and worked there for about a year.

In 1911, Ramanujan published the first of his papers in the

Journal of the Indian Mathematical Society. This paper made him popular in Madras. In 1913, he began corresponding with the British mathematician, Godfrey H. Hardy, who helped him obtain a special scholarship from the University of Madras and a grant from Trinity College, Cambridge. He went to England in 1914 and worked with Godfrey H. Hardy on mathematical problems.

In March 1916, Ramanujan received his bachelor's degree for his work on 'Highly Composite Numbers' which was published as a paper in the *Journal of the London Mathematical Society.*

In 1918, he became one of the youngest Fellow of the Royal Society of London. He was elected for his investigation in Elliptic Functions and the Theory of Numbers. In 1918, he also became the first Indian to be elected as Fellow of Trinity College, Cambridge.

Ramanujan was suffering from tuberculosis and passed away on 26 April 1920 in Chennai. He was only thirty-two years old.

GOOD TO KNOW

- Ramanujan's birth anniversary, 22 December, is celebrated as National Mathematics Day in India.
- Once, Godfrey took a taxicab to meet Ramanujan, and commented that the license plate number of the taxi was '1729, a rather dull number'. Ramanujan promptly remarked that it was the smallest number to be expressed in two different ways as the sum of two cubes: $1^3 + 12^3 = 1729$ and $9^3 + 10^3 = 1729$.
- In 1993, Shri P.K. Srinivasan founded the Ramanujan Museum in the Avvai Academy in Chennai.

QUIZ

1. Which year was declared as National Mathematics Year in India?

a) 2000
b) 2005
c) 2012

Answer: 2012

2. Bertrand Arthur William Russel wrote in a letter that G.H. Hardy and J.E. Littlewood had discovered a second _____ in Madras. Fill in the blank.
   a) Einstein
   b) Curie
   c) Newton

Answer: Newton

3. Which of these is also known as the Ramanujan Number?
   a) 1729
   b) 1730
   c) 1731

Answer: 1729

GLOSSARY

- Number Theory: is a branch of mathematics dealing with the properties and relationships of numbers, especially the positive integers
- Trigonometry: is a branch of mathematics dealing with the relationship between the angles and sides of triangles.
- Royal Society: is the oldest national scientific society in the world, and the leading national organization for the promotion of scientific research in Britain.

VIKRAM SARABHAI

Vikram Sarabhai is lovingly called the 'Father of Indian Space Program'. He contributed significantly to the field of space research and also worked in the fields of textiles, pharmaceuticals, nuclear power, electronics and many others.

Vikram Sarabhai was born on 12 August 1919 in Ahmedabad, Gujarat. As he was born into a family of successful industrialists, the Sarabhai home in Ahmedabad was frequented by many great minds of his day. This had great impact on his young mind, and shaped his future considerably.

At an early age, Sarabhai attended the family-run school, which was started by his mother. After completing his Intermediate Science Examination from Gujarat College in Ahmedabad he went to England. There, he attended St John's College under the University of Cambridge. He obtained his Tripos in Natural Sciences in 1940.

When the Second World War started, he returned to India and joined the Indian Institute of Sciences in Bangalore, under the supervision of Sir C.V. Raman. His area of research was cosmic rays, and he published his first research paper titled 'Time Distribution in Cosmic Rays'. After the war, he completed his PhD on cosmic rays from Cambridge. He returned to the newly independent India and persuaded charitable trusts to contribute in the formation of the Physical Research Laboratory in Ahmedabad.

In the next few years, Sarabhai set up various institutions

of which the most notable was the Indian Space Research Organisation (ISRO). Around that time, the erstwhile USSR had launched Sputnik 1, the first artificial Earth satellite. He convinced the government of India that the fledgling nation needed a dedicated organisation for space science. Dr Homi J. Bhabha, who was the secretary of Department of Atomic Energy at that time, both influenced and supported Sarabhai in setting up this project. In his capacity as the head of ISRO, he single-handedly set up the Space Centre at Thumba near Thiruvananthapuram from where India's first space launch a two-stage rocket, imported from the USA was made in 1963.

After Dr Bhabha passed away in 1966, the union government urged Sarabhai to take up the position of Chairman of the Atomic Energy Commission, which he accepted. In the field of nuclear research, he continued Bhabha's work, and played an important part in the establishment and development of India's nuclear power plants. He was also the driving force behind the development of nuclear technology for defence purposes in India.

Sarabhai was a multi-faceted personality who was responsible for the establishment of a number of institutes. Along with his wife, Mrinalini, he founded the Darpana Academy of Performing Arts in Ahmedabad. He played an important role in the establishment of the Indian Institute of Management in Ahmedabad. He set up the Variable Energy Cyclotron Centre in Calcutta, the Faster Breeder Test Reactor in Kalpakkam, the Electronics Corporation of India Limited in Hyderabad, the Uranium Corporation of India in Bihar, and many others.

Sarabhai died on 30 December 1971 in Kovalam, Thiruvananthapuram, Kerala.

GOOD TO KNOW

- Vikram Sarabhai was awarded the Padma Vibhushan posthumously in 1972.
- In the mid-1970s, the International Astronomical Union at Sydney decided to call the Moon Crater BESSEL in the Sea of Serenity as the Sarabhai Crater.

QUIZ

1. With which art form would you associate his daughter Mallika Sarabhai?
   a) Dancing
   b) Singing
   c) Painting

Answer: Dancing

2. What was Vikram Sarabhai's middle name?
   a) Ambalal
   b) Laxmikant
   c) Haridas

Answer: Ambalal

3. Aryabhata I was launched in 1975 from a cosmodrome belonging to...
   a) USA
   b) USSR
   c) Germany

Answer: USSR

GLOSSARY

- Cosmic Ray: is a highly energetic atomic nucleus or other particle travelling through space at a speed close to that of light.
- Sputnik: is a series of artificial satellites of the Soviet Union.

ART AND CULTURE

AMIR KHUSRAU

Hazrat Amir Khusrau was a thirteenth century scholar, poet, and Sufi musician.

Khusrau was born in AD 1253 in Patiali, in present-day Uttar Pradesh. His ancestors trace their lineage to Hazaras from Transoxiana which corresponds approximately with modern-day Uzbekistan, Tajikistan, Southern Kyrgystan and Southwest Kazakhstan. His father worked for Iltutmish, a ruler of the Slave dynasty.

Khusrau, all through his life, enjoyed the patronage of the Muslim rulers of Delhi, especially Sultan Ghiyas-ud-Din Balban and his son, Muhammad Khan of Multan. As a child he learnt theology, Persian and the Quran. He started composing poetry in 1262, when he was only nine years old.

Khusrau became popular when he acted as the private tutor to Prince Muhammad, the eldest son of Sultan Balban, a ruler of the Slave dyansty. Later, after the fall of the Slave dynasty, he became the court-poet to Alauddin Khalji. His prose work *Khaza-in-al-futuh* or *The Treasure Chambers of the Victories* contains an interesting account of the first few years of the reign of Alauddin Khalji. Alauddin Khalji took him along in his famous Chittor expedition, which he undertook in 1303 to capture the queen of Chittor, Rani Padmini. Later, as the Poet Laureate in Ghiyasuddin Tughluq's court, he received a sum of one thousand tankas(currency) per mensem(month).

As a composer, Khusrau used the local dialects of Khadi

Boli, Braj Bhasha and Hindawi, as well as the court languages like Persian, Arbaic and Turkish. Notable among his works are the five 'divans' compiled at different periods in his life, and his 'Khamsah', a group of five long pieces in the style of the 'Khamseh' (of the legendary Persian poet Nezami). Amir Khusrau's works revolve around general themes of Islamic literature. Apart from this, the historical poems 'Nuh Sipihr' and 'tughluq-namah' also earned him much fame.

Khusrau had a great command over languages and was always careful about his audience. For the masses he would select the local dialects like Hindawi or Braj Bhasha, but for the court he would select Persian. He believed in the equality of all religions and cultures.

Khusrau was influenced by the famous Sufi saint, Hazrat Nizamuddin Auliya. He contributed immensely to the evolution of various cultural elements of the time including Sufi music and Qawwali. The synthesis of Hindu and Muslim elements led to the term 'Ganga-Jamuni Tehzeeb' which denotes the mutually participatory co-existence of Hindus and Muslims in northern India. He is considered as the founder of this culture.

Khusrau passed away in AD 1325.

GOOD TO KNOW

- Today, the majority of the Sama Mehfils that are held, begin with Qaul and end with Rang, which are two of Amir Khusrau's famous compositions.
- Khusrau is said to have created a new system of musicology called 'Indraprastha Mata' or 'Chaturdandi Sampradaya'.
- Khusrau brought into circulation the two specific musical genres of 'tarana' and 'Kaul', which complemented the prevalent array of musical forms.

QUIZ

1. Who asked Amir Khusrau to write poetry in Hindi also, to popularise the language among Muslims?
   a) Iltutmish
   b) Ghiyasuddin Balban
   c) Hazrat Nizamuddin Auliya

Answer: Hazrat Nizamuddin Auliya

2. Who appointed Amir Khusrau the librarian of the Imperial library in Delhi?
   a) Razia Sultan
   b) Alauddin khalji
   c) Jalal-ud-din Khalji

Answer: Jajal-ud-din Khalji

3. *Khaliq-e-bari,* compiled by Amir Khusrau, is the oldest known printed...
   a) atlas
   b) dictionary
   c) encyclopedia

Answer: Dictionary

GLOSSARY

- 'Nuh Sipihr' or 'The Nine Heavens': is a historical poem which gives an account of the reign of Qutb-ud-din Aibak.
- *Tughluq-namah* or *The Book of Tughluq:* is a historical account of the reign of ghiyas-ud-din Tughlaq.
- Rubaab: is a string Instrument.
- Braj Bhasha: is a dialect of Hindi spoken around Mathura in U.P.

AMJAD ALI KHAN

Amjad Ali Khan is a classical musician who plays the sarod.

Amjad was born on 9 October 1945 in Gwalior, to Ustad Hafiz Ali Khan, a sarod player and court musician to the Maharaja of Gwalior. His forefathers were members of the Senia Bangash Gharana. Introduced to music by his father when he was only five years of age, he gave his first sarod recital when he was six.

When he was thirteen, he gave an outstanding performance at a Sangeet Sammelan in Calcutta. From then on, he was invited to perform in various important concerts across India and abroad. He has participated in numerous festivals including the Suresh Sangeet Sammelan, Nishit Sangeet Sammelan, Sadarang, Tansen and Haridas.

He has performed regularly at the Carnegie Hall, Royal Albert Hall, Royal Festival Hall, Kennedy Center, House of Commons, Victoria Hall in Geneva, Chicago Symphony Center, Palais des Beaux-Arts de Lille, Mozart Hall in Frankfurt, St James Palace and the Opera House in Australia.

He has collaborated with various musicians across the world. He composed a piece for the Hong Kong Philharmonic Orchestra conducted by Yoshikazu Fukumora titled Tribute to Hong Kong. He has been a visiting professor at the Universities of Yorkshire, Washington, Stony Brook, North Eastern and New Mexico.

He has won numerous awards and honours. He is the

recipient of the Padma Awards: Padma Shri (1975), Padma Bhushan (1991) and Padma Vibhushan (2001). He was awarded the Gandhi UNESCO Medal in 1995 for his composition titled Bapukauns. He received the Sangeet Natak Akademi Award for 1989 and the Sangeet Natak Akademi Fellowship for 2011.

In 2003, he received 'Commander of the Order of Arts and letters' by the French Government and the Fukuoka Cultural grand prize in Japan, the following year. In 2009, he was nominated for a Grammy Award in the Best Traditional World Music Album category.

Although he belonged to the traditional gharana of his father, he introduced his own innovations and improvisations in his work which made his style unique. He is equally proficient in playing Thumri, Bhatiali and other forms of folk music.

His sons Amaan Ali Khan and Ayaan Ali Khan have authored a book on their father titled *Abba-God's Greatest Gift to Us*.

GOOD TO KNOW

- In 1999, he inaugurated the World Festival of Sacred Music with His Holiness the Dalai Lama.
- He has received the Honorary Citizenship to the States of Texas (1997), Massachusetts (1984), Tennessee (1997) and the city of Atlanta, Georgia (2002).
- A documentary on him called *Strings for Freedom* won the Bengal Film Journalist Association Award and was also screened at the Ankara Film Festival in 1996.

QUIZ

1. In whose honour did Amjad Ali Khan create Raga Kamalashree?
   a) Indira Gandhi

b) Rajiv Gandhi
c) Kamala Nehru

Answer: Rajiv Gandhi

2. Amjad Ali Khan's wife Subhalakshmi Khan is an exponent of which Indian classical dance?
   a) Bharatnatyam
   b) Odissi
   c) Kathak

Answer: Bharatnatyam

3. In 1984, which state in the United States, declared April 20 as Amjad Ali Khan Day?
   a) California
   b) Massachusetts
   c) Texas

Answer: Massachusetts

GLOSSARY

- Gharana: in Hindustani Classical music, can be compared to a style or school of dance or music (vocal/ instrumental). These gharanas are generally named after the city, district or state that the founder lived in. Each gharana has a style of its own in terms of presentation, technique and repertoire.

BEGUM AKHTAR

Begum Akhtar, often referred to as the 'Queen of Thumri and Ghazal', was a singer. She was one of the most influential figures in Hindustani light, classical music of the 20th century. With her characteristic rich and deep voice with nasal intonations, she is believed to have contributed greatly in raising ghazals to the level of a classical form of Indian music.

Begum Akhtari Faizabadi, also known as Begum Akhtar was born on 7 October 1914 in Baradarwaja, Faizabad, to a musician mother, who was also her first trainer. Later, she was trained by Abdul Wahid Khan of Kirana gharana, Ramzan Khan of Lucknow, Barkhat Ali of Patiala and Ata Mohammad of Patiala.

She went to Calcutta with her mother in the early 1930s. In Calcutta, she had the opportunity of meeting Jaddanbai who provided her a chance to sing on the radio. Soon, the number of radio assignments increased and she was invited by the Megaphone Record Company to record an album.

Her first ghazal '*Woh asser-e-dam-e*' became a super hit, and within a short period of time she released a number of albums in different genres.

In 1934, she sang for Hindi films which were made in Kolkata at that time and also gave her first public performance.

Around that time she received and accepted an invitation from the Nizam of Hyderabad.

Later, she moved to Mumbai to try her luck as a playback singer in Hindi cinema industry.

In 1943, Begum Akhtar joined Raza Ali Khan's Rampur durbar, as a court singer. There, she met Barrister Ishtiaq Ahmed Abbasi and married him leading to a five-year hiatus from music. In 1948, she made her comeback with a recital from the Lucknow radio station and quickly made her name as the trendsetter of ghazals and thumris.

Begum Akhtar was mesmerised by the poetry of Ghalib, Dadh, Faiz Ahmed Faiz, Jigar Moradabadi, Shakeel Badayuni and Kaifi Azmi. She even patronized new and upcoming poets from time to time. She was revered across the country and not restricted to the Hindi or Urdu speakers. Her popularity was such that excerpts from one of her concerts appeared in a Satyajit Ray film.

She taught for a short while at the Bhatkhande College of Music in Lucknow.

Later stalwarts of classical music like Shanti Hiranand, Rita Ganguly, Vasundhara Pandit and Rekha Surya were her students at the institution.

Music was such an important part of her life that despite her ill health and doctor's advice she gave one last concert in Ahmedabad in late October of 1974, and passed away shortly after that.

GOOD TO KNOW

- Begum Akhtar performed in public for the first time when she was only eleven years old.
- In her gramophone records, at the end of each song, she announced her name as Akhtari Bai Faizabadi.
- She did playback singing for many films including *Roti, Naseeb ka Chakkar, Nala Damayanthi* and *Dana Paani.*

QUIZ

1. In which year was Begum Akhtar awarded the Padma Shri?
   a) 1968
   b) 1970
   c) 1973

   Answer: 1968

2. Who wrote the book *The Story of my Ammi* based on Begum Akhtar?
   a) Rita Ganguly
   b) Shanti Hiranand
   c) S Kalidas

   Answer: Shanti Hiranand

3. Which famous musician also made his debut along with Begum Akhtar at her first concert when she was eleven years old?
   a) Bismillah Khan
   b) Zakir Hussain
   c) Amjad Ali Khan

   Answer: Bismillah Khan

GLOSSARY

- Thumri: is a genre of semi-classical Indian music.
- Dadra: is a semi classical form of music.

HARIPRASAD CHAURASIA

Pandit Hariprasad Chaurasia is a flautist, who is revered globally for his mastery over the bansuri, a simple bamboo flute.

Chaurasia was born on 1 July 1938 in Allahabad. He did not belong to a family of musicians; his father was a professional wrestler, and wanted him to take up the sport.

Chaurasia took vocal lessons in Hindustani classical music from the noted vocalist Pandit Raja Ram of Varanasi, but kept it hidden from his father.

Inspired by one of Pandit Bholanath Prasanna's flute performances, Chaurasia became his disciple and underwent eight years of arduous training until 1958. Later, he became a regular staff artiste of All India Radio in Cuttack, Odisha, where he performed and composed.

In 1960, he was transferred to All India Radio, Mumbai. Though this move opened the doors to the film industry, he continued to perform at concerts. He also learnt to play the surbahar under the guidance of Annapurna Devi, daughter of the late Alauddin Khan of Maihar Gharana. Around this time he left AIR to concentrate on a career solely centered on music.

Once he gained repute as a flautist, he travelled around the world catering to audiences exposed to different kinds of musical tastes and tradition. He also started earning recognition from his seniors and peers in the world of music like Yehudi Menuhin, Jean-Pierre Rampal, among others.

He then went on to collaborate with the santoor player

Pandit Shiv Kumar Sharma and directed music for Hindi films. The duo gave the Indian audience some unforgettable music in films like *Silsila*, *Lamhe*, *Chandni*, *Faasle*, *Parampara*, *Sahibaan* and *Darr*.

Though a traditionalist, Chaurasia was not averse to experimenting with his style and technique. This paved way for endless possibilities with the bansuri. Like his contemporary Pandit Ravi Shankar, he collaborated with several artistes from the west including jazz musicians John McLaughlin, Jan Garbrek, and Ken Lauber. He released an album titled *Eternity* (1985) which mingled the North Indian classical form of music with western elements to create a fusion which became quite popular. In Indian forms he experimented with various types of music with great aplomb. His jugalbandis with Indian stalwarts like Pandit Shiv Kumar Sharma, Pandit Jasraj, Dr Balmurali Krishna and Ustad Zakir Hussain were hugely popular.

Chaurasia was awarded the Padma Bhushan and the Padma Vibhushan in 1992 and 2000 respectively. He also holds the position of Artistic Director of Indian Music Department at Rotterdam, the Netherlands.

GOOD TO KNOW

- *Bansuri Guru*, directed by Rajeev Chaurasia is a documentary that depicts the illustrious life of Pandit Hariprasad Chaurasia.
- In their album, *Call of the Valley*, Shivkumar Sharma, Brijbhushan Kabra and Hariprasad Chaurasia used their instruments to tell the story of a day in the life of a shepherd in Kashmir, using ragas associated with various times of the day.

QUIZ

1. What is the title of Hariprasad Chaurasia's biography written by Shri Surjit Singh?
   a) *The Fall of a Sparrow*
   b) *Woodwinds of Change*
   c) *Wisdom Song*

Answer: ***Woodwinds of Change***

2. Which of these films saw Shiv Kumar Sharma and Hariprasad Chaurasia debut as the composer duo known as Shiv-Hari?
   a) *Vijay*
   b) *Lamhe*
   c) *Silsila*

Answer: ***Silsila***

3. Who conferred the title Officer in the Order of Orange-Nassau (officier in de Orde van Oranje-Nassau) on Hariprasad Chaurasia?
   a) Queen Elizabeth
   b) The Dutch Royal Family
   c) Emperor Hirohito of Japan

Answer: The Dutch Royal Family

GLOSSARY

- Flautist: is a flute player.
- Surbahar: is a plucked string instrument used in Hindustani classical music. It is related to the sitar, but is larger in size and has a lower tone.
- Jugalbandi: is a performance in Indian classical music that features a duet of two solo musicians.

JAMINI ROY

Jamini Roy was one of the most significant and influential modern artists of India. He rejected the traditional practices of his time, and instead adopted themes and styles from Bengali folk art which marked a new epoch in Modern Indian Art. His depiction of rural life and women figures are popular with collectors around the world.

Roy was born on 15 April 1887 in Beliatore, West Bengal. In 1903, he joined the Government School of Art in Calcutta, where he was trained in the art of drawing, based largely on the academic traditions of Europe. This helped him become a good portraitist. In 1916, he graduated from Art School and made a career out of regular commissions that made him work mostly in the Impressionist style.

He was deeply inspired by the folk art and craft traditions of village life and thus changed his style. The Kalighat Pat painting style popularized by local painters outside the Kalighat temple in Kolkata, was a major source of inspiration to him. The creator in him always looked around for inspiration regardless of place and genre. He started representing village scenes and people, images he was familiar with and close to because of his upbringing in a rural set up.

Very soon his images reflected sweeping, calligraphic lines in them and his themes where drawn from everyday life like a child and mother, figures of women at work, singing bauls, etc. He also started painting on themes based on tales from the

Ramayana and *Mahabharata* and from folk literature. He drew inspiration from the life of Jesus Christ, and portrayed them in a simple manner.

Though Roy liked painting images from the countryside, his technique was very different from those of the folk artist. His method was meticulous and he made detailed drawings of his images. He simplified the forms, used bold, flat colours and drew his themes from local folk paintings. He replaced expensive canvas and oil paint with less expensive material, and used the medium of the folk artists. Jamini Roy is believed to have used only seven colours in his paintings: Indian red, yellow ochre, cadmium green, vermillion, grey, blue and white. These were mostly earthy or mineral colours.

Roy died on 24 April 1972.

GOOD TO KNOW

- The famous *Cat* series, was influenced by Roy's own apparitions of the cat family from his childhood days in the dense forests of Beletore in Bankura.
- Nissim Ezekiel, in one of his poems, refers to Jamini Roy as, 'He started with a different style,/ He travelled, so he found his roots./ His rage became a quiet smile/ Prolific in its proper fruits.'
- Roy abandoned the traditional canvas, and made his own painting surfaces out of cloth and wood, using earth and vegetable colours.

QUIZ

1. In which district in West Bengal is the Jamini Roy College located?
   a) Hooghly
   b) Bankura

c) Murshidabad

Answer: Bankura

2. What was the name of the technique of painting which was evolved by Jamini Roy?
   a) Flat Technique
   b) Square Technique
   c) Round Technique

Answer: Flat Technique

3. In which year was Jamini Roy awarded the Padma Bhushan?
   a) 1945
   b) 1955
   c) 1965

Answer: 1955

GLOSSARY

- Kalighat paintings: are popular folk paintings sold outside the Kalighat Temple in Calcutta.
- Impressionism: is a style or movement in painting which chiefly developed in France. The works in this style are characterized by an accurate and objective recording of the world around us, especially in terms of the shifting effect of light and colour.

MADURAI SHANMUKHAVADIVU SUBBULAKSHMI

M.S. Subbulakshmi, also known as M.S., was one of the leading exponents of Carnatic music. She was the first Indian musician to receive the Ramon Magsaysay Award in 1971. She was also the first musician to receive the Bharat Ratna in 1998.

Subbulakshmi was born as Kunjamma on 16 September 1916 in Madurai, Tamil Nadu. Her mother was the celebrated veena maestro Srimati Shanmukhavadivu. Subbulakshmi was exposed to the world of music right from her birth. She gave vocal support to her mother's recitals from a very young age.

Madurai Srinivasa Iyengar was her first teacher but she could not learn much as her guru passed away. In the absence of a teacher, she practiced hard and tried to learn as much as she could from her mother. Later, she was groomed by Musiri Subrahmanya Iyer and Semmangudi Srinivasa Iyer. Her zeal enabled her to give brilliant vocal recitals from the early age of sixteen. She recorded her first album in 1926.

In 1938, Subbulakshmi made her debut as an actor in the film *Sevasadanam,* which revolved around the theme of women's liberation. In 1940, she married Thyagaran Sadasivam, who became her mentor and guided her musical career. In 1941, she played the male role of Narada in the film *Savitri*, to raise money for her husband's nationalist Tamil magazine titled *Kalki.* In 1945, she portrayed the Rajasthani saint-poetess, Meera, in the film of the same name. It earned her national acclaim and was remade in Hindi in 1947.

Subbulakshmi has sung the compositions of the Carnatic music trinity Tyagaraja, Muthuswamy Dikshitar and Shyama Shastri. She also sang bhajans and slokas in different languages.

Her rendition of the bhajan 'Vaishnava Janato' is said to have moved Mahatma Gandhi to tears. The Meera bhajan, 'Hari Thuma Haro', was recorded by All India Radio before Gandhiji's birthday in 1947. On October 2, Gandhiji heard it during his evening prayer meeting

Subbulakshmi was the first woman to receive Chennai Music Academy's Sangita Kalanidhi award. She was honoured with the Padma Bhushan (1954), Padma Vibhushan (1975) and Kaalidas Sanman (1988), among others.

In 1982, the India Festival in London was inaugurated by her. She introduced Carnatic music to the western world at the 1963 Edinburgh Festival, and since then has performed in many places around the world. In 1966 she gave a recital of Indian songs in the General Assembly Hall, as part of the United Nations Day (24 October) celebrations.

Subbulakshmi was conferred the degree of Doctor of Letters by many universities. She donated large sums of money to different charitable organizations. Social and political stalwarts like Gandhiji, Jawaharlal Nehru and Chakravarti Rajagopalachari were her ardent listeners. Jawaharlal Nehru once said, 'Who am I, a mere Prime Minister, before the Queen of Song?'

M.S. Subbulakshmi passed away on 11 December 2004 in Chennai.

GOOD TO KNOW

- Tirupati Urban Development Authority (TUDA) installed a bronze statue of M.S. Subbulakshmi at the Poornakumbham circle in the temple town.

- Subbulakshmi's most unique contribution is her series of recordings of purely spiritual verses and chants of the Venkatesa Suprabhatam, Bhajagovindam of Adi Sankara, and Vishnu Sahasranamam.
- The royalty from Subbulakshmi's Venkatesa Suprabhatam goes to the Veda Patasala run by the Tirupati Tirumala Devasthanam.

QUIZ

1. A shade of which colour of Kancheepuram saris have been named after MS Subbulakshmi?
   a) Red
   b) Blue
   c) Green

   Answer: Blue

2. In which year was the Bharat Ratna awarded to M.S. Subbulakshmi?
   a) 1996
   b) 1997
   c) 1998

   Answer: 1998

3. All India Radio played which song recorded by Subbulakshmi after Mahatma Gandhi's assassination?
   a) Vaishnava janato
   b) Hari Thuma Haro
   c) Thumaka chalato Ramachandra

   Answer: Hari Thuma Haro

GLOSSARY

- Bhajan: a devotional song that comes from the Sanskrit word 'bhaj' meaning 'to honour' or 'adore'.
- Sloka: is a couplet of Sanskrit verse.

- Carnatic music: is a system of music commonly associated with the southern part of the Indian subcontinent.

MAQBOOL FIDA HUSAIN

Maqbool Fida Husain, also known as M.F. Husain, was a painter and film-maker.

Husain was born on 17 September 1915 in Pandharpur, Maharashtra. He was two years old when his mother passed away. His father remarried, and they moved to Indore, where he eventually completed his schooling.

Husain moved to Bombay in 1935 and joined Sir J.J. School of Art. Like many aspiring artists, he started his career by painting film posters. After a decade's struggle, his original works began to gain attention.

Husain got his break in 1947 when The Bombay Art Society arranged for his first exhibition. He was also a part of the Bombay Progressive Artists' Group that had S.H. Raza and F.N. Souza as its members. The Bombay Art Bazaar of 1950 provided him a platform by arranging a one-man show. Around this time, he established his identity by his choice of themes which were diverse in nature and, more often than not, came in a series.

Husain's first international show was held in Zurich in 1952. His paintings soon gained popularity, and attracted prices similar to that of his contemporaries. Suddenly, owning a 'Husain' had become a status symbol. Some of his influential works from this period are: *Man* (1951), *Vishwamitra* (1973) and *Passage Through Human Space* (year), a series of forty-five watercolour paintings that he completed in the mid-1970s.

Around the 1960s, Husain broadened his creative base and

used the medium of film-making to express his views. His first film, *Through the Eyes of a Painter,* made in 1967, earned him a prestigious award at the International Film Festival in Berlin—the Golden Bear for short films. In due course, he made two more films, one titled *Gaja Gamini*, with Madhuri Dixit in the leading role, whom he admired and described as his muse. In fact, when Husain did a series of paintings inspired by Madhuri, he signed them as 'Fida' which is the Urdu word for devoted. The other film was titled *Meenaxi: A Tale of Three Cities*. Critics commented that it was somewhat a semi-autobiographical film by him.

By the 1990s Husain's work became the highest selling Indian art in the international market earning him millions of dollars. In fact around 2010-11, three of his paintings were auctioned for ₹2.32 crore.

The Government of India honoured him with the Padma Shri (1955), the Padma Bhushan (1973) and the Padma Vibhushan (1991). He was also nominated as member of the Rajya Sabha in the 1980s.

The last years of Husain's life were marred by controversies. Right-wing Hindu groups accused him of being malicious in depicting Hindu deities. Many of his exhibitions were vandalised, and his paintings were banned. Having faced a series of lawsuits and death threats, a hurt Husian left India. He went on a self-imposed exile, and lived in London, Dubai and Doha. The Museum of Islamic Art in Doha, Qatar, included ninety-nine of his specially commissioned paintings in its collection, when it opened in 2008. He accepted Qatar's offer of citizenship in 2010.

M.F. Husain passed away on 9 June 2011 in London.

GOOD TO KNOW

- Husain's refusal to wear footwear became his signature trademark, and he was known as the 'Bare Foot Painter'.
- Husain was a special invitee along with Pablo Picasso at the Sao Paulo Biennial in 1971.
- In one of his interviews, he said, 'I don't have a studio anywhere. I am like a folk painter, paint and move ahead.'

QUIZ

1. In 2010, Husain obtained the citizenship of...
   a) Qatar
   b) Yemen
   c) United Kingdom

   Answer: Qatar

2. What is the name of Husain Museum of Art and Cinema in Hyderabad?
   a) Cinema Ghar
   b) Chitrakar Ghar
   c) Kalakar Ghar

   Answer: Cinema Ghar

3. Who played the female lead in *Meenaxi: A Tale of Three Cities*?
   a) Tabu
   b) Kajol
   c) Sridevi

   Answer: Tabu

GLOSSARY

- Golden Bear: is the highest prize for any film that is shown in the Berlin International Film Festival.
- Auction: is a public sale in which goods or property are sold to the highest bidder.

RAJA RAVI VARMA

Raja Ravi Varma, a 19th century painter, is considered as one of the greatest artists of India. He contributed greatly to the growth of both painting and printing in the country.

He is known to be the first Indian painter to adapt European realist style of painting (that focused on perspective and composition) to various Indian themes, using oil paints and canvas as his media. He made significant contributions by introducing iconography and lithographs in the Indian art scene.

Ravi Varma was born on 29 April 1848 in Kilimanoor, modern-day Kerala. As a child, he showed great interest in drawing. Raja Raja Varma, his uncle, noticed his talent and gave him elementary lessons in painting,

Ravi Varma was taken to the palace of the Maharajah of Travancore, to learn from the court artists. The great court artist Rama Swamy Naidu taught him to paint with watercolours. He then studied oil painting under Theodore Jensen, a British painter, who was invited by the maharajah in 1863 to paint a few portraits; thus introducing him to European realist techniques.

In 1866, by virtue of his position he married the maharajah's younger sister and became an important member of the royal household.

Under the patronage of the royal households of Mysore and Travancore, he flourished in painting mythological themes. His portraits and landscapes inspired by Hindu mythology were noted for the use of bright colours. Gradually, he became very popular with royalty. Among the works that stood out from the rest was the composition of Shakuntala writing a letter and the non-mythological *The Miser*, *Lady with the Mirror*, *Yasodha* and *Krishna* are also critically acclaimed. Even in the 19th century, he commanded sums over thousands of rupees for his life size paintings. In fact, a private collection that he had done for the Maharajah of Baroda, which was a series of 14 paintings, fetched him ₹50,000.

At this juncture, his friend the Dewan of Baroda, Sir Madhav Rao's idea caught his attention and he set up an oleographic printing press in Bombay, named Ravi Varma Oleographic and Chromolithographic Printing Workshop brackets, which enabled him to reproduce his own paintings in greater numbers and sell them to the masses.

Ravi Varma's active years coincided with various movements across the world which enriched and modified art in all forms. It fostered a change in artistic expressions and ushered in a new perspective of viewing themes. In his case, he adapted western technique to portray solely Indian themes and landscapes. He became a popular artist by making oleograph copies of his own works and sold more copies than any other artist from his time.

By 1894, Ravi Varma had become so important that he looked after the affairs of the state as the guardian of the young Maharaja of Travancore. He passed away on 2 October 1906 in Tiruvananthapuram.

GOOD TO KNOW

- Raja Ravi Varma is perhaps responsible for single-handedly giving modern form and colour to Hindu Gods and Goddesses. He painted them all in vivid colours, with an European tinge in his brush.
- Raja Ravi Varma is said to have signed his paintings in

three types of signature—R.V., Ravi Varma and Ravi Varma with the 'V' underlined.

- At Chennai, Raja Ravi Varma's paintings, which are considered as National Treasures, have been placed in a gallery with fibre optic lighting in order to avoid the deterioration due to heat and radiation.

QUIZ

1. In which present-day state was Raja Ravi Varma born?
   a) Kerala
   b) Tamil Nadu
   c) Kranataka

   Answer: Kerala

2. In 1873, Ravi Varma won the Governor's Gold medal for which of these paintings?
   a) *Jatayu Vadha*
   b) *Nair Lady at Toilet*
   c) *Shakuntala*

   Answer: *Nair Lady at Toilet*

3. In 1940, what title was conferred on Ravi Varma by the British?
   a) King of Painting
   b) Master Painter
   c) Kaiser-e-Hind

   Answer: Kaiser-e-Hind

GLOSSARY

- Lithography: The process of printing from a flat surface treated so as to repel the ink except where it is required for printing.
- Oleograph: A print textured to resemble an oil painting.

RASIPURAM KRISHNASWAMY IYER LAXMAN

Rasipuram Krishnaswamy Iyer Laxman or R.K. Laxman, is a cartoonist who is best-known as the creator of the comic strip *You Said It.* He is R.K. Narayan's younger brother.

Laxman was born on 24 October 1921 in Mysore. The youngest among his siblings, he started drawing at an early age, and spent hours sketching the activity around him.

While studying at Maharaja's College in Mysore, Laxman illustrated the stories written by R.K. Narayan in *The Hindu* newspaper. He was influenced by the British cartoonist, Sir David Low, whose cartoons also appeared in *The Hindu.*

Laxman graduated with a degree in philosophy, economics and politics; a mix of subjects that would lay the basis for many of his cartoons that were to come.

Laxman began his career as a self-employed political cartoonist in Mysore, but hoped to work in Delhi, to capture the political action. In 1946, he joined *The Free Press Journal* in Bombay with Bal Thackeray, who was a cartoonist before founding the Shiv Sena. In 1947 he shifted to *The Times of India,* where he would work for over fifty years. There, he created *You Said It*, a satirical strip that portrayed the numerous problems faced by average Indians through the point-of-view of a character called the 'Common Man'. Forever in the same dhoti and checked coat, the Common Man was a small figure with caterpillar eyebrows, dishevelled hair and a toothbrush moustache.

Laxman published many short-stories, essays, and travel articles, some of which were compiled in *The Distorted Mirror* in 2003. He also wrote the novels *The Hotel Riviera* in 1988 and *The Messenger* in 1993, the short-story collection *Servants of India* in 2000, and an autobiography, *The Tunnel of Time* in 1998. Additionally, many collections of Laxman's cartoons have also been published.

Laxman was honoured with the Ramon Magsaysay Award for Journalism in 1984. He was also awarded the Padma Vibhushan in 2005.

GOOD TO KNOW

- The Common Man featured on a stamp brought out to commemorate the 150th anniversary of the *Times of India*.
- When Laxman sent a few of his cartoons to the Dean of Bombay's J.J. School of Art, asking for admission, the Dean wrote back, 'I see no talent whatsoever. Please continue your studies.'
- There is a chair named after R.K. Laxman at Symbiosis International University. It is called the R.K. Laxman Chair for research and studies in media and communication, and focuses on thought leadership, guiding research and policy formation in media and communication.

QUIZ

1. In which city can you find the statue of the Common Man?
   a) Lucknow
   b) Hyderabad
   c) Pune

Answer: Pune

2. What is the name of R.K. Laxman's autobiography?
   a) *The English Teacher*

b) *The Tunnel of Time*
c) *The God of Small Things*

Answer: *The Tunnel of Time*

3. Fill in the blank to complete the quote by R.K. Laxman, 'They are the most intelligent creatures. I like nothing better than watching a ________'
   a) parliament of owls
   b) murder of crows
   c) gaggle of geese

Answer: murder of crows

GLOSSARY

- Philosophy: is the study of the fundamental nature of knowledge, reality and existence, especially when considered as an academic discipline.
- Comic strip: is a sequence of drawings in boxes that tell an amusing story, typically printed in a newspaper or magazine.

RAVI SHANKAR

Pandit Ravi Shankar was a sitar player, who was instrumental in introducing Indian classical music to the west.

Ravi Shankar was born as Robindro Shaunkor Chowdhury on 7 April 1920 in Varanasi. At the age of ten, he accompanied his brother Uday Shankar, to Paris. He spent the next few years with Uday's dance troupe called Company of Hindu Dance and Music, touring in India and Europe. He soon learnt to dance and play music, and was made a part of the troupe when he turned thirteen. While in Europe, he was introduced to Western classical music, jazz, and cinema.

Uday invited Baba Alladuddin Khan, an exponent of the Maihar Gharana who played several instruments, to join the troupe for a European tour. An inspired Ravi Shankar returned to India in 1938 to train further under Baba Allauddin.

Baba Alauddin, a hard taskmaster, trained Ravi Shankar to play the sitar, surabhar and a few other instruments. After completing his training in 1944, he joined the Indian People's Theatre Association in Mumbai and composed music for their ballets. He served as the music director of All India Radio from 1948 until 1956, after which he toured Europe and the United States playing for small audiences. In the United States, he found an admirer in George Harrison of the British band called The Beatles; this association would last till Harrison's death in 2001. He performed at the Monterey Pop Festival, the Woodstock festival, and the iconic Concert for Bangladesh which George Harrison had arranged. He also collaborated with the American violinist Yehudi Menuhin; in 1967, they won a Grammy Award for Best Chamber Music Performance for their album *West Meets East.* During these years, he had become a household name in the west.

He also composed music for the Satyajit Ray's *Apu Trilogy*. The music for the Bengali film *Kabuliwala,* earned him the Silver Bear Extraordinary Prize of the Jury at the 1957 Berlin International Film Festival.

In 1986, he was nominated as a member of the Rajya Sabha.

His albums *West Meets East* (1966), *The Concert for Bangladesh* (1971) and for *Full Circle* (2001) were Grammy award winners. In 2001, his performance with his daughter Anoushka Shankar at the Carnegie Hall titled *Full Circle* also won a Grammy Award.

Ravi Shankar has written two autobiographies: *My Life, My Music* (1969) and *Raga Mala* (1999).

Pandit Ravi Shankar passed away on 11 December 2012 in San Diego, California, at the age of ninety-two. He was posthumously awarded his fourth Grammy Award in 2013 for *The Living Room Sessions Part 1,* and was honoured with the Lifetime Achievement Award by the Recording Academy.

GOOD TO KNOW

- Ravi Shankar's second daughter is the Grammy Award-winning singer-songwriter, Norah Jones.
- George Harrison was fascinated with the sitar and played the instrument with a Western tuning on the song *Norwegian Wood.*
- Ravi Shankar had created many melodic ragas like the Gangeshwari Raga, dedicated to Goddess Durga and Mohan Kauns, in memory of Mahatma Gandhi

QUIZ

1. In 1982, Ravi Shankar's score for which film earned him an Oscar nomination?
   a) *Pather Panchali*
   b) *Gandhi*
   c) *Do Bigha Zameen*

Answer: ***Gandhi***

2. Ravi Shankar smeared his palms with which of these to get a sheen that would reflect when he played?
   a) Sandalwood paste
   b) Alta (a red dye)
   c) Milk

Answer: Alta (a red dye)

3. Who called Ravi Shankar 'the Godfather of World Music'?
   a) Yehudi Menuhin
   b) George Harrison
   c) Amjad Ali

Answer: George Harrison

GLOSSARY

- Maihar Gharana: is a school of Hindustani Classical music founded by Ustad Alauddin Khan in the city of Maihar, Madhya Pradesh.
- Jazz: a type of music of black American origin which emerged at the beginning of the 20th century, characterized by improvisation and usually a regular or forceful rhythm.
- Saxophone: a member of a family of metal wind instruments with a reed like that of a clarinet, used especially in jazz and dance music.

TANSEN

Tansen was a Hindustani classical music composer, musician and vocalist. He was proficient in playing many musical instruments, and is credited with improving and popularizing the plucked rabab, which is a bowed or plucked stringed instrument of Arab origin.

It is believed that Tansen was born in 1493, in the tiny village of Behat, to a Brahmin named Makarand Pande. He was named Ramtanu at birth. He started his early training at a school founded by Raja Man Singh Tomar of Gwalior. He was trained under the tutelage of two talented singers in his youth: Saint Haridas and the Pir of Gwalior, Mohammed Ghaus.

Besides them, the king of Bihar, Sultan Mohammad Adil, and Govind Swami also played an important role in his growth. Before coming to Akbar's court, Tansen was the chief court musician in the court of King Ramachandra of Rewa in central India. The fame he acquired there attracted the attention of Akbar, who had a reputation of selectively collecting and employing the best musicians of his age. At Akbar's request, Tansen shifted to his court in Delhi. Tansen was selected to be one of the Navaratnas (Nine Jewels) of Emperor Akbar's court. It was in 1562 that Tansen entered Emperor Akbar's court and stayed there until his death. One of the main sources of information about music in Akbar's court comes from Abul Fazl's *Ain-i-Akbari*. Akbar was famous for identifying talent from different places and dividing them into seven orders, one for each day of the week. There were nineteen vocalists who performed under the guidance of Tansen accompanied by the instrumentalists. Sarmandal, bin, nay, karna and tanpura were the leading instruments of that time.

Legend has it, that once he was asked to perform *Deepak Raga* by Akbar, a raga that could actually produce heat when sung properly. Tansen sang it with such perfection that his whole body started burning up. It was only when his daughter sang *Megh Malhar*, a raga that causes rain, that his body became cool.

According to sources, Tansen was responsible for the treatise titled Ragamala, the Shri Ganesh Stotra and the Sangeet Saar. He is also credited with reducing the number of ragas and raginis to 400 from an astronomical figure of 4000 in his time. With his expertise, he also reduced the number of talas from 92 to a mere 12. The ragas 'Miyan Malhar' and 'Miyan ki todi' are said to be his creation. His gharana of music is remembered as the 'Senia Gharana', which after his death was led by two stalwarts and digressed into two directions. The elder son Bilas Khan took the responsibility of heading the rabab players and the second son Suratsen took up the sitar players.

The date of his death remains uncertain. It is said that he wished to be buried in Gwalior on the event of his death; this was rightfully done and his tomb is now a tourist attraction.

GOOD TO KNOW

- Tansen Samman is the highest award in the field of classical music instituted by the Madhya Pradesh Government.
- Tansen Samaroh is the largest and the oldest Samaroh in the field of classical music. Samaroh means a congregation or gathering of people.

QUIZ

1. What was Tansen's original name?
   a) Ramtanu Pande
   b) Mahesh Das
   c) Shekhar Gupta

Answer: Ramtanu Pande

2. In which state is the Tomb of Tansen located?
   a) Madhya Pradesh
   b) Uttar Pradesh
   c) Andhra Pradesh

Answer: Madhya Pradesh

3. Which actor played the role of Tansen in the 1943 film of the same name?
   a) K.L. Saigal
   b) V Shantaram
   c) Sohrab Modi

Answer: K.L. Saigal

GLOSSARY

- Pir: is a Muslim saint or holy man.
- Gharana: is any of the various specialist schools or methods of classical music or dance, like Gwalior and Lucknow.
- Raga: is each of the six basic musical modes which express different moods in certain characteristic progressions.
- Navaratnas: is also known as Nine Jewels, they were nine courtiers in Akbar's court, all of whom excelled in their own specialised fields.

TYAGARAJA

Tyagaraja was a saint-composer who is often regarded as one of the most important musicians in the history of Southern India's classical music. Tyagaraja's works are rendered in almost every modern-day concert in the region. He composed ragas and songs of the genre kirtana or kriti, which are devotional songs. He was one among the trinity of Carnatic music, the other two being Muthuswami Dikshitar and Syama Sastri.

Tyagaraja was born on 4 May 1767 in Tiruvarur, Tamil Nadu, into a Telugu Brahmin family. He was named after Thyagaraja, principal deity of the Thyagaraja Swamy Temple in Tiruvarur. At an early age, he became a disciple of Sonti Venkatramaiah, a renowned scholar.

He did extensive research on Sanskrit and Telugu, and acquired a thorough knowledge of the Valmiki Ramayana. He composed his first song 'Namo Namo Raghavayya' at the age of thirteen. One of his ragas, called 'Jagadanandakaraka', contains the 108 most famous names of Lord Rama. For composing his kritis, Thyagaraja preferred his mother tongue Telugu, a language which was more easily understandable than Sanskrit by the majority of people of the region.

Tyagaraja's songs were generally spread through word of mouth. One of the most important aspects of his performance was his ability to improvise during rendition.

About 700 of the reported 24,000 songs he has sung, still survive. It is often believed that his disciples wrote down the songs on palm leaves which are now mostly lost.

Thyagaraja attained samadhi on Pushya Bagula Panchami day in 1847. His mortal remains were interred in Tiruvayaru.

GOOD TO KNOW

- A saint named Ramakrishnananda taught Tyagaraja the Ramasadakshari mantra. It is said that after Tyagaraja chanted Rama Nama 96 crore times, Lord Rama appeared before him, accompanied by Sita, Lakshmana and Hanuman.
- Tyagaraja Aradhana is an annual Carnatic music festival held at Thiruvaiyaru in Tamil Nadu, India. The aradhana is observed on Pushya Bagula Panchami day when the saint attained samadhi.

QUIZ

1. Most of Tyagaraja's songs were in honour of...
   a) Rama
   b) Krishna
   c) Arjuna

Answer: Rama

2. After Tyagaraja's death, his remains were interred at a spot on the left bank of which river?
   a) Ganga
   b) Yamuna
   c) Cauvery

Answer: Cauvery

3. It is believed that Tyagaraja was the incarnation of...
   a) Valmiki
   b) Ved Vyas
   c) Thiruvalluvar

Answer: Valmiki

GLOSSARY

- Kirtan: is a devotional song
- Ramayana: a great Sanskrit epic written by Valmiki. It describes how Rama, aided by his brother and the monkey Hanuman, rescued his wife Sita from Ravana, the ten-headed demon king of Lanka.
- Kriti: is a more formalized pattern of the kirtana. It has evolved from the kirtana, has more technicalities and higher musical value.

LANGUAGE AND LITERATURE

BANKIM CHANDRA CHATTOPADHYAY

Bankim Chandra Chattopadhyay was an author and journalist, who is best-known as the composer of the national song 'Vande Mataram'. His works were a great source of inspiration to the people during the struggle for independence. His novels have been translated into multiple regional Indian languages and English.

Bankim Chandra Chattopadhyay was born on 27 June 1838 in Kanthalpara (in present-day Bangladesh). Shortly after his birth, his father was posted in Midnapur, a small town in West Bengal, as Deputy Collector.

Chattopadhyay joined the Mohsin College in Hooghly and studied there for a few years. During this period, he developed a passion for reading books, especially in Sanskrit which greatly influenced his literary style.

In 1856, Chattopadhyay joined the Presidency College in Calcutta. He passed the BA examination in 1859, and was appointed as Deputy Collector the same year. In recognition of his outstanding service, he received the titles of Rai Bahadur in 1891 and Companion of the Most Eminent Order of the Indian Empire (CMEOIE) in 1894. He retired in 1891 after thirty-two years in service.

Chattopadhyay began his literary journey as a poet but eventually became a novelist. Though he wrote his novel, *Rajmohan's Wife*, in English, he went on to write more than twelve novels in Bengali. *Rajmohan's Wife* appeared in the *Indian Field* in 1864 and is generally accepted as the first novel in English by an Indian. While he worked as a deputy magistrate in 24 Parganas, in West Bengal he wrote two of his famous novels, *Durgeshnandini* (1865) and *Kapalkundala* (1866). His other popular novels include *Mrinalini* (1869), *Vishbriksha* (1873), *Chandrasekhar* (1877), *Rajani* (1877), *Rajsimha* (1881), and *Devi Chaudhurani* (1884). His most famous novel was *Anandamath* (1882), which is possibly his last notable literary work. *Anandamath* is a political novel and contains the song 'Vande Mataram', which was later adopted as the National Song of India.

In 1872, to bring about a cultural revival in Bengal, Chattopadhyay launched the monthly magazine *Bangadarshan.* He regularly contributed novels, stories, humorous sketches, political and other essays, religious discourses, and literary criticisms to the magazine. *Vishbrikhsha* was his first novel to appear serially in *Bangadarshan*.

Besides his novels, he is also popular for his humourous sketches. *Kamalakanter Daptar* contains half-humourous and half-serious sketches on many issues including political, religious and social. He passed away on April 8 1894 in Kolkata.

GOOD TO KNOW

- 'Bankim Chandra' in Bengali means 'the moon on the second day of the bright fortnight'.
- His brother Sanjeeb Chandra Chattopadhyay was also an eminent writer whose most famous work was on the jungles of Palamau.

QUIZ

1. On which of these real life movements was the novel

Anandamath based?

a) French revolution
b) Sannyasi rebellion
c) Santhal rebellion

Answer: Sannyasi rebellion

2. Which was the last novel written by Bankim Chandra Chattopadhyay?
   a) *Sitaram*
   b) *Durgeshnandini*
   c) *Kapala Kundala*

Answer: *Sitaram*

3. In 1896, who first sang the song 'Vande Matram' in public, in a political arena?
   a) Swami Vivekananda
   b) Rabindranath Tagore
   c) Bankim Chandra Chattopadhay

Answer: Rabindranath Tagore

GLOSSARY

- Companion of the Most Eminent Order of the Indian Empire: was an order of chivalry founded by Queen Victoria in 1878.
- Magistrate: is a civil officer who administers the law, especially one who conducts a court that deals with minor offences and holds preliminary hearings for the more serious ones.

KABIR

Kabir was a mystic poet-saint, reformer, critic, and spiritual leader who spread the notion of equality and love among different communities in India. He used songs called dohas as the primary medium for communicating his thoughts and beliefs. His works have lived on for more than 500 years, spreading orally through song and music, and resulting in a rich array of folk and classical form in numerous regional styles.

The details of his birth, life and death are unclear. Some believe that he was born in 1440 and died in 1518. It is also believed that he was born to a Brahmin woman who abandoned him at birth, and was eventually raised by a Muslim couple.

He was greatly influenced in later life by a Hindu ascetic, Ramananda. Kabir preached a religion of love, promoted unity amongst different sections of the society and rejected religious rites and rituals. He believed that the path to salvation was through Bhajan or devotional worship, together with the freedom of the soul from dishonesty, greed, violence, selfishness and cruelty.

Kabir is equally revered by Hindus, Muslims and Sikhs. The Sikhs often regard him as a precursor to Guru Nanak. 541 hymns in the Guru Granth Sahib, the holy book of Sikhism, were written by him. While in Islam, he is placed in the lineage of Sufis, Hindus regard him as a Vaishnava who encouraged universalism. He was an oral poet whose works were written down by others.

Kabir's humble upbringing and social status helped give shape to the Kabir Panth, which was a sect found across north and central India. This sect mostly drew its followers from the lower classes, who were earlier perceived as untouchable. This sect regards Kabir as its principal leader, or guru. The *Bijak* is the sacred book of the Kabir Panth.

GOOD TO KNOW

- In the 1881 census conducted by the British authorities in India, Kabir-panth was recognized as a separate religion.
- Kabir and his followers named his poetic utterences, banis, which means 'utterances'.

QUIZ

2. Sant Kabir Nagar is a district in which state?
   a) Uttar Pradesh
   b) Tamil Nadu
   c) Bihar

Answer: Uttar Pradesh

1. In the early 20th century, who translated Kabir's poetry into English?
   a) Sri Aurobindo Ghosh
   b) Rabindranath Tagore
   c) Vivekananda

Answer: Rabindranath Tagore

3. Fill in the blank to complete this doha by Kabir: 'Bada hua to kya hua jaise ped ______, Panthi ko chhaya nahin phal lagey ati door'.
   a) khajoor
   b) amrood
   c) kela

Answer: Khajoor

GLOSSARY

- Doha: is another term for rhymed couplets.
- Vaishnava: is a devotee of the god Vishnu.
- Ramananda: Saint Ramanand or Swami Ramanand, a Vaishnava saint.

KALIDASA

Kalidasa was a Sanskrit poet and dramatist. He is credited with writing more than forty poems and plays, and many of these works are popular even today. His works have inspired many poets and authors around the world. He is also referred to as Kavikulaguru, Kavikulashiromani, Dipashikha Kalidasa and the Shakespeare of India.

Many theories place Kalidasa between 200 BC and AD 600. Some scholars believe that he lived during the reign of King Vikramaditya, around 57 BC, while others believe that he may have lived around 1 BC.

Kalidasa, according to tradition, was a foolish man who became a literary genius after Goddess Gauri gave him a boon as an answer to his prayers.

There are about forty-one works which are credited to Kalidasa. *Meghaduta*, *Raghuvamsham* and *Abhijnanashakuntala* are among the best-known.

Ritusamhara is considered as Kalidasa's first work. It is a lyrical poem that describes the six seasons: grishma (summer), varsha (rainy), sharad (autumn), hemanta (dewy), shishira (winter) and vasanta (spring).

'Kumarasambhava' is a classical poem, based on the myth of Lord Shiva and Parvati's marriage, and the birth of their son Kumara Karttikeya, who killed demon Taraka.

Meghaduta, one of his most famous works, is a lyrical love poem dealing with the story of a yaksha who asks a cloud to take a message to his love, living in the Himalayan city of Alaka.

Abhijnanashakuntala is considered the best play in the Sanskrit language. Adapted from Hindu mythology, it tells the story of Shakuntala and King Dushyanta. The story is important because their child Bharata is believed to be the source of the name of 'Bharat', another name for the Republic of India.

Among his other works are *Malavikagnimitram* and *Vikramorvashiyam*.

Kalidasa had profound knowledge not only in philosophy, law, economics and zoology, but also in music and fine arts.

Kalidasa's contribution to Sanskrit poetry remains unparalleled. With his simple and lucid style of writing, he brought Sanskrit poetry to a level which has seldom been surpassed in Indian history.

GOOD TO KNOW

- It is said that Kumaradasa, the king of Ceylon and the author of the work *Janakiharana,* threw himself on the funeral pyre of his friend Kalidasa.
- The name Kalidasa literally translates to 'Servant of Kali'.

QUIZ

1. Which of these works composed by Kalidasa is a play?
   a) *Malavikagnimitram*
   b) *Meghduta*
   c) *Ritusamhara*

Answer: *Malavikagnimitram*

2. Which of Kalidasa's characters was originally called Sarvadamana?
   a) King Dushyanta
   b) Taraka
   c) Bharata

Answer: Bharata

3. Which Indian state awards the Kalidasa Samman, every year, to people from the creative fields?
   a) Assam
   b) Haryana
   c) Madhya Pradesh

Answer: Madhya Pradesh

GLOSSARY

- Lyric: is an expression of the author's feelings, which is usually brief and in stanzas.

MIRZA GHALIB

Mirza Asadullah Baig Khan, popularly known as Mirza Ghalib, was a poet and writer, writing in both Urdu and Persian. He wrote in different literary styles, and is as famous for his poems and letters as he is for his prose pieces. A contemporary of the last Mughal emperor in India, Bahadur Shah Zafar, he is considered to be one of the most influential and renowned poets of the Urdu language.

Ghalib was born on 27 December 1797 in Agra, into a well-to-do family of army officers. His father, Mirza Abdullah, had died in a battle when he was just five years old. He was raised at his maternal great granduncle's house with his numerous cousins. The time he spent there shaped his personality.

Ghalib studied in a Maktab, which was run by a scholar named Muhammad Mu'azzam. There, he dabbled in classical Persian prose and poetry. He was also influenced by a Persian traveller, Abdus Samad, who stayed with his family for some time.

Though his education did not go beyond his classes with Abdus Samad and Muhammad Mu'azzam, he read extensively and worked very hard to make up for his lack of formal training.

Ghalib wrote his first Urdu ghazal at the age of nine, and composed his first Persian Masnavi when he was eleven.

Mirza Ghalib first visited Delhi when he was seven years old. He would eventually settle in the city after his marriage, and remain there till his death.

Delhi at the time was a hub of activities. He met powerful and accomplished people from different fields. He developed a lasting friendship with many of them. He was facing monetary problems when Bahadur Shah Zafar commissioned him to write the history of the Royal House of Timur at a salary of ₹600 per annum.

In early 1850s, he was appointed Poet Laureate to Bahadur Shah II.

Ghalib produced works in both Urdu and Persian. Though his Urdu diwan has around 5,000 couplets, his writings in Persian, with around 11,000 couplets, are more extensive. He also wrote numerous letters which were discovered after his death and have since become a part of various collections. *Panj-Ahang* (Persian grammar and vocabulary, a selection from his poems and letters), *Mihr-i-nimroz* (volume I of the history of Mughal dynasty), *Dastanboo* (an account of Delhi during the mutiny), and *Kati Burhan* (criticism of the Persian lexicon *Burhan-i-kati)* are some of his most important works in Persian.

Ghalib was open to western ideas, and so was never at odds with the British. He even showed a keen interest in learning the English language.

During his last years he was associated with the Rampur Darbar, and had turned to mysticism. He died on 15 February 1869 in Delhi.

In the year 2000, a museum was set up at the haveli of Mirza Ghalib at Gali Qasim Jaan, Chandni Chowk, to honour his memory.

GOOD TO KNOW

- Ghalib was actually Mirza Asadullah Khan's pen name. He also used the pen name 'Asad' in some of his writings.
- Ghalib was displeased with Sir Syed Ahmed Khan's idea

of carrying out a scholarly research on *Ain-i-Akbari* and reproached him. Syed Ahmed Khan was a Muslim educator, jurist and author, who founded the Anglo-Mohammedan Oriental College at Alīgarh.

QUIZ

1. During a visit to which of these cities did Ghalib compose his poem 'Chiragh-i-Dair'?
   a) Benaras
   b) Ajmer
   c) Lahore

Answer: Benaras

2. Who among these was considered to be Ghalib's closest rival?
   a) Sheikh Shahbai
   b) Zauq
   c) Abul Fazl

Answer: Zauq

3. Mirza Ghalib was portrayed by which of these actors in the biographical television drama titled *Mirza Ghalib*?
   a) Amitabh Bachchan
   b) Om Puri
   c) Naseeruddin Shah

Answer: Naseeruddin Shah

GLOSSARY

- Maktab: is a Muslim elementary school where boys were instructed in Quran recitation, reading, writing and grammar.
- Lexicon: is the vocabulary of a person, language or branch of knowledge.
- Diwan: is a term for a collection of poems.

MUNSHI PREMCHAND

Premchand was an author, social reformer and thinker, who used the medium of literature to address social issues. He was the first writer in Hindi to use realism in his works. His works focused on life around him and made his readers aware of the problems plaguing the society. He is credited with writing nearly 300 stories and novels in Hindi and Urdu. Some of his best-known novels are *Sevasadan*, *Rangmanch*, *Gaban*, *Nirmala,* and *Godan*. The anthology, *Manasarovar,* is a treasure trove of around 250 of his short-stories. His short-story, 'Shatranj ke Khiladi', was made into a film by Satyajit Ray.

Premchand was born as Dhanpat Rai Srivastava on 31 July 1880 in Lamahi near Varanasi, Uttar Pradesh. When he was young, he studied in a madarasa under a maulvi, which accounted for his complete command over Urdu.

Premchand's mother died when he was only eight and his father, too, passed away when he was in his teens. He had to give up studying after his intermediate in order to support his family. He got a job as a teacher in the primary school. In the year 1919, he passed his B.A. with History, English and Persian, while working as a teacher. He got a number of promotions in quick succession, after which he was raised to the rank of Deputy Inspector of schools.

In response to Gandhiji's call for non-cooperation against the British in 1921, Premchand quit his job. This helped him concentrate on his writing.

Premchand's literary style was simple and lucid, and carried notes of satire and humour. His first story was featured in a magazine called *Zamana.* Many of his stories revolved around patriotism, and he often used Mahatma Gandhi's revolutionary ideas as themes. *Soz-e-Watan* was a collection of patriotic stories published in 1907.

Premchand is sometimes referred to as the 'Father of Urdu short-stories'. 'Qaatil Ki Maan', 'Zewar Ka Dibba', 'Gilli Danda', 'Eidgaah', 'Namak Ka Daroga', and 'Kafan' are some of his well-known short stories (also known as afsanas in Urdu). Some of his Urdu anthologies are *Prem Pachisi*, *Prem Battisi, Wardaa*t, and *Zaad-e-Raah*.

Premchand died on 8 October 1936 in Varanasi.

On his 125th birth anniversary, Sahitya Akademi started a fellowship that was named after him. It is called Premchand Fellowship. This fellowship is awarded to scholars involved in research on Indian literature or to creative writers from the countries of the SAARC region other than India.

GOOD TO KNOW

- Munshi Premchand wrote some of his works under the pseudonym Nawab Rai.
- After Munshi Prenmchand's death, his wife, Shivarani Devi, wrote a book on him titled *Premchand Ghar Mein* (*Premchand in House*).

QUIZ

1. Which was the last story by Premchand, which was published in 1937, after his death?
   a) Cricket Match
   b) Football Match
   c) Hockey Match

Answer: Cricket Match

2. In the 1980s, who made a feature film based on Munshi Premchand's short-story *Sadgati*?
   a) Satyajit Ray
   b) Bimal Roy
   c) Girish Karnad

Answer: Satyajit Ray

3. Munshi Premchand published a translation of which of these author's stories?
   a) Shakespeare
   b) PB Shelley
   c) Leo Tolstoy

Answer: Leo Tolstoy

GLOSSARY

- Sahitya Akademi: is an organisation dedicated to the promotion of literature in Indian languages.
- SAARC: an acronym of the South Asian Association for Regional Cooperation. It is an organisation of South Asian nations with Bangladesh, Bhutan, India, Maldives, Nepal, Pakistan and Sri Lanka as participating countries.

PANINI

Panini is considered as one of the greatest grammarians in the world. He unified and codified the Sanskrit language into a composite whole, the rules which are followed to this day. His work on grammar has remained important for its correct usage ever since.

Panini is believed to have lived between 520 BC and 460 BC. He was born in Shalatula, a town near Taxila (now in Pakistan). According to various sources, the names of his parents have been deduced to have been Panin and Dakshi. He is said to have studied at Takshashila University.

Ashtadhyayi is the oldest and most definitive book on Sanskrit grammar. It is characterized by precision, maturity, and attention to detail. The text, luckily, has been preserved in its original form. In creating this work, he drew inspiration from some of the greatest grammarians of the past, such as Apishali, Kashyapa, Gargya, Galava, Chakraverman, Bharadwaj, Shakatayana, Shakalya, Shonaka, and Sphotayana.

The four major components of Sanskrit grammar as mentioned by him are: *Astadhyayi or Astaka, Sivasutras, Dhatupatha, and Ganapatha.*

Ashtadhyayi is written in the style of the sutras. It has 4000 sutras and eight chapters. A sutra is short, definite and clear statement, and is understood and interpreted keeping in mind the context in which it appears. Therefore, a sutra cannot be looked upon as an independent fact but as a part of a larger whole.

The book starts with the Maheshwara Sutras, where sounds have been divided into three basic parts: Swara, Antastha and Vyanjanaand, and have been explained in great scientific detail.

Panini has also discussed the topic of the formation of words in great detail. He said that a sentence is an indivisible unit, and that the word does not make any sense without the context.

The reason why his work is so highly regarded around the world among linguists and scientists is the scientific manner in which he has described Sanskrit morphology.

Panini treated Sanskrit as a living language. He even discussed the difference of usage among people in the east and those in the north of India.

GOOD TO KNOW

- The Department of Posts released a postage stamp on Panini in 2004 to commemorate India's heritage in grammar and mathematics.
- Panini's *Ashtadhyayi* has been a great source of inspiration to later grammarians like Katyayana and Patanjali.

QUIZ

1. Panini was born in the present-day North-West Province of which country?
   a) Bangladesh
   b) Sri Lanka
   c) Pakistan

Answer: Pakistan

2. In which city in Madhya Pradesh is the Maharshi Panini Sanskrit evam Vedic Vishwavidyalaya located?
   a) Gwalior
   b) Ujjain
   c) Bhopal

Answer: Ujjain

3. What was categorized by Panini into two main groups, that is, Subanta and Tinganta?
   a) Words
   b) Sentences
   c) Poetry

Answer: Words

GLOSSARY

- Morphology: in linguistics, is the study of the various forms of words.

PATANJALI

The great sage Patanjali, sometimes referred to as the 'Father of Yoga', lived more than 2000 years ago. He is known by the names Gonardiya, Phani, Adhipati, and Sheshraja. He is often regarded as the incarnation of Sheshanaga, the king of all serpents.

He has contributed towards the three branches of science: Ayurveda (medicine), Vyakarana (grammar), and Yoga (meditation).

Patanjali was from a place called Gonarda, which was either a part of Uttar Pradesh or Jammu and Kashmir. Though his parentage is obscure, scholars believe that he was educated at the ancient university of Takshashila, and is said to have become a teacher at Pataliputra. In many sources, he is referred to as a contemporary of King Pushyamitra, who lived around 2 BC.

Many pioneering works are attributed to Patanjali, including *Yogasutra*, *Mahabhashya* and *Nidan Sutras* or *Samvediya-Nidan Sutra*.

As the name suggests, *Yogasutra* is a systematic compilation of the various aspects of yoga. It forms the basis of the Ashtanga yoga philosophy. Patanjali preached the eightfold path of Yoga. Hesaid that the way to improve physical and mental health, was through certain restraints and observances such as physical discipline, breath regulations, restraining the sense organs, contemplation, meditation and samadhi.

Mahabhashya, on the other hand, is a unique book on

Sanskrit grammar. It is believed to be the first and oldest existing commentary on Panini's famous work *Ashtadhyayi*. It has helped in answering any questions or doubts that may have arisen from *Ashtadhyayi*, and forms a definitive work on grammar. Written in conversational style, in the question and answer format, it has more than seven hundred outstanding quotations. The book is also one of the earliest works to introduce the theory of gravity.

Another important work that has been credited to Patanjali is the *Nidan Sutras* or *Samvediya-Nidan Sutra* which is a work on medicine.

Mahanada, *Charak Parishkara*, *Siddhanta Sarawali*, *Paramartha sar* and *Lok shastra* are some of the other works that have been credited to him.

GOOD TO KNOW

- Patanjali's *Mahabhashya* was lost almost three hundred years after he died. The Kashmiri king Jayaditya searched for it and found one copy. From that he made several copies.
- In India, Sanskrit Diwas or Sanskrit Day is observed every year on the Shravan Purnima.

QUIZ

1. Patanjali is believed to be an incarnation of who among these?
   a) Garuda
   b) Sheshnaga
   c) Jatayu

Answer: Sheshnaga

2. Which of Patanjali's eight angas of yoga controls the regulation of the breath through certain techniques and exercises?

a) Yama
b) Asana
c) Pranayama

Answer: Pranayama

3. In which of these places did Patanjali receive his formal education?
   a) Nalanda
   b) Takshashila
   c) Pataliputra

Answer: Takshashila

GLOSSARY

- Ashtanga yoga philosophy: dwells on the eight angas—Yama, Niyama, Asana, Pranayama, Pratyahara, Dharana, Dhyana and Samadhi. Yoga dwells on the control of the senses and the states of chitta.
- Ayurveda: is a traditional Hindu system of medicine and a part of the Atharva Veda, the last of the four Vedas.

RABINDRANATH TAGORE

Rabindranath Tagore, also known as Gurudev, was a Bengali poet, short-story writer, song composer, playwright, essayist and painter. He played an important part in introducing various aspects of Indian culture to the West.

He also wrote the national anthem of India and Bangladesh. He was awarded the Nobel Prize in Literature in 1913.

Tagore was born on 7 May 1861 in Jorasanko, Kolkata. He was the youngest son of Sarala Devi and Debendranath Tagore, a leader of Brahmo Samaj.

Sarala Devi died when Tagore was young. He showed an aversion to traditional forms of education from a very young age, and preferred to roam around in his mansion in Kolkata, and also in places like Bolpur and Panihati. At the age of eleven, he left Kolkata to tour India with his father for several months. Their first stop was in Shantiniketan, followed by a brief stop in Amritsar, before heading off to the Himalayan hill station of Dalhousie. During this period, he read a lot on history, astronomy, modern science and Sanskrit.

With the intention of becoming a barrister, Tagore joined a public school in Brighton, England, in 1878 but soon left to study Shakespeare and other authors. He returned to Bengal without finishing school, in 1880. He married Mrinalini Devi on 9 December 1883, and they had five children. Sadly, however, two of them died at a young age. Tagore released his *Manasi* poems, which are among his most loved works, in 1890. These poems were followed by other works, including a large number of stories of the three-volumed *Galpaguchchha*, written in the early 1890s during what is often referred to as Tagore's sadhana period.

Tagore went to Shantiniketan in 1901 with the aim of founding an ashram. There, he published *Naivedya* (1901) and *Kheya* (1906), and translated his poems into free verse. He wrote a number of articles on the problems of education in India and drew up a comprehensive programme of work for the National Council of Education.

Tagore won the Nobel Prize in Literature in 1913 for his work *Gitanjali* (*Song Offerings*). He became the first Asian to win a Nobel Prize. He was knighted by the British Crown in 1915, but he relinquished the knighthood following the Jallianwala Bagh Massacre. He formally laid the foundation stone of Viswa Bharati University in 1918.

Tagore, together with the economist, Leonard Elmhirst, set up the Institute for Rural Reconstruction that was later renamed Shriniketan. The next few years, he travelled extensively and visited England, France, USA, Holland, Germany, Sweden and Austria among other places. He stayed in Buenos Aires as Victoria Ocampo's guest, in Italy as Benito Mussolini's guest, and met Romain Rolland in Switzerland.

Tagore's health deteriorated rapidly in the final years of his life. As a result of his ill health, Oxford University held a special convocation at Shantiniketan in 1940, to confer Doctorate on him. His final lecture, 'Crisis in Civilisation' was read on his eightieth birthday. He passed away on the 7 August 1941 in Kolkata.

Tagore was proficient in many literary genres. Among his fifty odd volumes of poetry are, *Sonar Tari* (1894) [*The Golden Boat*], *Gitanjali* (1910) [*Song Offerings*], *Gitimalya* (1914) [*Wreath of Songs*], and *Balaka* (1916) [*The Flight of Cranes*]. He wrote numerous plays including *Raja* (1910) [*The King of the Dark Chamber*], *Dakghar* (1912) [*The Post Office*], *Achalayatan* (1912) [*The Immovable*], *Muktadhara* (1922) [*The Waterfall*], and *Raktakaravi* (1926) [*Red Oleanders*]. He is the author of several volumes of short stories and a number of novels, among them are *Gora* (1910), *Ghare-Baire are* (1916) [*The Home and the World*] and *Yogayog* (1929). He also wrote musical dramas, dance dramas, essays of all types, travel diaries, and two autobiographies.

GOOD TO KNOW

- 'The Child' is Tagore's one and only original English poem.
- In 1905, when partition was announced, Rabindranath initiated the Rakhsha Bandhan ceremony as a symbol of unity in Bengal.
- Tagore had lost the manuscript of *Gitanjali* in the underground railway in London, but later found it in the lost-property office of the railway.

QUIZ

1. Which of these is the national anthem of Bangladesh?
   a) Amar Desher Mati
   b) Banglar Mati Banglar Jol
   c) Amar Shonar Bangla

Answer: Amar Shonar Bangla

2. Which of these commemorates the 150th birth anniversary of Rabindranath Tagore?
   a) Godan Express
   b) Sanskriti Express
   c) Vivek Express

Answer: Sanskriti Express

3. Rabindranath Tagore renounced his knighthood in protest against which event?
   a) Jallianwala Bagh massacre
   b) Moplah Rebellion
   c) Bengal Famine

Answer: Jallianwala Bagh Massacre

GLOSSARY

- Knighthood: is the title, rank, or status of a knight. It is one of the highest honours an individual in the United Kingdom can achieve.

RASIPURAM KRISHNASWAMY NARAYAN

R.K. Narayan is one of the leading and most influential Indian authors writing in English. His simple and lucid writing style appealed to both children and adults. He created the fictional town of Malgudi, where he set most of his works.

Narayan was born on 10 October 1906 in Madras and started his studies in Lutheran Mission School. However, he had to travel quite often with his father to various towns where his father taught in schools. Soon his father became the headmaster of Maharaja's Collegiate High School in Mysore. As his father's job was transferable, Narayan spent most of his childhood with his maternal grandmother. During this time, he had a monkey and a peacock as pets. After finishing school, Narayan studied at Maharajah College in Mysore and graduated in 1930.

After he had finished college, he worked as a school teacher for a short period, and wrote articles for various magazines and newspapers. It was during this time that he also wrote his first novel *Swami and Friends*, the story of two cricket-loving friends and their adventures in the fictional town of Malgudi. In 1933, he married a girl named Rajam and subsequently started working for a Madras based paper called *The Justice*.

He sent *Swami and Friends* to many publishers but they refused to publish it. Narayan had also sent a copy of the manuscript to a friend in Oxford, London, where the noted author Graham Greene chanced upon it. It was Greene who first showed an active interest in Narayan's writing, and eventually got it published. This marked the beginning of a strong relationship between the two authors which they maintained for the next fifty years. It was Greene who advised Narayan to shorten his name to R.K. Narayan, under which the book was published.

His next two books were *The Bachelor of Arts* and *The Dark Room.*

In 1939, his wife died of typhoid and it affected him deeply. This brought about a significant change in his life and was the subject of his next novel, *The English Teacher*, followed by *Mr Sampath, The Financial Expert* and *Waiting for the Mahatma*. Later, he wrote the iconic novel *The Guide*, that many consider to be his masterpiece. In 1953, his works were published in the United States for the first time. Some of his other famous works include *The Man-Eater of Malgudi*, *The Vendor of Sweets, Malgudi Days* and *The World of Nagaraj*.

He was nominated to the Rajya Sabha in 1989. In his six year term as a nominated member of the Rajya Sabha he spoke only once, commenting on the hardships children face when they carry heavy schoolbags. He received the Sahitya Akademi Award in 1958 for his novel *The Guide*, which was later made into a film starring Dev Anand.

In 1964, he was awarded the Padma Bhushan for his distinguished service to literature. He passed away on 13 May 2001.

GOOD TO KNOW

- R.K. Narayan had sent the manuscript of *Swami and Friends* to a friend in London, and told him to throw the manuscript into the Thames if the publisher returned it.
- Graham Greene once said that Narayan was 'the novelist I most admire in the English language.'

- He was a firm believer of the fact that a book should never be more than 200 pages long and tried to follow the rule.

QUIZ

1. Who played the male lead in the film *Guide*, based on R.K. Narayan's novel?
   a) Dilip Kumar
   b) Dev Anand
   c) Raj Kapoor

Answer: Dev Anand

2. What was the name of his memoir?
   a) My Life
   b) My Days
   c) Swami and I

Answer: My Days

3. Which of these works is not set against the backdrop of Malgudi?
   a) *The English Teacher*
   b) *Mr Sampath*
   c) *The Grandmother's Tale*

Answer: *The Grandmother's Tale*

GLOSSARY

- Padma Bhushan: is the third highest civilian award in the Republic of India, after the Bharat Ratna and the Padma Vibhushan, but comes before the Padma Shri.

THIRUVALLUVAR

Thiruvalluvar was a Tamil poet-saint, whose impact on Tamil literature remains unparalleled. He is the author of the *Thirukkural* (meaning 'Sacred Couplets' in Tamil), the most famous of the *Patiren-kirkkanakku (Eighteen Ethical Works)* in Tamil literature. It is considered a masterpiece of human thought and an enduring example of the literature from the Sangam period of Tamil Nadu. This classic work provides a unique code of conduct for a person to follow during the course of his life. It gives an insight into a range of topics that include family, love, virtue, wealth and administration.

The details about his birth, life, and death are shrouded in obscurity. He is believed to have lived around 1 BC or 6 AD. While some scholars are of the opinion that he was born in Madurai as a Valluvar (meaning a devotee of the Valluva caste), others argue that he was born in Mylapore, Chennai.

Researchers have also recently unearthed evidence that he was born in Tirunayanarkurichi in the erstwhile Valluva Nadu. However, historians have not been able to arrive at a consensus so far.

The core concept that Thiruvalluvar dwelt on was that a man did not have to lead the life of an ascetic (Sanyasi) to be deemed pure; citing his own life as an example, that one could be a sage as well as a householder (Grihastha).

Thirukkural has 1,330 couplets, divided into 133 chapters in three sections.

The three sections are: Arathupaal, Porutpaal and Kaamathupaal.

Arathupaal deals with aram, or ethical behavior. The correct manner of conducting worldly affairs is taught in the Porutpaal. Kaamathupaal teaches inbam, or love.

Thirukkural is also known by the following names: *Uttaravedam*, *Poyyamozhi*, *Vayurai Vazhthu*, *Deyvanool*, *Poth umarai*, *Muppal* and *Tamil Marai*.

There are many legends surrounding his life which have raised him from the stature of a mere mortal to that of a saint. One such legend states that upon completing *Thirukkural*, he took it to Madurai where it was customary to read out literary works in public in front of peers and critics alike. As a measure of the purity of the work, it was also customary to place the work on a plank of wood in the water tank of Madurai Meenakshi Temple. During this particular instance, it is widely believed that not only did the *Thirukkural* keep the plank afloat, but the plank shrunk in size as well to only hold the manuscript, while all the other scripts fell into the water.

The memorial statue of Thiruvalluvar is in Kanyakumari. The pedestal stands at a height of 38 feet and the statue over it is 95 feet tall. (The height of the pedestal represents the 38 chapters in the *Book of Aram* in *Thirukkural*, and the height of the statue and the pedestal together represents the total number of chapters in *Porul* (70 chapters) and *Inbam* (25 Chapters).

Therefore, the statue symbolizes the various aspects of the Thirukkural, by combining all its elements.

GOOD TO KNOW

- P. Chidambaram, the finance minister, is known to end most of his speeches in Parliament by quoting from *Thiruvalluvar*.

- The Thiruvalluvar University is located in Vellore, Tamil Nadu

QUIZ

1. On which day does the Tamil Nadu government celebrate Thiruvalluvar Day as part of the Pongal celebrations?
   a) January 15
   b) February 15
   c) June 15

Answer: January 15

2. The Thirukkural Express is a weekly train running between H. Nizamuudin in Delhi and which other place?
   a) Mumbai
   b) Mangalore
   c) Kanyakumari

Answer: Kanyakumari

3. In the eighteenth century, Constanzo Beschi translated *Thirukkural* into which language?
   a) English
   b) Latin
   c) Spanish

Answer: Latin

GLOSSARY

- Madurai Meenakshi Temple: is a historic Hindu temple in Madurai which on some days has as many as 25,000 visitors.
- Couplet: is a pair of successive lines of verse, typically rhyming and of the same length.

FILMS

ALLAH RAKHA RAHMAN

A.R. Rahman, sometimes referred to as the 'Mozart of Madras', is a music composer and playback singer. He has been awarded the Academy Award (Oscar) twice and has been nominated five-times for the same.

Rahman was born A.S. Dileep Kumar on 6 January 1967 in Madras (now Chennai). He began learning the piano at the age of four. His father passed away when he was nine years old. He joined Ilayaraja's troupe as a keyboard player to support his family. As a result, he dropped out of school and travelled all around the world with various orchestras. He also accompanied the tabla maestro, Zakir Hussain, on a couple of world tours. He won a scholarship to attend the Trinity College of Music in Oxford University, where he studied Western classical music. He later converted to Islam and came to be known as A.R. Rahman.

Rahman was passionate about music and after helping popular musicians in India, he went on to compose jingles and scores for Indian television features. He set up his own in-house studio called 'Panchathan Record-Inn' in Chennai.

In 1991, prominent film-maker Mani Ratnam offered Rahman a chance to compose music for his film *Roja*. He accepted the offer and won the National Award for Best Music Director. This was the first time the award was given to a debutant. In a career spanning more than two decades, he has composed music for numerous films including *Bombay, Dil Se, Taal, Lagaan, Jodhaa Akbar* and *Slumdog Millionaire*.

In 1997, to commemorate fifty years of Indian Independence, Rahman worked with Sony Music to produce the album *Vande Mataram* which became the largest selling non-film album. In 2001, he composed music for Andrew Lloyd Webber's musical, *Bombay Dreams*. A few years later, Rahman composed the score for the stage production of Tolkein's *The Lord of the Rings*. Subsequently, he undertook many concert tours in over fifty international destinations, which also included one at the prestigious Hollywood Bowl in 2006 and the Royal Festival Hall in 2010.

Many of Rahman's tracks are featured in films, such as *The Lord of War*, *Inside Man* and *The Accidental Husband*. He has composed music for several Hollywood productions, including *Elizabeth—The Golden Age, Slumdog Millionaire, Couples Retreat, 127 Hours* and *People Like Us.* He has also scored the music for the Chinese film, *Warriors of Heaven and Earth,* produced by Sony Pictures. His composition 'Bombay Theme' holds the distinction of being featured in over fifty international compilations.

In 2008, Rahman's work gained global acclaim with the exemplary success of his music for *Slumdog Millionaire* that won 8 Academy Awards, including two for Rahman, for Best Score and Best Song.

Rahman was awarded the Padma Bhushan and the Padma Shri, in recognition of his contribution to music. He has also won 4 National Film Awards and 28 Filmfare Awards.

Rahman has been conferred with honorary doctorates from the Trinity College of Music, Aligarh Muslim University, Anna University, and the Middlesex University.

The classical adaptations of Rahman's works have been performed by the London Philharmonic Orchestra, Los Angeles Philharmonic Orchestra and Babelsberg Film Orchestra. He has also collaborated with several other international artistes, including Nusrat Fateh Ali Khan, Michael Jackson, Michael Bolton, MIA, Vanessa Mae, The Pussycat Dolls, Sarah Brightman, Dido, Hossam Ramzy, Hans Zimmer and Akon.

Time magazine rated the soundtrack of *Roja*, in their list of Top Ten best film soundtracks in the world.

GOOD TO KNOW

- In 2009, he was named by *Time* magazine as one of the 100 most influential people in the world.
- In 2011, Rahman joined a band called SuperHeavy, comprising of Mick Jagger, Joss Stone, Damian Marley and Dave Stewart.
- *The Guardian* listed the soundtrack of *Bombay* in '1000 Albums to Listen Before You Die'.

QUIZ

1. Released in 2007, which was Rahman's first English single?
   a) 'Rockstar'
   b) 'Pray for Me Brother'
   c) 'People Like Us'

   Answer: 'Pray For Me Brother'

2. Name the first Hindi film for which A.R. Rahman composed music score.
   a) *Rangeela*
   b) *Bombay*
   c) *Sapnay*

   Answer: *Rangeela*

3. For which song did A.R. Rahman win an Oscar in 2009?
   a) 'Dil Hain Chhotasa'
   b) 'Barso Re Megha'
   c) 'Jai Ho'

   Answer: 'Jai Ho'

GLOSSARY

- Mick Jagger: is an English musician, singer, songwriter and actor. He is best-known as the lead vocalist and a founder member of the band, Rolling Stones.
- London Philharmonic Orchestra: founded by Sir Thomas Beecham in 1932, it is one of the major orchestras in the United Kingdom.
- Mozart: was a prolific and influential composer of the Classical era.

AMITABH BACHCHAN

Amitabh Bachchan is an icon of Indian cinema. He has appeared in over one hundred and eighty Indian films. In a career spanning more than four decades, he has played a variety of roles a variety. He is known for introducing the character of the 'angry young man' in Hindi films.

Born on 11 October 1942 in Allahabad, Amitabh Bachchan's father was the famous Hindi poet Harivansh Rai Bachchan. He studied in Sherwood College, Nainital, and later completed his formal education from Kirori Mal College in Delhi with double Master of Arts degrees from Delhi University. He worked as a freight broker in the shipping firm, Bird and Co. in Calcutta, but quit to devote himself to acting.

Amitabh Bachchan won the National Film Award for Best Newcomer for his debut film *Saat Hindustani.* After playing acclaimed roles in many films including *Anand* (alongside Rajesh Khanna), *Saudagar* and *Bombay To Goa,* it was his role in *Zanjeer* that catapulted him stardom. A series of action films followed, including *Deewar*, *Abhimaan* and *Don*. The 1975 film *Sholay,* made him a cult figure. It became the highest grossing film of all time in India. In 1999, BBC India declared it the 'Film of the Millennium'.

His first foray into playback singing came with the song for the film *Mr Natwarlal.*

In 1982, Amitabh Bachchan faced a near fatal injury while filming a fight scene for *Coolie* with co-star Puneet Issar. Mass prayers and messages flooded in from all over India, and truly showcased how well-loved he was across the country. However, his subsequent films did not do well at the box office. He entered politics in 1984 and contested the Lok Sabha seat for his hometown, Allahabad. He won by the highest victory margin in general election history (68.2 per cent of the votes). However, he resigned after three years.

Amitabh Bachchan returned to acting with the film *Agneepath*, which garnered huge critical acclaim and won him the National Award for his portrayal of a mafia don. He then established a film production and event management company called Amitabh Bachchan Corporation Ltd. However, the business was fraught with monetary trouble and he once again returned to films. In the 2000s, he acted in numerous films; his performances in *Black* (a film based on the life of Helen Keller, where he plays a teacher who develops Alzheimer's disease) and *Paa* (where he plays Auro, a 12 year old boy who suffers with the rare genetic disorder called progeria) received critical acclaim. His first experiment with English language films came with Rituparno Ghosh's *The Last Lear* (2007), which garnered rave reviews.

Amitabh Bachchan is also the host of the television show *Kaun Banega Crorepati,* modelled on the British show *Who Wants to Be a Millionaire?* He featured with Bally Sagoo on the album *Aby Baby* in 1996. He also appeared in Adnan Sami's song 'Kabhi Nahi'.

Amitabh Bachchan was awarded the Padma Shri in 1984 and the Padma Bhushan in 2001 for his contribution to Arts. In June 2000, his wax sculpture was installed at London's Madame Tussauds Wax Museum. He was conferred with the 'Légion d'honneur' (Legion of Honour) by the French Republic in 2007.

Amitabh Bachchan is married to actress Jaya Bhaduri. His son Abhishek Bachchan is also an actor.

GOOD TO KNOW

- He was going to be named Inquilab, which means 'revolution' before his father Harivansh Rai Bachchan decided on Amitabh, which means 'brilliance unlimited'.
- BBC Online voted Amitabh Bachchan 'Star of the Millennium', above Laurence Olivier, Charlie Chaplin and Marlon Brando.
- Amitabh Bachchan failed an audition for a newsreader's job at All India Radio.
- While shooting for Mukul Anand's *Khuda Gawah*, Najibullah, the then president of Afghanistan, provided Amitabh Bachchan with half the Air Force of the country for his protection. The film became one of the most-watched Indian films in Afghanistan.

QUIZ

1. Which character did Amitabh Bachchan portray in the 2013 film *The Great Gatsby*?
   a) Meyer Wolfsheim
   b) Jay Gatsby
   c) George Wilson

Answer: Meyer Wolfsheim

2. What was his name in the films *Agneepath, Shehenshah* and *Shakti*?
   a) Amit
   b) Vijay
   c) Ajay

Answer: Vijay

3. In which of these films did he play a double role?

a) *Aakhree Raasta*
b) *Pukar*
c) *Namak Halaal*

Answer: ***Aakhree Raasta***

GLOSSARY

- Madame Tussauds: is a wax museum in London with branches in a number of major cities displaying waxworks of historical and royal figures, film stars and sports stars.
- Légion d'honneur: is a French order established by Napoleon Bonaparte on 19 May 1802. The Order is the highest decoration in France and is divided into five degrees—Knight, Officer, Commander, Grand Officer and Grand Cross.

ASHA BHOSLE

Asha Bhosle is a playback singer, who has sung more than twelve thousand songs over a period of sixty years in many languages, including Hindi, Urdu, Bengali, Tamil, Gujarati, Assamese, Punjabi, English, Czech, Russian, Marathi, Telugu, Nepali, Malay and Malayalam. She is known for her vocal range and has sung songs in many genres of music like folk, film, pop, ghazal, qawwali, bhajan, Indian classical and Rabindra Sangeet, to name a few. Lata Mangeshkar is her elder sister.

Asha Bhosle was born on 8 September 1933 in Sangli, Maharashtra. After her father, Dinanath Mangeshkar passed away in 1942, the family moved from Pune to Kolhapur and eventually to Bombay.

Asha was trained in classical music by her father. At the age of ten, she sang her first film song for a Marathi film called *Majha Bal*. Her first song in Hindi was for the film *Chunariya* (1948). She worked very hard for many years before becoming successful.

Asha has sung songs for many music directors, including O.P. Nayyar, Khayyam, S.D. Burman and Ravi, among others. Her best-known early works are with the music director O.P. Nayyar, in films such as *Naya Daur* and *Tumsa Nahin Dekha*. She collaborated with S.D. Burman for films such as *Paying Guest* and *Nau Do Gyarah*.

Asha went on to sing more songs than any other singer in the 1950s, mainly for small-budget films. Some of her famous songs include 'Jaiye Aap Kahan Jayenge', 'Aaja Aaja Main Hoon Pyar Tera', 'Yeh Hai Reshmi Zulphon Ka Andhera' and 'Tanha Tanha Yahan Pe Jeena'.

In the 1970s, she sang many duets with Kishore Kumar, many-a-time composed by R.D. Burman.

Besides singing for Hindi films, Asha has recorded a few studio albums as well. In 1987, together with R.D. Burman and Gulzar, she recorded a double album called *Dil Padosi Hai*. Ten years later, she recorded an Indipop album titled *Janam Samjha Karo,* with Leslie Lewis. In 2002, she composed music for an eight-song music and video album called *Aap Ki Asha*. She sang a duet with Adnan Sami in his album *Kabhi to nazar milao*. She has collaborated with musicians from different countries including Robbie Williams, Boy George, Code Red, Nelly Furtado and The Black Eyed Peas. She recorded the song 'The Way You Dream' with Michael Stipe, which was used in the film *Bulletproof Monk.*

In 2001, the CD single of Nelly Furtado, 'I'm Like A Bird', included a Nelly vs Asha remix. In 2005, parts of her songs 'Ae Naujawan Sab Kuchh Yahan' and 'Yeh Mera Dil Pyar Ka Diwana' were used by the Black Eyed Peas for their their single 'Don't Phunk With My Heart'. 'A Brimful Of Asha' by the British band Cornershop is a tribute to her.

Asha has also remixed many R.D. Burman classics in a posthumous tribute album called *Rahul & I.*

The Government of India honoured her with the Dadasaheb Phalke Award in 2000. She also received the Padma Vibhushan in 2008. In 2011, Asha entered the *Guinness Book of World Records* for the most number of songs recorded.

Asha married R.D. Burman in 1980.

GOOD TO KNOW

- In 2006, she sang the duet 'You're The One For Me', with Australian cricketer Brett Lee.
- Asha Bhosle has sung in virtually every Indian language, as well as in Russian and Malay.
- Asha is a brilliant cook herself and owns a chain of restaurants called Asha's in different parts of the world.

QUIZ

1. With which film did Asha make her Hindi film debut?
   a) *Dadi*
   b) *Mai*
   c) *Chachi*

   Answer: ***Mai***

2. With which of the following bands did Asha sing 'We Can Make It'?
   a) Code Red
   b) Code Blue
   c) Code Green

   Answer: Code Red

3. Which Hindi film was based on the relationship between Lata Mangeshkar and Asha Bhosle?
   a) Saaz
   b) *Awaaz*
   c) *Sur*

   Answer: ***Saaz***

GLOSSARY

- Ghazal: is a lyric poem with a fixed number of verses and a repeated rhyme, typically on the theme of love, and normally set to music.
- Remix: is a new or different version of a recorded song that

is made by changing or adding to the original recording of the song.

- Qawwali: is a style of Muslim devotional music, now associated particularly with Sufis.

DEVIKA RANI

Devika Rani is widely recognized as the 'First Lady of the Indian Screen'. She was a true artiste, who was adept at handling the various processes of film-making in front of the camera as well as behind it. In 1934, she founded the studio Bombay Talkies along with her husband and film-maker, Himanshu Rai.

Devika Rani was born on 30 March 1908 in Vishakhapatnam (now in Andhra Pradesh). Her father was Colonel M.N. Choudheri, the first Indian Surgeon-General of Madras, and her mother was Leela Choudheri.

Devika Rani was educated in England. She studied applied arts, specializing in textile designing and decor, and also architecture. In 1928, while working as a textile designer at a prominent art studio in London, she met the Indian producer Himanshu Rai, who convinced her to join his production unit. She was initially hired as a set and costume consultant. In 1929, she married Rai and went with him to Germany. At the U.F.A. Studios in Berlin, she took classes in make-up, costume designing, and other related branches of film production. She was also trained to become an actor.

When the world was transitioning from the silent era of films to the talkie era, Devika Rani was still working at U.F.A. which gave her the opportunity to study and experiment with the various techniques that were developed. She debuted as an actor in *Karma* (1933) opposite her husband Rai. It was a black-and-white bilingual film, made primarily for international audiences. It was also the first Indian film released in English.

They returned to India and decided to establish their own studio. In 1934, they set up a studio called Bombay Talkies in Malad, Bombay. With technical expertise being provided by German director Franz Osten and cameraman Carl Josef Wirsching, and excellent equipment brought from abroad, the studio soon emerged as one the best in the country. The studio was responsible for launching the careers of future stalwarts of Bollywood, such as Ashok Kumar, Dilip Kumar and Raj Kapoor.

Arguably, Devika Rani was the jewel in the crown of Bombay Talkies Ltd. Her innovative approach to acting and inimitable style were later emulated by numerous other actors. Many of her films have become classics of Indian cinema. *Javani Ki Hawa* (1935), holds a special place in the history of Hindi films, as it was the first film that was shot entirely on a train, as it travelled between Bombay and Lonavala. Some of her other famous films were, *Jeevan Nayya, Achoot Kanya, Savitri, Jeevan Prabhat, Durga, Vachan, Nirmala* and *Izzat.*

Even after Himanshu Rai's death in 1940, Devika Rani upheld the high standards of the company, as chief producer and controller of production. This period was marked by successful films such as: *Punarmilan, Kangan, Bandhan, Basant, Kismat* and *Hamari Baat*. She met Svetoslav Roerich, an artist, in 1944. A year later they married, and she decided to retire.

Devika Rani received the Padma Shri from the Government of India in 1958. In 1969, she became the first recipient of the Dadasaheb Phalke Award, for her contribution to Indian cinema. She was also awarded the coveted Soviet Land Nehru award in 1989.

Devika Rani passed away on 9 March 1994 in Bangalore.

GOOD TO KNOW

- In 2011, a postage stamp, bearing her photo, was released in her honour.
- After its release, the film *Karma* was specially screened for the royal family at Windsor.

QUIZ

1. Which of these actors worked as a lab assistant in Devika Rani's film studio?
   a) Dilip Kumar
   b) Ashok Kumar
   c) Raj Kapoor

   Answer: Ashok Kumar

2. What was Devika Rani's nickname?
   a) Iron Lady
   b) Dragon Lady
   c) Princess

   Answer: Dragon Lady

3. Devika Rani was related to which Nobel laureate?
   a) C.V. Raman
   b) Amartya Sen
   c) Rabindranath Tagore

   Answer: Rabindranath Tagore

GLOSSARY

- Talkie: is a film with a soundtrack, as distinct from a silent film.

DHUNDIRAJ GOVIND PHALKE

Dhundiraj Govind Phalke, also known as Dadasaheb Phalke and referred to as the 'Father of Indian cinema', was a producer and director of the early 20th century. He is credited with directing the first Indian feature film, Raja Harishchandra, in 1913. A major part of work from that period that still survives, is associated with him. His life was devoted to making silent films. Popularly known as Dadasaheb Phalke, he made 95 films and 26 short films in less than two decades.

Dadasaheb Phalke was born in Trimbakeshwar, about 30 kilometres away from Nashik, on 30th April 1870, to a Sanskrit scholar who wanted his son to follow in his footsteps. When his father shifted to Bombay as a teacher, he joined Sir J.J. School of Art, and later went to Kalabhavan in Baroda. It was in Baroda that he first became interested in photography. During this time, he demonstrated a keen interest in various fields like lithography, photography, architecture and amateur dramatics. He started training as an amateur magician and later worked as a photographer, a scene painter, a portrait photographer, stage make-up man and as an assistant to a German magician. In 1901, he joined Raja Ravi Varma's press in Lonavala. After working for a few years, he started an independent venture named Phalke's Engraving and Printing Works. In 1909, he went to Germany to learn the new three-colour technology. He returned and upgraded his press which was then called the Lakshmi Art Printing Works. This was one of the rare presses at that time which dealt with colour printing. But later he gave up working at the press.

In 1910, Phalke had the opportunity to watch the French silent film *Vie et Passion du Christ (Life and Passion of the Christ)*. It was a life changing moment for him, as it made him decide that he wanted to be involved in film-making. He made a few short films and then travelled to London in 1912 to buy better equipment. There, he also spent time with the British film director Cecil Hepworth of Walton Studios.

The film that Phalke is most famous for, *Raja Harishchandra*, premiered in 1913 at the Coronation Cinema in Bombay and ran for twenty-three days. After that, he shifted from Bombay to Nashik and made *Mohini Basmasur* and *Satyavan Savitri*. *Mohini Bhasmasur* is an important film, as it was the first Indian film that featured a woman in its cast. Some of his later films include *Lanka Dahan* (1917), *Shri Krishna Janma* (1918) and *Kaliya Mardan* (1919).

Phalke died on 16 February 1944 in Nashik.

The then Government of India introduced Dadasaheb Phalke Award in 1969, to recognize and acknowledge the contribution of people who have worked towards the development of Indian cinema.

GOOD TO KNOW

- Phalke's daughter, Mandakini Phalke, acted in the film *Kaliya Mardan*.
- Phalke was a trained magician. He even shot a film performing magic tricks himself.

QUIZ

1. What was the name of the magazine that Phalke wrote for?
   a) *Navyug*

b) *Kalyug*
c) *Satyug*

Answer: ***Navyug***

2. Who was the first recipient of the Dadasaheb Phalke Award?
   a) Prithviraj Kapoor
   b) Uttam Kumar
   c) Devika Rani

Answer: Devika Rani

3. In 1901, Phalke joined a printing press in Lonavala which was originally owned by a famous person. Who was he?
   a) Rabindranath Tagore
   b) Raja Ravi Varma
   c) Jawaharlal Nehru

Answer: Raja Ravi Varma

GLOSSARY

- Lithography: is a method of printing from a flat surface (such as a smooth stone or a metal plate) that has been prepared so that the ink only sticks to the design that is to be printed.
- Silent film: is a film with no sound.

DILIP KUMAR

Dilip Kumar is a former Hindi cinema actor, who was referred to as the 'Tragedy King' of Bollywood. He was the first actor to receive the Filmfare Award for Best Actor in 1954.

Dilip Kumar was born as Muhammad Yusuf Khan on 11 December 1922 in Peshawar (now in Pakistan). His father, Ghulam Sarwar, was a fruit merchant. Their family moved to Mumbai in the 1930s and in the early 40s he moved to Pune, where he eventually owned a canteen and supplied dry fruits.

Dilip Kumar got his first break in films when he accidentally met the actress Devika Rani in Nainital. His debut film was *Jwar Bhata*, but it was not until a few years later that he received great acclaim for his role in the film *Jugnu*. He starred alongside Raj Kapoor in the 1949 hit film *Andaaz*, which firmly cemented his place as a superstar. Incidentally, it was the only film in which they acted together. Throughout the 1950s, he was extremely popular and shared this space only with Raj Kapoor and Dev Anand. He was well-known for playing tragic roles in films like *Deedar, Amar, Devdas,* and *Madhumati* which led Bimal Roy and B.R. Chopra to call him a 'Tragedy King'. He changed his 'Tragedy King' image with his roles in *Aan*, *Azaad* and *Insaniyat*. He also portrayed comic characters in *Ram Aur Shyam, Leader* and *Kohinoor*. He is often regarded as the finest method actor in Bollywood.

Dilip Kumar married the actress, Saira Banu in 1966, when she was just twenty-two years of age. In 1962, the famous British director David Lean offered him the role of Sherif Ali in the film *Lawrence of Arabia,* but he rejected it.

The character of Amarnath Singh in *Qila* (1998) was Dilip Kumar's last role in any film. He has acted in more than fifty films in his lifetime and won eight Filmfare Best Actor Awards.

Dilip Kumar was awarded the Padma Bhushan in 1991, Filmfare Lifetime Achievement Award in 1993 and the Dadasaheb Phalke Award in 1995. He served as a member of Rajya Sabha from the year 2000 to 2006.

GOOD TO KNOW

- Dilip Kumar is said to have spent one and a half years learning to play the sitar for the sequence of the song 'Madhuban mein Radhika nache re' for the film *Kohinoor.*
- Satyajit Ray described Dilip Kumar as the ultimate method actor.
- When he was looking for a screen name, some of the names suggested were Jehangir and Vasudev.

QUIZ

1. Who gave the name Dilip Kumar to Yusuf Khan?
   a) Bhagwati Charan Verma
   b) Mahadevi Verma
   c) Harivansh Rai Bachchan

   Answer: Bhagwati Charan Verma

2. So far, which is the only film in which Amitabh Bachchan and Dilip Kumar acted together?
   a) *Dharam Adhikari*
   b) *Shakti*
   c) *Karma*

   Answer: ***Shakti***

3. In which of these films did Dilip Kumar play a triple role?

a) *Bairaag*
b) *Shakti*
c) *Ganga Jumna*

Answer: *Bairaag*

GLOSSARY

- Method acting: is a technique of acting developed by Russian actor, theoretician and producer Konstantin Stanislavsky. In this method, the actor tries to have a complete emotional identification with the part he is playing.

KISHORE KUMAR

Kishore Kumar was a singer, lyricist, music director, actor, director and producer. He has sung in many languages, including Bengali, Hindi, Bhojpuri, Kannada, Assamese, Marathi, Gujarati, Oriya and Malayalam. He is also distinctly remembered for his yodelling.

Kishore Kumar was born on 4 August 1929 in Khandwa (present-day Madhya Pradesh), to Kunjalal Ganguly and Gouri Devi. He was born Abhas Kumar Ganguly and was the youngest of Kunjalal's children. His siblings were Ashok Kumar, Anoop Kumar and Sati Devi. He wanted to be a singer from a young age and so, he left for Mumbai from Khandwa when he was only eighteen years old. He changed his name to Kishore Kumar and began his career as a chorus singer at Bombay Talkies. He sang his first solo song for the film *Ziddi*, composed by Khemchand Prakash.

The song failed to establish him as a singer and Kishore started acting in films. Kishore's first successful film as an actor was *Ladki* (1953) followed by many comedy films including *New Delhi* (1956) and *Asha* (1957), making him a popular comic hero. He also appeared with his brothers Ashok and Anoop in the hit films *Badhti Ka Naam Dadhi*, *Chalti ka Naam Gadi* and *Chalti Ka Naam Zindagi.*

With *Jhumroo* (1961), he became a music director. He made his directorial debut with the film *Door Gagan Ki Chhaon Mein (1964).*

In 1969, Kishore sang two of S.D. Burman's songs, 'Mere Sapnon Ki Rani' and 'Roop Tera Mastana', for the film *Aradhana.* They became a huge hit, and he had established himself as a leading playback singer.

Some of Kishore Kumar's most popular songs include: Ek ladki bheegi bhaagi si (*Chalti Ka Naam Gaadi*), Gaata rahe mera dil (*Guide),* Pal bhar ke liye koi (*Johny Mera Naam),* Yeh shaam mastani (*Kati Patang*) and Khaike paan Banaraswala (*Don*).

Kishore Kumar holds the Guinness World Record for winning the most number of Filmfare Best Singer Awards. He has won the Filmfare Award for Best Male Playback Singer eight times, a record in that category.

On the night before Kishore died of a heart attack, he recorded a duet with Asha Bhosle. He died on 13 October 1987 in Mumbai, at the age of fifty-eight.

GOOD TO KNOW

- Kishore Kumar sang in more than 90 films for Rajesh Khanna.
- Kishore Kumar learnt yodelling by listening to his brother Anoop Kumar's Austrian records.
- As he was very busy, Kishore Kumar had to let Mohammed Rafi playback for him for the song 'Ajab Hai Dastaan Teri' in the 1959 film *Shararat*.

QUIZ

1. On which actor was Kishore Kumar's first solo song picturised?
   a) Raj Kapoor
   b) Dev Anand
   c) Dilip Kumar

Answer: Dev Anand

2. From which film is the song 'Paanch Rupaiyah Barah Anna'?
   a) *Padosan*
   b) *Chalti Ka Naam Gaadi*
   c) *Half Ticket*

Answer: *Chalti Ka Naam Gaadi*

3. Which state awards the Kishore Kumar Awards?
   a) Uttar Pradesh
   b) West Bengal
   c) Madhya Pradesh

Answer: Madhya Pradesh

GLOSSARY

- Yodelling: is a form of singing or calling, marked by rapid alternation between the normal voice and falsetto.

LATA MANGESHKAR

Lata Mangeshkar, also referred to as the 'Nightingale of India', is a playback singer whose career has spanned over seven decades.

Lata Mangeshkar was born on 28 September 1929 in Indore (now in Madhya Pradesh). Her father, Pandit Deenanath Mangeshkar, was a classical singer and actor. She was named Lata, after the character 'Latika' in one of her father's plays. She was the eldest child, and her music lessons started at the age of five under the guidance of her father. However, her father passed away when she was just thirteen.

Vinayak Damodar Karnataki, the owner of Navyug Chitrapat Film Company and a close family friend, helped the family in this time of need. He also helped Lata begin her career as a singer. Though her first recorded song was for the Marathi film *Kiti Hasaal* (1942), it was edited from the final cut. When Vinayak moved to Bombay in 1945, the Mangeshkar family moved with him. It was here that she took music lessons from Ustad Amanat Ali Khan. She and her younger sister, Asha, also played minor roles in Vinayak's first Hindi-language film, *Badi Maa* (1945). She also sang a melodious bhajan called 'Maata Tere Charnon Mein' for the film.

After Vinayak's death in 1948, music director Ghulam Haider mentored Lata. She received her first breakthrough with the song 'Dil Mera Toda' from the film *Majboor*. The song 'Ayega Aanewaala' from the 1949 film *Mahal* became a hit; after which music directors vied with one another to sign her. Legends like Shankar-Jaikishan, Naushad Ali, S.D. Burman, Hemant Kumar and Salil Chowdhury worked with her and produced successful songs. Films like *Tarana, Baiju Bawra, Mughal-E-Azam, Kohinoor, Aag, Shree 420* and *Chori Chori* brought out numerous hit songs. She won the Filmfare Award for Best Female Playback Singer in 1958 for the song 'Aaja Re Pardesi' from the film *Madhumati.*

During the Sino-Indian War, she sang the song 'Aye Mere Watan Ke Logo', which is said to have moved Jawaharlal Nehru to tears.

In the early 1970s, Lata recorded songs for Meena Kumari's last film *Pakezaah* and also S.D. Burman's last couple of films like *Sharmeelee* and *Abhiman*. In the subsequent years, she recorded songs with both new and veteran music directors. She has sung in many of Yash Chopra's films, including *Chandni* (1989), *Lamhe* (1991), *Darr* (1993), *Yeh Dillagi* (1994), *Dilwale Dulhaniya Le Jayenge* (1995), *Dil To Pagal Hai* (1997), *Mohabbatein* (2000), *Mujhse Dosti Karoge* (2002) and *Veer Zaara* (2004).

Lata and A.R. Rahman have collaborated for several films, including *Dil Se, Zubeidaa, Rang De Basanti* and *Lagaan.*

Lata was nominated as a member of the Rajya Sabha in 1999. She was awarded the Bharat Ratna in 2001. She founded the Master Deenanath Mangeshkar Hospital in Pune, which is managed by the Lata Mangeshkar Medical Foundation.

GOOD TO KNOW

- In 1969, Lata made the unusual gesture of giving up her Filmfare Award in order to promote fresh talent. She was later awarded the Filmfare Lifetime Achievement Award in 1993.
- The state of Madhya Pradesh honours eminent musicians

with the prestigious award 'Lata Mangeshkar Samman Alankaran'.
- Lata was named 'Hema' at her birth.

OUIZ

1. Which was the first film of R.D. Burman in which Lata Mangeshkar sang?
   a) *Majboor*
   b) *Chhote Nawab*
   c) *Kagaaz ke Phool*

   Answer: *Chhote Nawab*

2. Who directed the 1990 film *Lekin*, produced by Lata Mangeshkar?
   a) Gulzar
   b) Laxmikant Pyarelal
   c) Kishore Kumar

   Answer: Gulzar

3. In 2005, what did Lata Mangeshkar design which was called 'Swaranjali'?
   a) Benarasi saree
   b) Filmfare award statue
   c) Jewellery collection

   Answer: Jewellery collection

GLOSSARY

- 'Aye Mere Watan Ke Logo': is a patriotic Hindi song, written by Kavi Pradeep.

MOHAMMED RAFI

Mohammed Rafi was an Indian playback singer who sang over twenty-five thousand songs in various Indian languages, in his career which spanned almost four decades.

Mohammed Rafi was born on 24 December 1924 in Kotla Sultanpur, near Amritsar (now in Pakistan). His family moved to Lahore when he was young. He showed interest and enthusiasm in music from a very early age. As a child, he was influenced by a 'Fakir' who sang folk songs in his village. Though his father was against his decision to pursue singing as a career, his elder brother encouraged him.

He was trained by prominent singers like Ustad Abdul Wahid Khan, Pandit Jiwanlal Matto, Ghulam Ali Khan and Firoz Nizami.

The turning point in his life was when, at the age of fifteen, he was asked to perform in public. As fate would have it, noted composer Shyamsunder was in the audience, and impressed by his talent invited him to Bombay to sing in films.

The first song Rafi recorded was for the Punjabi film *Gul Baloch*. Some of his earlier recordings in Bombay were for films like *Gaon Ki Gori, Samaj Ko Badal Dalo* and *Jugnu.* Naushad was the composer who first recognized his talent and gave him his first solo assignment, which was the song 'Tera khilona toota balak' in the film *Anmol Ghadi* (1946), and later the song 'Is duniya mein aye dilwalon' in the film *Dillagi* (1949) which turned out to be extremely popular. *Baiju Bawara,* later, established

Rafi's credentials as a talented singer.

Rafi was a born perfectionist, and he rehearsed his songs well before the final take, which accounts for the high-level of quality each of his songs achieved.

The following years saw Rafi in great demand, with composers using his unmatched voice quality and vocal range to great advantage. Another quality that set him apart was that he could change his voice to match that of the character who was singing it on screen. Therefore, he was equally comfortable with singing 'Tere husn ki kya tariff karoon' for Dilip Kumar in the film *Leader*, 'Yeh duniya agar mil bhi jaaye to kya hai' for Guru Dutt in *Pyaasa* and 'Yahoo' for Shammi Kapoor in the film *Junglee*. He also excelled in classical songs like 'Madhuban mein Radhika' and light numbers like 'Aaja Aaja'. His duets with contemporary playback singers are popular to this day.

Two very important features of Rafi's personality that few know about were his humility and generosity. He would often sing at a very low price for producers who could not afford the normal fee.

Rafi was awarded the Padma Shri in 1965 and the Rajat Kamal in 1977. He also received six Filmfare Awards in his lifetime.

Mohammed Rafi passed away on 31 July 1980.

GOOD TO KNOW

- Mohammed Rafi sang 'Chanda Ka Dil Toot Gaya Ha' for Nissar Kaazmi, in the film *Khoj,* just for ₹1.
- Rafi has sung more duets with Asha Bhosle than any other playback singer.
- Rafi could sing ghazals, bhajans, classical songs, folk tunes and quawalis.

QUIZ

1. Mohammed Rafi sang for which singer-actor in films such as *Raagini*, *Baaghi*, *Shehzaada* and *Shararat*?
   a) Manna Dey
   b) Kishore Kumar
   c) Talat Mahmood

   Answer: Kishore Kumar

2. For which film did Mohammed Rafi sing the song 'O Duniya Ke Rakhwale'?
   a) *Baiju Bawra*
   b) *Pyasaa*
   c) *Junglee*

   Answer: *Baiju Bawra*

3. Mohammed Rafi sang 'Bar bar dekno, hazar baar dekho' for which of these actors?
   a) Dilip Kumar
   b) Shammi Kapoor
   c) Shashi Kapoor

   Answer: Shammi Kapoor

GLOSSARY

- Playback singer: (Especially in Indian cinema) a singer who records songs to be mimed by actors in films.
- Fakir: is a Muslim (or, loosely, a Hindu) religious ascetic who lives solely on alms.

RAHUL DEV BURMAN

Rahul Dev Burman, also referred to as R.D. Burman or Pancham, was a legendary music director and singer. He is credited with composing music for more than two hundred and fifty Hindi films and many Bengali films. He has composed music in many languages, including Oriya, Assamese, Tamil, Telugu and English.

R.D. Burman was born on 27 June 1939 in Calcutta, to the music director Sachin Dev Burman. He was fond of playing the mouth organ and helped his father in films like *Pyaasa* (1957) and *Aradhana*. But it was his friend and actor Mehmood, who gave him a break as an independent music composer in his 1961 production *Chhote Nawab*. Burman had to wait for four years before he was signed for his next film, which was Mehmood's *Bhoot Bangla* (1965). He was also cast in a comic role in the same film.

Burman's first box office hit was his music for Nasir Hussain's film *Teesri Manzil* (1966). He went on to produce music for many successful films like *Caravan, Yaadon Ki Baaraat* and *Hum Kisi se Kam Nahin*.

In the early 1970s, Burman reached his zenith composing a list of songs in films starring in films like *Kati Patang* and *Namak Haram,* Rajesh Khanna. His image received a boost with songs such as 'Hare Rama Hare Krishna' and 'Yeh Jawani Hai Diwani', which made him a pop icon. A new dimension of his versatility found expression when he collaborated with Gulzar to produce soulful songs like 'Tum Aa Gaye Ho' for the film *Aandhi* and 'Naam Ghum Jayega' for the film *Kinara.*

Burman is also credited with introducing electronic rock into Hindi film music. He used such music in films like Narendra Bedi's *Jawani Diwani.* He also introduced the Brazilian bossa nova rhythm with the song 'Maar dalega dard-e-jigar' for the film *Pati Patni.*

R.D. also produced independent albums, which includes one based on the samba and one with British pop star Boy George. He sang songs in a unique grunting bass.

The trio of Rajesh Khanna, R.D. Burman and Kishore Kumar worked together in more than 30 films.

Burman married the legendary singer Asha Bhosle in 1980. *1942: A Love Story*, his last film, was released after his death, and was a major musical success.

R.D. Burman passed away on 4 January 1994 in Mumbai.

GOOD TO KNOW

- Mehmood says he gave his friend, Rahul, his break as a music director in *Chhote Nawab* in 1961 because he got tired of Rahul denting his car with the persistent drumming of his fingers.
- *Pancham Unmixed: Mujhe Chalte Jaana Hai* by Brahmanand and S. Singh, is a documentary on R.D. Burman.
- In the film *Khushboo*, for the song 'O Manjhi Re,' R.D. used soda bottles with water filled at different levels to create a 'phook' sound by blowing into them. This sound was used with the orchestra.

QUIZ

1. For which of these films did R.D. Burman win his first Filmfare Award?

a) *Aradhana*
b) Sanam Teri Kasam
c) 1942: A Love Story

Answer: ***Sanam Teri Kasam***

2. According to R.D., if Amitabh Bachchan was a Bollywood Legend, who was a Permanent Superstar?
   a) Dilip Kumar
   b) Raj Kapoor
   c) Rajesh Khanna

Answer: Rajesh Khanna

3. R.D. Burman composed his first song at the age of nine for which of these films?
   a) *Fantoosh*
   b) *Khushboo*
   c) *Sanam Teri Kasam*

Answer: ***Fantoosh***

GLOSSARY

- Sachin Dev Burman: was a Bengali singer and composer. He was also a music composer of Hindi films.
- Bossa nova: is a kind of music that is originally from Brazil.

RAJ KAPOOR

Raj Kapoor was a Hindi film director and actor, whose films were popular in India, the Middle East, the Soviet Union and China. He was also known as the 'Showman' of Hindi cinema.

Raj Kapoor was born on 14 December 1924 in Peshawar (now in Pakistan), to Prithvi Raj Kapoor. His first brush with Bollywood came when he started working as a clapper boy for Bombay Talkies and also acted in small roles for Prithvi Theatres; both companies being owned by his father. His popularity soared after the 1947 film *Neel Kamal* in which he played the lead role.

When Raj Kapoor was just twenty-four years old, he set up his own studio called RK Films and produced and directed his first film, *Aag*. It was his first film with Nargis, but did not generate much success. The studio's second film *Andaz*, in which he was paired opposite Nargis, struck gold at the box office. This was his first major success as an actor. He starred in successful films such as *Barsaat*, *Shree 420*, *Jagte Raho* and *Mera Naam Joker*. He became immensely popular in Russia after *Awaara* and *Shri 420,* as the films attained cult status in the country.

In 1964, Raj Kapoor produced, directed and starred in the first colour film of his career, *Sangam*. It also marked his last major success as an actor. In 1973, he produced and directed *Bobby*, through which he also launched the acting career of his second son, Rishi Kapoor. The film turned out to be a huge success.

Kapoor's style of acting has often been compared to that

of Charlie Chaplin's. He depicted the story of a common man in his films and they appealed to every section of the society. Music was an integral part of his films, and the songs were popular not only in India, but abroad as well.

He won numerous awards during his career in Hindi films. In 1985, Raj Kapoor's film *Ram Teri Ganga Maili* won the Filmfare Award for Best Film and Best Director. His film *Awara* was nominated for the Grand Prix at the 1953 Cannes Film Festival.

Raj Kapoor was awarded the Padma Bhushan in 1971. He also won the Dadasaheb Phalke Award for his indispensable contribution to Indian cinema.

Raj Kapoor was to receive the Dadasaheb Phalke award when he suffered an acute asthma attack and passed away on 2 June 1988.

GOOD TO KNOW

- The actors Ranbir Kapoor, Karisma Kapoor and Kareena Kapoor are all his grandchildren.
- *Kal Aaj Aur Kal* (1971) featured three generations of the Kapoor family: Prithviraj Kapoor, Randhir Kapoor, and Raj Kapoor and Randhir Kapoor.

QUIZ

1. From which film did the scene featuring Nargis, Raj and a violin become the RK Films' logo?
   a) *Aag*
   b) *Barsaat*
   c) *Mera Naam Joker*

Answer: ***Barsaat***

2. Which of these films was released in Russia under the name *Brodigaya*?
   a) *Awara*

b) *Shree 420*
c) *Sangam*

Answer: ***Awara***

3. Which of these films was Raj Kapoor's last, as an actor?
    a) *Naukri*
    b) *Vakil Babu*
    c) *Teesri Kasam*

Answer: ***Vakil Babu***

GLOSSARY

- Prithvi Theatres: is one of Mumbai's best known theatres, it was built by Shashi Kapoor in memory of his father Prithviraj Kapoor.
- Grand Prix at the Cannes Film Festival: is an award of the Cannes Film Festival bestowed by the jury of the festival on one of the competing feature films.

RAJINIKANTH

Rajinikanth is an actor who has worked in more than one hundred and fifty films. He is known most for his action sequences and his particular way of delivering dialogues.

Rajinikanth was born as Shivaji Rao Gaekwad on 12 December 1950 in Bangalore, Karnataka.

As a youngster, he worked as a bus conductor for the Bangalore Transport Service.

His friend, Raj Bahadur, persuaded him to join the Madras Film Institute. His theatre performances were noticed by the film director K. Balachander. On his suggestion, Rajinikanth learnt to speak Tamil, and Balachander cast him in his very first role. This proved to be the turning point in his career.

Rajinikanth mostly played negative roles early in his career. Some of the films of the period were: *Apoorva Raaganga* and *Moondru Mudichu*. The first film where he appeared as a hero was the Tamil film *Bairavi*, released in 1978. He also appeared with N.T. Rama Rao in the film *Tiger*. Though he tried to quit acting, he was coaxed back. He made a comeback with the Tamil film *Billa*, which was a remake of the Bollywood film *Don* (1978). In the 80s, he acted in more than 90 films in Tamil, Hindi, Telugu and Kannada, and became a popular actor in South India.

Rajnikanth then starred in his first full-length comedy film called *Thillu Mullu*. He made his Bollywood debut in 1983 with the film *Andha Kanoon*, in which Amitabh Bachchan was his co-star. He also acted in an English film called *Bloodstone,* directed by Dwight H. Little.

In 1991, he shared the screen with Amitabh Bachchan yet again in the film *Hum*. He also acted alongside Mammooty in the film *Thalapathi*, directed by Mani Ratnam. He even wrote screenplays for the films *Valli* and *Baba* in 2002.

Chandramukhi (2005) was Rajinikanth's comeback film after his 2002 film *Baba* did not become a hit. The film set a record of being the longest-running Tamil film of its time. In 2007, his film *Shivaji* was enlisted in the box office list of the top ten best released films in the United Kingdom and South Africa. In 2010, his film *Endhiran* was considered as the most expensive and highest-grossing Tamil film in India at the time of its release.

He has received numerous awards and honours including the Kalaimamani Award (1984), the M.G.R. Award (1989) and the Padma Bhushan (2000).

Rajnikanth is married to Latha Rangachari, and they have two daughters named Aishwarya Rajinikanth and Soundarya Rajinikanth.

GOOD TO KNOW

- The story of Rajnikanth's life is taught to students of CBSE affiliated schools. The chapter is titled 'From Bus Conductor to Superstar'.
- He has nicknames like 'Superstar' and 'Thalaivar'.
- The song 'Lungi Dance' from the film 'Chennai Express' is dedicated to Rajnikanth.

QUIZ

1. Name the book written by P.C. Balasubramanian and Ram N. Ramakrishnan, which discusses Rajinikanth as a brand.
   a) *Rich Brand Rajini*

   b) *Value Brand Rajini*
   c) *Grand Brand Rajini*

Answer: *Grand Brand Rajini*

2. In his 100th film, Rajinikanth played the role of which saint?
   a) Saint Raghavendra
   b) Saint Tukaram
   c) Saint Tyagaraja

Answer: Saint Raghavendra

3. In the 1995 film *Aatank Hi Aatank*, Rajinikanth shared screen space with which of these Bollywood heroes?
   a) Shah Rukh Khan
   b) Amitabh Bachchan
   c) Aamir Khan

Answer: Aamir Khan

GLOSSARY

- Debut: is a person's first appearance or performance in a particular capacity or role.
- Box office: is a place at a theatre and cinema, where tickets are bought or reserved. It is also used to refer to the commercial success of a film, play or actor in terms of the audience size or takings that they command.

SATYAJIT RAY

Satyajit Ray was a film-maker who, even today, is considered as one of the greatest in the field, both in India and the world. He established India firmly on the map of international cinema with his very first film *Pather Panchali,* that won numerous awards. He was not only a film director but was also adept at other aspects of film-making, like scriptwriting, composing, and producing.

Ray was born on 2 May 1921 in Calcutta, to Sukumar Ray and Suprabha Ray. He belonged to a family that was devoted to the arts. His grandfather, Upendra Kishore Ray Chowdhury, was a famous writer of children's literature, renowned painter and composer of great repute. Upendra Kishore was also the founder of one of the finest presses in the country, U. Ray & Sons. His father was a famous poet, story writer and playwright. Before joining Ballygunj Government School at the age of eight, he was homeschooled by his mother. Ray was fascinated by films from an early age.

Ray graduated from Presidency College in 1940. While he was in college, he was passionate about watching films and listening to Western classical music. When he was eighteen, he gave up the idea of studying further to become a commercial artist, even though he was not formally trained. However, his mother insisted that he should do a course in painting at Shantiniketan and he obliged.

Ray came back to Calcutta after a few fruitful years in Shantiniketan, and in April 1943 he joined the British-run advertising agency called D.J. Keymer, as a junior visualiser. It was during his stint here that he came across a copy of Bibhuti Bhushan Bannerjee's *Pather Panchali*, a novel which would prove to be a turning point in his life. He worked in the agency for twelve years, till the film *Pather Panchali* became a reality.

Ray co-founded Calcutta's first film society in 1947. Thereafter, he began both writing and publishing various articles on cinema, in newspapers and magazines. The work *Our Films, Their Films,* is a compilation of such articles, which were written from 1948 to 1971.

1949 was Ray's most momentous year. He met the famous French film director, Jean Renoir. Initially, he was supposed to help Renoir find locations for his film *The River* but they eventually ended up having long discussions about the various aspects of film and film-making. Soon, he was sent by his advertising agency on a trip to London. On the way to the city and his journey back, he made detailed notes on *Pather Panchali*. During his stay there, he saw numerous films, which included experimental films made in the avant garde and nouvelle vague styles. *The Bicycle Thieves*, a film directed by Vittorio De Sica, influenced him greatly.

Ray returned to Calcutta in 1950, and began shooting *Pather Panchali*. He formed a team of technicians to assist him and obtained the rights for filming the novel. Even though he tried hard, he couldn't find a producer to back his film. Finally, he approached the chief minister of Bengal, Dr B.C. Roy, who granted him funds. As he had to work in outdoor locations with inexperienced actors, he had to face many difficulties while shooting the film.

Pather Panchali was released on 26 August 1955 in Calcutta. Ray drew on his experience from his advertising days and he himself designed five billboards for the film. The film went on to become a huge success, earning accolades from around the world. Dr B.C. Roy was so moved by the film that he ensured Pandit Jawaharlal Nehru watched it on his visit to Calcutta; Nehru was so touched by the film that he ensured its entry into the Cannes Film Festival in 1956.

The enormous success of the film allowed Ray to have total control over his subsequent films. He worked on the various aspects of his later films in the capacity of writer, director, casting director and even composer. Two sequels based on the novels *Aparajito*, or *The Unvanquished* (1956) and *Apur Sansar*, or *The World of Apu* (1959), completed the universally acclaimed *Apu Trilogy*. He would go on to make a feature-length film every year till 1981.

Some of Ray's later films include, *Parash Pathar* (*The Philosopher's Stone*, 1958), *Jalsaghar* (*The Music Room*, 1958), *Devi* (*The Goddess*, 1960), *Teen Kanya* (*Two Daughters*, 1961), *Kanchenjungha* (1962), *Charulata* (*The Lonely Wife*, 1964), *Pratidwandi* (*The Adversary*, 1970), *Shantranj Ke Khilari* (*The Chess Players*, 1977) and *Ghare-Baire* (*Home and the World*, 1984).

In 1961, Ray revived the children's magazine *Sandesh*, which was founded by his grandfather, and contributed stories, poems and illustrations for its publication. He also wrote numerous short stories, articles and novels in Bengali. He was also the creator of the detective character called Feluda.

Ray was awarded an Honourary Oscar for Lifetime Achievement in 1992. He was also awarded the Bharat Ratna shortly before his death.

Satyajit Ray died on 23 April 1992.

GOOD TO KNOW

- Ray's designs of two typefaces 'Ray Roman' and 'Ray Bizarre' won an international competition in 1971.

- Acclaimed film-maker Akira Kurosawa once said about Ray, 'Not to have seen the cinema of Ray means existing in the world without seeing the sun or the moon.'

QUIZ

1. Which of these films was Satyajit Ray's last?
   a) *Agantuk*
   b) *Ghare Baire*
   c) *Ganashatru*

Answer: ***Agantuk***

2. Satyajit Ray composed music for which of these Merchant Ivory films?
   a) *Shakespeare Wallah*
   b) *The Night of Counting the Years*
   c) *A Room with a View*

Answer: ***Shakespeare Wallah***

3. For which film had Jean Renoir come to Calcutta when he met Satyajit Ray?
   a) *The River*
   b) *The Lake*
   c) *The Sea*

Answer: ***The River***

GLOSSARY

- Avant–garde films: are films which use new and experimental ideas and methods.
- Nouvelle vague: is a term given to a group of French film directors of the late 1950s and 1960s who reacted against established French cinema and sought to make more individualistic and stylistically innovative films. Some of the directors were Jean-Luc Godard, Alain Resnais and François Truffaut.

SHAH RUKH KHAN

Shah Rukh Khan is an actor famous for his romantic roles, and is often referred to as the 'Badshah of Bollywood', 'King Khan' and 'King of Romance'. He has won numerous Filmfare Awards for roles in various capacities.

Shah Rukh Khan was born on 2 November 1965 in Delhi. His father, Meer Taj Mohammed, was a lawyer and freedom activist. He studied at St Columba's School, Delhi. As a student, he excelled in studies as well as in sports, especially hockey and football. He was given the 'Sword of Honour', an award for the student who best represents the spirit of the school. He earned a bachelor's degree in economics from Hansraj College.

Shah Rukh Khan enrolled with Barry John to study theatre. His first acting stints were in television serials like *Fauji* and *Circus*, aired on Doordarshan. However, the turning point in his career was when he won the Filmfare Award for Best Male Debut, for his role in the film *Deewana.*

Shah Rukh Khan's initial success was derived from playing negative roles in films like *Baazigar, Anjaam* and *Darr*. However, in subsequent films he took on the mantle of the hero with his talent and charisma, and created blockbusters like *Dilwale Dulhania Le Jayenge*, *Karan Arjun*, *Dil to Pagal Hai*, *Kuch Kuch Hota Hai*, *Devdas* and *Kal Ho Naa Ho*. He was also lauded for his offbeat roles in films like *Chak De! India* and *Swades*, where he shed the image of the glamourous hero. He was equally successful in portraying comical characters in films such as

Chamatkar, *Yes Boss* and *Duplicate.*

Shah Rukh Khan has also hosted two television based game shows: *Kya Aap Paanchvi Pass Se Tez Hain* and *Kaun Banega Crorepati.*

Shah Rukh Khan along with his friend and actress Juhi Chawla, established Dreamz Unlimited, a production company, in 1991. In 2004, he founded Red Chillies Entertainment, which produced the highly successful *Main Hoon Na.* He is also the owner of the Indian Premier League cricket team, Kolkata Knight Riders, that won the league title in 2012.

He also ranked first, in the very first edition of *Forbes* (India) Celebrity 100 list.

Shah Rukh Khan is married to Gauri Chibber since 1991.

GOOD TO KNOW

- In 2011, Shah Rukh Khan received the *UNESCO* award 'Pyramide con Marno' for his charity engagements and social commitment towards providing education for kids.
- In 2008, Shah Rukh became the first Indian film star to be conferred the prestigious Malaysian title 'Datuk'.

QUIZ

1. What is the name of the bungalow where Shah Rukh Khan lives?
   a) Mannat
   b) Jannat
   c) Khubsurat

Answer: Mannat

2. After which of these films did the sale of hockey sticks shoot up by 30 per cent?
   a) *Chamatkar*
   b) *Dil to Pagal Hai*

c) *Chak De! India*

Answer: ***Chak De! India***

3. In which TV serial did he play the role of Abhimanyu Rai?
   a) *Fauji*
   b) *Circus*
   c) *Wagle ki Duniya*

Answer: ***Fauji***

GLOSSARY

- UNESCO: United Nations Educational, Scientific and Cultural Organization is a specialized agency of the United Nations, and its purpose is to contribute to peace and security by promoting international collaboration through education, science and culture.

SPORTS

ABHINAV BINDRA

Abhinav Bindra is a shooter who became the first Indian to win an Olympic gold medal in the individual category when he won the 10 metre air rifle event at the 2008 Beijing Olympic Games.

Abhinav Bindra was born on 28 September 1982. He studied at Doon School and in St Stephen's School, Chandigarh. He was the youngest Indian to participate in the 1998 Commonwealth Games and the 2000 Olympic Games. He was also the youngest person to receive the Rajiv Gandhi Khel Ratna Award from the Government of India.

At the 2002 Manchester Commonwealth Games, Bindra won the gold medal in 10 metre air rifle team event partnering Sameer Ambekar, and the silver medal in the individual category. At the 2004 Athens Olympic Games, Abhinav broke the then Olympic record to qualify for the final stage but faltered and was the only shooter to score below 100. In 2006, he became the first Indian shooter to win a World Championship gold medal. The same year, he won the gold medal in the Commonwealth Games 10 metre air rifle team event and a bronze medal in the individual event.

At the 2008 Beijing Olympic Games, Bindra again qualified for the final stages, but this time he was in the lead with two others, with a score of 597. In a nerve-wracking climax, he was tied with Henri Hakkinen just before the final shot. This time he held his nerves while the others faltered and he created Indian sporting history by winning the coveted Gold medal. In the team event, India missed another medal by only 2 points. It was India's first Olympic gold after 1980. Bindra was the flag bearer of the Indian contingent at the 2010 New Delhi Commonwealth Games. He also had the honour of taking the oath on behalf of all the participants. He won the gold medal in the team event, but unexpectedly lost the individual event to Gagan Narang. However, at the 2012 London Olympics, Bindra failed to qualify for the final stage.

Before the 2008 Olympic Games, Bindra was supported by the Mittal Champions Trust for importing ammunitions and various other factors which contributed to his win. In 2008, he became a MCT board of trustee himself to closely involve himself with the development of sports in India and produce more champions.

GOOD TO KNOW

- Abhinav Bindra's mentor and physical trainer, Dr Amit Bhattacharjee, has completed three doctorates just to help Abhinav keep at his best.
- Apart from Lt Col Jagir Singh Dhillon and Dr Amit Bhattacharjee, expert coaches like Gaby Buehlmann, Heinz Reinkemier and Dr Uwe Riesterer have worked with Abhinav as his guides.
- Apart from sports, he is also the Director of two companies, one of which is the sole distributor of a German gunmaker in India.

QUIZ

1. How many Asian Games medals has Abhinav Bindra won?
   a) Three
   b) Two
   c) One

Answer: One—Silver at Guangzhou

2. What is the title of Abhinav Bindra's biography, co-authored with journalist and sports writer Rohit Brijnath?
   a) *A Shot at History: My Obsessive Journey to Olympic Gold*
   b) *Open*
   c) *The Race of my Life: An Autobiography*

Answer: *A Shot at History: My Obsessive Journey to Olympic Gold*

3. In 2011, along with which sportsperson was Abhinav Bindra conferred the rank of honorary Lieutenant Colonel by the Territorial Army?
   a) M.S. Dhoni
   b) Arjun Atwal
   c) Saina Nehwal

Answer: M.S. Dhoni

GLOSSARY

- 10 metre air rifle: is an international shooting event, where competitors shoot over a distance of 10 metres from a standing position with a 4.5mm caliber air rifle.
- Flag bearer: are designated sports persons who carry the flags of the countries in the opening and closing ceremonies in multi-sports events like Olympic Games.

BAICHUNG BHUTIA

Baichung Bhutia is a former footballer who played as a striker. Nicknamed the 'Sikkimese Sniper' for his ability to score goals, he is considered as one of the greatest representatives of Indian football in the international arena.

Baichung was born on 15 December 1976 in Tinkitam, Sikkim. He was a versatile athlete, and represented his school in badminton, basketball, football and athletics. His uncle, Karma Bhutia, who managed a football club for boys in Gangtok, encouraged him to seriously take up the sport. He attended the Tashi Namgyal Academy in Gangtok, after he won a football scholarship from the Sports Authority of India (SAI).

Baichung won the 'Best Player' award in the 1992 Subroto Cup, the premier Indian football tournament for schools, after he had impressed many with his skills. Bhaskar Ganguly, the former Indian international goalkeeper, recognized his potential and offered him a spot in East Bengal Football Club.

In 1993, Baichung left school and joined East Bengal F.C. in Kolkata, where he spent two years. Later, he joined JCT Mills in Phagwara and helped them win the 1996-97 National Football League (later changed to I-League) title. He finished as the top goalscorer in the league that season, and returned to East Bengal F.C. in 1997. He was promoted as the captain of the team, and East Bengal F.C. finished second, under Salgaocar, during the 1998-99 season.

Baichung signed a three-year contract with the English club,

Bury F.C., in 1999. Though he managed only a limited number of appearances due to recurring injuries, he became only the second Indian footballer to play in Europe. He scored his first goal for the club on 15 April 2000, in a match against Chesterfield. He was released in 2001 after the club was placed in administration. Once again, he returned to East Bengal F.C. in 2003, after an unsuccessful-injury-prone stint with Mohun Bagan.

East Bengal won the 2003 ASEAN Club Championship, after beating Tero Sasana 3-1 in the final. Baichung was awarded the 'Man of the Match', and he also finished as top scorer of the tournament with 9 goals. Between 2003 and 2005, he played for two Malaysian sides: Perak F.C. and Selangor MK Land. Back in India, he played for Mohun Bagan from 2006 to 2009, and formed a formidable attacking partnership with the Brazilian striker Jose Ramirez Barreto. He quit the club amidst controversies and, for the final time, moved to East Bengal F.C. in 2010.

Baichung scored a goal on his international debut for India in a match against Uzbekistan in the 1995 Nehru Cup, becoming the youngest Indian goalscorer at the age of nineteen. His international titles, while playing for the country, include three South Asian Football Federation (SAFF) Championship titles, the Nehru Cup, the LG Cup, and the AFC Challenge Cup. He played a vital role in India's 2008 AFC Challenge Cup victory, and was picked as the 'Most Valuable Player' of the tournament. This victory helped India to automatically qualify for the 2011 AFC Asian Cup in Qatar, for the first time since 1984. He earned his 100th cap for India during the 2009 Nehru Cup, and was adjudged 'Player of the Tournament'. Injury prevented him from playing in the Asian Cup, and he announced his retirement shortly after India's early exit from the tournament. His record of 42 goals for the country was eclipsed by Sunil Chhetri in November 2013, after he scored his 43rd goal in a match against Nepal.

Baichung donned the Indian colours for the last time on 10 January 2012, in his farewell match against the German club Bayern Munich.

Bhaichung won 'Indian Player of the Year' award twice, in 1996 and 2008. He was honoured with the Ajuna Award in 1999 and the Padma Shri in 2008.

GOOD TO KNOW

- The name 'Baichung' literally means 'little brother'.
- Baichung founded the Bhaichung Bhutia Football Schools in Delhi, Chandigarh, Mumbai and Jammu.
- In Baichung's honour, the Sikkimese government built a stadium called 'Baichung Stadium' in Namchi.

QUIZ

1. In 2012, Baichung Bhutia was appointed as the interim manager of which football team?
   a) Salgaocar
   b) United Sikkim
   c) Dempo

   Answer: United Sikkim

2. Baichung Bhutia was a part of which team that won the 2003-04 National Football League title?
   a) East Bengal
   b) Mohun Bagan
   c) Mohammedan Sporting Club

   Answer: East Bengal

3. In the 2003 ASEAN Cup, against which team did Baichung Bhutia score five goals in a single match?
   a) BEC Tero Sasana

b) Los Angeles Galaxy
c) Philippine Army

Answer: Philippine Army

GLOSSARY

- ASEAN: Association of Southeast Asian Nations, is a geo-political and economic organisation of ten countries located in Southeast Asia. It was formed on 8 August 1967 by Indonesia, Malaysia, the Philippines, Singapore and Thailand.
- AFC Asian Cup: held by the Asian Football Confederation, every four years since 1956, is the second oldest continental football championship in the world.
- Nehru Cup: is an international association football tournament organized by the All India Football Federation (AIFF) that was launched in 1982.

DHYAN CHAND

Dhyan Chand, also known as Major Dhyan Chand and 'the Wizard of hockey', was a field hockey player who, even today, is considered as one of the greatest players of the game.

Dhyan Chand was born on 29 August 1905 in Allahabad, Uttar Pradesh. Since his father, Subedar Sameshwar Dutt Singh, was in the British Army, his family relocated several times before they finally settled in Jhansi. As a youngster, he was not particularly interested in any sport, but was known to have liked wrestling. He was formally introduced to the game of hockey after he joined the Indian Army in 1922. He regularly played in army hockey tournaments, and was a part of the Indian Army team that toured New Zealand in 1926. He sought permission from the army and played for United Provinces in the Inter-Provincial Tournament organized by the Indian Hockey Federation (IHF); the tournament was to select the team that would represent India at the 1928 Amsterdam Olympic Games. He was chosen as the centre-forward of the Indian team because of his stellar performance in the tournament.

At Amsterdam, the Indian team trounced Austria, Belgium, Denmark and Switzerland by convincing margins and without conceding a goal, to reach the final. By virtue of Dhyan Chand's hat-trick alone, India beat the Netherlands 3-0, and won the gold medal. He had netted 14 goals, that included 4 hat-tricks, in 5 matches.

After the Olympic Games, Dhyan Chand was posted in

Waziristan in the Northwest Frontier Province (now in Pakistan). As a result, he was away from competitive hockey for a long time. But given his talent, the IHF ignored the formalities involved in the selection process, and included him in the Indian squad for the 1932 Los Angeles Olympic Games. With only three teams participating in the event that year, the much superior Indian team beat Japan 11-1 and USA 24-1, to clinch its second Olympic gold medal. Out of the 35 goals that the team had scored, Dhyan Chand and his brother Roop Singh accounted for 25 of them.

Dhyan Chand focused on domestic hockey in the years that followed. In 1933, his home side Jhansi Heroes won the prestigious Beighton Cup held in Kolkata; subsequently, they defended the title in 1935. Later, in his 1952 autobiography *Goal!*, he would express his satisfaction in leading a young unheralded side to win a big competition. He captained the Indian team that toured Australia, New Zealand and Ceylon (now Sri Lanka) in 1935. He played in 43 out of 48 matches, and scored 201 goals. The legendary cricketer Don Bradman, who had watched him play, remarked, 'He scores goals like runs in cricket.'

At the 1936 Berlin Olympic Games, Dhyan Chand captained the Indian team that routed Hungary, USA, Japan and France, to face Germany in the final. Having lost the practice match to the Germans, the wary but confident Indians beat them 8-1 to win the gold medal for the third consecutive time. Dhyan Chand's hat-trick in the final took his tally of goals in three Olympic tournaments to 33. It is said that upon being impressed by his hockey skills, Hitler offered him German citizenship and a job in the German Army which the prolific striker politely turned down.

The next Olympic Games was only held in 1948, three years

after the Second World War had ended. By that time Dhyan Chand had mostly stopped playing competitive hockey. He retired from the army in 1956, and later became Chief Hockey Coach at the National Institute of Sports in Patiala, a post that he held for a long time. He spent his last days in Jhansi, and passed away on 3 December 1979.

Dhyan Chand was awarded the Padma Bhushan in 1956. His son, Ashok Kumar Singh, is a former field hockey Olympian who played for India in the '70s.

GOOD TO KNOW

- People in Vienna erected a statue of Dhyan Chand that had four hands and four sticks, as a tribute to his great ball control.
- 29 August, Dhyan Chand's birthday, is celebrated each year as the National Sports Day in India.
- The highest award for lifetime achievement in sports in India is called the Dhyan Chand Award.

QUIZ

1. Pankaj Gupta, who was one of his first coaches, predicted that Dhyan Chand would shine like what in his later playing days?
   a) Sun
   b) Stars
   c) Moon

   Answer: Moon. That's how he got the surname 'Chand'.

2. Against which team did Dhyan Chand play his last hockey match in 1948?
   a) Bengal
   b) Rest of India
   c) Pakistan

   Answer: Bengal

3. What is the title of Dhyan Chand's autobiography?
   a) *Goal!*
   b) *Score*
   c) *Shot*

Answer: ***Goal!***

GLOSSARY

- United Provinces: was a province in British India which roughly corresponds to present-day Uttar Pradesh and Uttarakhand.
- Subedar: is a rank in the Indian Army which is below the senior commissioned officers but above the non-commissioned officers.

KAPIL DEV

Kapil Dev Ramlal Nikhanj, also known as 'the Haryana Hurricane', is a former cricketer who is considered as one of the greatest fast bowlers and all-rounders to have played for India. He was the captain of the Indian team that lifted the 1983 Cricket World Cup.

Kapil Dev was born on 6 January 1959 in Chandigarh. He was coached by Desh Prem Yadav to become a pace bowler. He quickly earned the distinction of being an impact bowler within Haryana, and made his debut for the state in 1975 in a Ranji Trophy match against Punjab. His consistent all-round performance in major domestic tournaments, including the Irani Trophy, the Duleep Trophy and the Deodhar Trophy, earned him a place in the national squad.

Kapil Dev made his One-day International and Test cricket debut for India in 1978, in a series against Pakistan. His bowling figures weren't spectacular, but he startled the Pakistani players with his speed and bounce. In the third Test match, he also scored the fastest Test half-century by any Indian batsman. His first Test century was against the West Indies, when he slammed 126 runs. He picked up his first 5-wicket haul during the English tour in 1979. He followed this up with two 5-wicket hauls in a series at home against Australia, and soon was dubbed as the first ever genuine pace bowler from India.

In the home series against Pakistan, Kapil Dev picked up his first 10-wicket haul in a Test match in Chennai. During the same series, he became the youngest player to take 100 wickets and score 1,000 runs in just 25 matches. During the tour of Australia in 1980-81 in a Test match in Melbourne, he scalped 4 wickets as India successfully defended a small total of 143 runs. In the next few series against England, Sri Lanka and Pakistan, his success story with the bat and ball continued as he picked up several 5-wicket hauls and scored runs consistently. He was made the captain of the Indian team for the tour of the West Indies in 1983. Though he had a good series, his side only managed a lone but famous ODI victory. That particular victory was the harbinger of India's campaign in the 1983 Cricket World Cup.

Before the World Cup, Kapil Dev's ODI figures were ordinary compared to his Test career figures. The India team stunned everybody when they beat the West Indies, again, in their first match. Following a victory against Zimbabwe, India lost to Australia and the West Indies. Facing Zimbabwe in the next match, India was reduced to 17 for 5. Kapil Dev almost single-handedly led India to an improbable victory when he plundered 175 runs to set up a respectable total. The Zimbabweans were later bowled out, and India won the match by 31 runs. India beat Australia and entered the semi-finals to face the host nation, England. He took 3 wickets to restrict the English total to 213, and the Indian middle-order batsmen ensured a comfortable win to enter the final to face the West Indies who were looking to win the World Cup for a third consecutive time.

The West Indians restricted India to a paltry total of 183 runs before coming in to bat. They looked steady with a score of 57 for 2, but the course of the game changed completely when Kapil Dev ran twenty yards backwards from his deep square leg position to catch a straying shot from the in-form batsman Vivian Richards. They suddenly slumped to 76 for 6, and were bowled out for 140 runs handing India its maiden World Cup.

When the West Indians toured India right after the World Cup, despite some heroic individual performances India lost the Test series 0-3 and the ODI series 0-6. Following the loss, Kapil Dev lost his captaincy to Gavaskar, but was reappointed in March 1985. In 1986, he led India to a remarkable Test series victory in England. He also led India to the semi-finals of the 1987 Cricket World Cup, but it lost the match to England. He faced the blame for the unexpected loss, and did not captain the team again. In the following few years, he significantly contributed as a pinch-hitter in ODI matches. He retired in 1994 as the highest wicket-taker in ODIs with 253 wickets and in Tests with 434 wickets; both these records were later broken by the Pakistani Wasim Akram (in 1994) and the West Indian Courtney Walsh (in 1999), Pakistani and west Indian Cricketers, respectively.

Kapil Dev served as the coach of the national team for a brief period of ten months. In 2002, he won the 'Wisden Indian Cricketer of the Century' award.

On 24 September 2008, he joined the Indian Territorial Army as an honorary officer after he was commissioned as a Lieutenant Colonel.

GOOD TO KNOW

- Kapil Dev once hit four consecutive sixes off the English bowler Eddie Hemmings in a Test match to avoid follow-on.
- Kapil Dev led Haryana to their maiden Ranji Trophy triumph during the 1990-91 season, after it beat Mumbai in the final match.
- Kapil Dev has written three autobiographies: *By God's Decree* (1985), *Cricket My style* (1987) and *Stright from the Heart* (2004).

QUIZ

1. In 1994, against which team did Kapil Dev break the then world record tally of Test wickets?
   a) Sri Lanka
   b) West Indies
   c) England

Answer: Sri Lanka

2. Against which team did Kapil Dev play his last Test match?
   a) Australia
   b) New Zealand
   c) Zimbabwe

Answer: New Zealand

3. What is the name of his autobiography?
   a) *Straight from the Heart*
   b) *Cricket and I*
   c) *Of Fours and Sixes*

Answer: *Straight from the Heart*

GLOSSARY:

- Haul: is the number of points, medals or titles won by a person or team in a sporting event. In this case, five-wicket haul means getting five or more wickets in one innings.
- Pinch-hitter: is a batsman promoted up the order to score runs quickly.
- Follow-on: In first-class and Test matches, if a team batting second score less than 200 runs (in some cases less than 150 runs) than the team batting first, then, the team batting first can enforce the other team to bat again. This is known as follow-on.

KHASHABA DADASAHEB JADHAV

Khashaba Dadasaheb Jadhav was a wrestler, who won the freestyle wrestling bronze medal at the 1952 Helsinki Olympic Games and became the first Indian from independent India to win an individual Olympic medal.

Jadhav was born on 15 January 1926 in a village called Goleshwar in Maharashtra. His father, Dadasaheb, who was a wrestling coach introduced him to the sport and subsequently trained him. He often travelled to the neighbouring villages and watched wrestling matches held at fairs.

Jadhav recorded his first victory in 1934, when he beat a much acclaimed opponent in just two minutes, in a match held at Rethare village. He was trained at the village akhada for a few years, before being professionally trained and mentored at Tilak College by coaches Baburao Balwade and Belapure Guruji.

While studying at Rajaram College in Kolhapur, Jadhav's professional career took shape as he won several inter-collegiate and inter-university competitions. He had made a name for himself in the national circuit with his achievements, and qualified to compete in the 1948 London Olympic Games.

Jadhav was different from the other wrestlers of his time in the sense that he was fleet-footed. Rees Gardner, an English coach who had spotted his talent, offered to train him for the Olympics. He finished sixth in the flyweight category despite disparity between the Indian and international wrestling rules; he had wrestled on a mat for the first time. He did not let the sixth-place standing dishearten him, and trained vigorously after returning to India.

Jadhav had accused the officials of favouritism in a match that determined the qualifying wrestler for the next edition of the Olympics. He appealed to the Maharaja of Patiala, who later arranged another match where he emerged victorious and qualified for the 1952 Helsinki Olympic Games.

Jadhav's travel to Helsinki, was aided by contributions from the villagers. In fact, the principal of Rajaram College, Mr Khardekar, even mortgaged his house for ₹7,000. He competed in the bantamweight category and beat wrestlers from Canada, Mexico and Germany to win the bronze medal.

After Jadhav returned, there was a small felicitation for him at Mumbai's Shivaji Mandir auditorium in Dadar and later, a cavalcade of bullock carts welcomed him to his village. He joined the Maharashtra Police Force as a sub-inspector in 1955 and retired as an Assistant Superintendent of Police in 1983.

Jadhav's wish to participate in the 1956 Melbourne Olympics remained unfulfilled, but he later coached young wrestlers. He passed away in 1984.

GOOD TO KNOW

- Though Baburao Kashid (Gold medallist in Asian Games, Manila, 1954) and Sampat Phadtare (national champion in 1962), both Jadhav's wards, did a commendable job, they were unable to excel at the Olympic level.
- He was posthumously awarded the Meghnath Nageshwar Award in 1990 and the 1993 Chatrapati Shivaji Award from Government of Maharashtra.
- His wish to go abroad and study sports medicine remained unfulfilled.
- In 2010, the newly-built wrestling venue in the Indira

Gandhi Sports Complex in New Delhi was named as the K.D. Jadhav Stadium.

QUIZ

1. After his Olympic heroics, what name did Jadhav gave to his home?
   a) Olympica Niwas
   b) Patiala House
   c) Commonwealth Niwas

Answer: Olympica Niwas

2. When was KD Jadhav awarded the Arjuna Award, posthumously?
   a) 2001
   b) 2002
   c) 2003

Answer: 2001

3. Who was the Maharaja of Patiala in 1952 who helped K.D. Jadhav to participate in the Olympic Games?
   a) Maharaja Ranjit Singh
   b) Maharaja Yadavindra Singh
   c) Raja Bhoj

Answer: Maharaja Yadavindra Singh

GLOSSARY

- Bantamweight: In Jadhav's time, wrestlers weighing between 52-57kg competed for the Bantamweight class.
- Freestyle wrestling: was added in the 1904 olympic games where wrestlers can use their legs for pushing, lifting and tripping, and they can hold opponents above or below the waist. Previous to that, the Greco-Roman style (still in vogue today) competitors used only their arms and upper bodies to attack.

LEANDER PAES

Leander Paes is a professional tennis player who won the bronze medal at the 1996 Atlanta Olympic Games and became only the second Indian, after K.D. Jadhav, to win an individual Olympic medal. He is also one of the most successful doubles player in the world, with eight doubles and six mixed doubles Grand Slam titles to his credit.

Leander was born on 17 June 1973 in Goa, to the hockey Olympian Vece Paes and the basketball player Jennifer Paes. He moved to Chennai in 1985 and joined the Britannia Amritraj Tennis Academy. Watching him practice in his teens, Vijay Amritraj was quoted as saying, 'Leander is extremely tenacious, hard-working, determined and athletic...all the qualities that make a champion. I have no doubt that he will make a great tennis champion.'

Leander's first notable exploit in the international tennis circuit was when he won the 1990 Wimbledon Junior title. He was also briefly ranked the number-one junior player in the world. He joined the Indian Davis Cup team the same year, and turned professional in 1991.

Leander played an important role in the Indian Davis Cup team that played in the World Group stage from 1991-98. He was known to put up inspiring performances in his singles and reverse singles matches, beating players like Goran Ivanisevic, Wayne Ferreira and Jan Siemernik, among others, who were ranked much higher than him. He first played in the Davis Cup in 1990, when he partnered Zeeshan Ali in a doubles match against the Japanese team. By 1992, he had helped India beat stronger opponents like Great Britain, Brazil and Switzerland, among other nations. In the 1993 World Group quarter-finals, Leander with the veteran Ramesh Krishnan defeated the much fancied French team of Arnaud Boetsch and Henri Leconte in Frejus, France, to reach the semi-final, where they eventually lost to Australia.

Leander received a wild-card entry to play in the singles event at the 1996 Atlanta Olympic Games. He reached the semi-final where he lost to the eventual American gold medallist Andre Agassi, but later beat Brazil's Fernando Meligeni to win the bronze medal. In Andre Agassi's autobiography, he observed Leander as 'a flying jumping bean, a bundle of hyper-kinetic energy, with the tour's quickest hands.'

In the professional circuit, Leander succeeded in reaching the men's doubles semi-final of the 1993 US Open with Sebastian Lareau. His partnership with Mahesh Bhupathi began in 1994, and in a few years with several ATP doubles titles to their credit, they became one of the most respected doubles team in the world. Out of the 406 matches that they played together throughout their careers, they won 303. They also hold the record of twenty-three consecutive victories in Davis Cup doubles matches. In 1999, they reached the finals of all the four Grand Slams while winning the French Open and the Wimbledon titles. Nicknamed the Indian Express, the duo was ranked the number-one doubles team in the world that year, but personal problems between the two affected their full-time professional relationship. While they played together only occasionally in the professional circuit, they continued to appear together for India.

Around the same time he decided to focus more on his doubles and mixed doubles tournaments, as the only ATP singles title that he had won was at Newport in 1998. He won his maiden US Open doubles title with Martin Damm in 2006, and completed a career Grand Slam when he won the Australian Open doubles title with Radek Stepanek in 2012. In 2003, he won the Australian Open and the Wimbledon mixed doubles titles with the legendary Martina Navratilova.

Leander has also won several ATP titles with David Rikl, Martin Damm, Lukas Dlouhy and Radek Stepanek, among others. At the 2006 Doha Asian Games, he won two gold medals, at the men's doubles and the mixed doubles events with Mahesh Bhupathi and Sania Mirza, respectively.

Leander received the Arjuna Award in 1990, the Rajiv Gandhi Khel Ratna award in 1996-97 and the Padma Shri in 2001.

In early 2013, Leander made his debut as an actor in the Hindi film *Rajdhani Express*.

GOOD TO KNOW

- At the age of forty, Leander Paes became the oldest man to win a Grand Slam title after winning the 2013 US Open doubles title.
- In 2003, Leander Paes was diagnosed with neurocysticercosis, a parasitic infection.
- Leander Paes is the descendent of the Bengali poet Michael Madhusudan Dutta.

QUIZ

1. Which World Tennis team does Leander Paes represent?
   a) Washington Kastles
   b) Philadelphia Freedoms
   c) Boston Lobsters

Answer: Washington Kastles

2. Leander Paes won the 1999 mixed doubles Wimbeldon title with which of the following players?
   a) Martina Navratilova
   b) Martina Hingis
   c) Lisa Raymond

Answer: Lisa Raymond

3. In 2003, Leander Paes was hospitalized in an emergency condition with parasitic infection in which part of his body?
   a) Brain
   b) Heart
   c) Kydney

Answer: Brain

GLOSSARY

- ATP: Association of Tennis Professionals are the main organization which runs the ATP World Tour, the ATP Challenger Tour and the ATP Champions Tour for various level of male players.
- David Cup: started as the tennis competition between USA and Great Britain in 1900. It is now an annual team competition, with 130 nations participating in 2013.
- Grand Slam: The four major tennis tournaments of the world (Australian Open, French Open, Wimbledon and US Open) are referred to as Grand Slam tournaments. Any player winning any of the titles at these tournaments in said to have won a Grand Slam.

MAHENDRA SINGH DHONI

Mahendra Singh Dhoni is a cricketer, who is presently the captain of the Indian Test, One-day International and Twenty20 teams. He holds the distinction of being the first captain to win all three premier ICC (International Cricket Council) limited overs tournaments: the ICC World T20, the ICC Cricket World Cup, and the ICC Champions Trophy.

Dhoni was born on 7 July 1981 in Ranchi, Jharkhand (previously in Bihar). While in school he was the goalkeeper of the football team, and he also excelled in badminton. When he was given the chance to play cricket, he showed sufficient talent as a wicketkeeper. He regularly played as a wicketkeeper for a local club, and soon graduated to age-group cricket.

Dhoni made his Ranji Trophy debut for Bihar during the 1999-2000 season and later played for Jharkhand.

His contributions as a hard-hitting lower order wicketkeeper/ batsman during the 2003-04 domestic season, earned him a place in the East Zone team that eventually won the Deodhar Trophy but lost in the final of the Duleep Trophy.

Based on Dhoni's efforts in first-class cricket, the Indian cricket board picked him to play for India 'A'. With back-to-back centuries and decent performances behind the wicket, he caught the attention of the then captain Sourav Ganguly. He made his debut for the senior team during the tour of Bangladesh in 2004-05. After a mediocre tour, he scored 148 runs in his fifth international match in a home series against Pakistan. In 2005, he hammered an unbeaten 183 runs against Sri Lanka, setting a record for the most number of runs scored by any wicketkeeper, as India chased down a target of 299. He also made his Test debut during the Sri Lankan tour, and scored a half-century in his second Test match. In 2006, he scored his maiden century against Pakistan at Faisalabad.

After India's first-round exit from the 2007 ICC Cricket World Cup, Dhoni was named the vice-captain of the Indian ODI team for the England tour. He was also elected to lead Indian team at the inaugural ICC World T20 in South Africa. The inexperienced Indian team, quite surprisingly, put up some incredulous performances against much fancied oppositions, to reach the final. In a cliffhanger, India beat Pakistan by 5 runs, making Dhoni the second Indian captain after Kapil Dev to lift any premier ICC trophy. He was promoted as the captain of the ODI team and the Test team in September 2007 and November 2008 respectively. Under him, India became the number-one ranked Test team in the world for the first time in the history of cricket, after it registered a 2-0 victory over Sri Lanka in 2009.

Dhoni is known for his ability to handle pressure, and getting the team out of difficult situations while scoring fast runs off his unorthodox shots. Having done the same several times in the past, the final of the 2011 Cricket World Cup was no more different. India entered the competition as favourites, and some good all-round performances had seen it reach the final for the title clash against Sri Lanka at the Wankhede Stadium in Mumbai. The Sri Lankans posted a decent total of 274 runs, as Mahela Jayawardene scored a century. India slowly inched towards the target but lost wickets at crucial times. Dhoni, who had had a low-scoring tournament thus far, came out to bat ahead of the in-form middle-order batsman Yuvraj Singh. He steadied the innings and accelerated the run-rate when required with regular boundaries. With 4 runs required from 11 balls, he finished off in style with a six over long-on as India won the match by 6 wickets. His unbeaten score, 91 runs from 79 balls, proved to be invaluable as India lifted the World Cup for the second time since 1983.

In March 2013, Dhoni became the most successful Indian Test captain with 24 Test victories, when he surpassed Sourav Ganguly's tally of 21 victories. Later in June, he propelled a young Indian team to win the 2013 ICC Champions Trophy in England and Wales, and became the first captain to win all three of the major ICC tournaments.

In 2008, Dhoni was signed by the Chennai Super Kings for the inaugural season of the Twenty20 tournament, the Indian Premier League (IPL). Since then, he has led the team to two consecutive IPL titles (2010 and 2011) and the 2010 Champions League Twenty20 title.

GOOD TO KNOW

- *Forbes* magazine ranked Dhoni as the sixteenth highest paid athlete in the world, as of June 2013.
- Dhoni is the founder of 'Mahi Racing Team India'; it competes in the FIM Supersport World Championship.

QUIZ

1. Which of the following players did Dhoni replace as the Test captain of India?
   a) Sourav Ganguly
   b) Rahul Dravid
   c) Anil Kumble

Answer: Anil Kumble

2. Against which team did M.S. Dhoni become the first captain to score a century in an ODI after coming to bat at number

7 position?

a) Sri Lanka
b) Pakistan
c) Australia

Answer: Pakistan

3. In 2013, a Test win against which team made Dhoni the most successful Indian Test captain?

a) Pakistan
b) Sri Lanka
c) Australia

Answer: Australia

MANGTE CHUNGNEIJANG MARY KOM

Mangte Chungneijang Mary Kom, or M.C. Mary Kom as she is generally referred to, is the first Indian female boxer to win an Olympic medal in 2012. She is also a five-time world boxing champion and carries the distinction of being the first woman boxer to win six medals at World Championships.

Mary was born on 1 March 1983 in Churachanpur, Manipur. Her parents, Mangte Tonpa Kom and Mangte Akham Kom, were jhum agriculturists. The success of fellow Manipur-born Asian Games gold medallist Dingko Singh, inspired her to become a boxer in 2000. Realising her potential in the sport, M. Narjit Singh, the state boxing coach of Manipur, trained her.

In 2001, Mary lost in the final of the AIBA World Championship and had to be satisfied with the Silver medal. In 2002, she started her domination at the same World Championships where she won her first Gold. Her dominance in her weight category stretched to 2006. After that she went off the sport for two years as she gave birth to her twins. But by 2008, she was back at the top and won her fourth World Championship Gold. Her achievement was so inspiring that even the AIBA conferred her with the title of 'Magnificent Mary'.

Mary was awarded the Arjuna Award in 2004, the Padma Shri in 2006 and the Rajiv Gandhi Khel Ratna Award in 2009.

At the 2012 AIBA Women's World Boxing Championship,

Mary lost the semi-final match in the 51 kg category, but automatically qualified for the 2012 London Olympic Games. In fact, women's boxing was officially made a part of the Olympic Games only in 2012. In London, however, her coach Charles Atkinson was not allowed to join her, as he did not posses the required 3 Star Certification issued by International Boxing Association (AIBA). Despite that setback, she beat Karolina Michalczuk of Poland and Maroua Rahali of Tunisia, to qualify for the semi-finals. Though she lost the match to Nicola Adams of the UK, she was guaranteed a bronze medal.

GOOD TO KNOW:

- In 2013, M.C. Mary Kom gave birth to her third son (the first two are twins) and named her baby Prince Chungthanglen Kom.
- When she was young, Mary Kom said in an interview that she loved to watch action films, especially, Jackie Chan films.
- On 3 October 2010, she, along with Vijender Singh, had the honour of bearing the Queen's Baton in its opening ceremony run in the stadium at the 2010 Commonwealth Games in Delhi.

QUIZ

1. Where did M.C. Mary Kom first become the world champion in 2002?
   a) Anatalya, Turkey
   b) Paris, France
   c) London, England

Answer: Anatalya, Turkey

2. M.C. Mary Kom's husband, Onler Kom, played which sport?
   a) Tennis

b) Football
c) Basketball

Answer: Football

3. Which medal did Mary Kom secure at the 2012 London Olympics?
    a) Gold
    b) Silver
    c) Bronze

Answer: Bronze

GLOSSARY:

- AIBA World Championships: are amateur boxing competitions organized by International Boxing Association (AIBA). The men's and women's events are held separately.
- Dingko Singh: is an Indian boxer who has won a Gold Medal at the 1998 Asian Games.

PILAVULLAKANDI THEKKEPARAMBIL USHA

P.T. Usha is a former athelete who was referred to as the 'Queen of Indian track and field'.

Usha was born on 27 June 1964, in the village of Payyoli, Kerala. As a youngster, she was coached by O.M. Nambiar. She shined at the 1979 National School Games, and subsequently was selected for the 1980 Moscow Olympic Games. At the 1982 Delhi Asian Games, she won silver medal in the 100 and 200 metres sprint. At the1983 Asian Track and Field Championship in Kuwait, she won the gold medal in the 400 meter race, setting a new Asian record.

The 400 metres hurdles was introduced into the list of track races for the first time at the 1984 Los Angeles Olympic Games. Having qualified to compete in this race, Usha finished first in the semi-finals. In the final, she lost out on a podium finish by 1/100th of a second. Undaunted by the loss, she continued to train harder.

Usha won five gold medals at the 6th Asian Track and Field Championship held at Jarkarta in 1985. Her hard work continued to pay off when at the 1986 Seoul Asian Games, she won four gold medals and a silver medal in the track events losing only the 100 metres final to Lydia de Vega of Philippines. She became the first athlete in the history of Asian Games to win medals in all the events that she had participated in. In her career, she participated in all the Olympic Games from 1980 to 1996, except the 1992 Barcelona Olympics, since she retired briefly for a period after the 1990 Asian Games.

Usha was employed by the Indian Railways and was once adjudged the Best Railway Athlete in the world. She was awarded the Padma Shri and Arjuna Award in 1985.

After retirement, Usha started an academy called 'Usha School of Atheletics'. Several young athletes like Tintu Luka, who qualified for the women's 800 metres semi-finals at the 2012 London Olympic Games are mentored by her.

GOOD TO KNOW

- At the 1986 Seoul Asian Games, Usha won the Adidas Golden Shoe Award for the best athlete.
- She was the youngest athelete to participate in the 1980 Moscow Olympic Games.
- Her School of Athletics is situated at Koyilandi near Kozhikode.

QUIZ

1. How many international medals has P.T. Usha won in total?
   a) 100
   b) 101
   c) 102

Answer: 101

2. What is the name of the autobiography P.T. Usha published along with Lokesh Sharma?
   a) *The Champion*
   b) *The Golden Girl*
   c) *Sprint Queen*

Answer: *The Golden Girl*

3. Which of these athletes beat P.T. Usha for the third place

at the 1984 Los Angeles Olympic Games?

a) Ann-Louise Skoglund
b) Cristieana Cojocaru
c) Debbie Flintoff-King

Answer: Cristieana Cojocaru

GLOSSARY

- 400 metres hurdles: is a track event where runners clear a total of ten hurdles placed over a distance of 400 metres.

PRAKASH PADUKONE

Prakash Padukone is a former badminton player, who is the first Indian to win the All England Championship.

Prakash Padukone was born on 10 June 1955 in Bangalore, Karnataka. His father, Ramesh Padukone, was a badminton aficionado and also a long-time secretary of the Mysore Badminton Association. Prakash first played in an official tournament in 1962 in his state's junior championship. With gradual exposure to competitions, Prakash went on to win the National Junior Championship in 1970. In 1971, he won the junior and senior National Championships at the age of sixteen. He went on to win the senior nationals for nine straight years. Immediately after his first win, he was inducted into the Indian team. He won the bronze medal in the team event at the 1974 Tehran Asian Games.

At the 1978 Edmonton Commonwealth Games, Prakash beat Derek Talbot of England to clinch the gold medal. Between 1979-80, he won a series of titles including the English Masters Championship, the Danish Open and the Swedish Open. Then came the highest point of his career when he beat the defending champion Liem Swie King of Indonesia in the final of the All England Championship. This victory took him to the number one spot in the world rankings. In 1981, Prakash went on to win the first ever Badminton World Cup held at Kuala Lumpur, Malaysia.

Prakash moved to Denmark in the early 1980s to avail

better training and playing facilities. In 1982, he won the Dutch Open and the Hong Kong Open. At the 1983 World Badminton Championship in Copenhagen, he won the bronze medal. Prakash continued his association with the game even after retirement, coaching several young players and teams. Badminton Association of India

GOOD TO KNOW

- In the Swedish Open tournament of 1980, Prakash got a chance to play against his idol, Rudy Hartono in an early round of the tournament. Prakash beat Rudy 9-15, 15-12 and 15-1, and even though he could easily have won by 15-0 in the last set, he didn't want to embarrass his idol. He was quoted as saying, 'I could have beaten him 15-0 in that last game but I couldn't do that to my idol, I conceded a point and finished the game'.
- Dev S. Sukumar published a biography on Prakash Padukone titled *Touch Play*.
- His daughter, Deepika Padukone, played badminton in her younger days but after that she concentrated on modeling and acting, and left the sport altogether.

QUIZ

1. Which of these sporting awards did Prakash Padukone receive in 1972?
   a) Rajiv Gandhi Khel Ratna Award
   b) Dronacharya Award
   c) Arjuna Award

Answer: Arjuna Award

2. Who was the next Indian to win the All England Championship after Prakash Padukone?
   a) Saina Nehwal

b) Pullela Gopichand
c) Jwala Gutta

Answer: Pullela Gopichand

3. Which was the first prize money tournament in Badminton that Prakash Padukone won?
   a) English Masters
   b) Augusta Masters
   c) Sultan Azlan Shah Cup

Answer: English Masters

GLOSSARY

- All England Championship: first played in 1898, is one of the world's oldest and most prestigious badminton tournaments. It was considered the unofficial world badminton championship till the late 1970s.
- English Masters Championship: in 1979, became the first open badminton tournament in the world where prize money was given to the winners.

SACHIN TENDULKAR

Sachin Tendulkar, the Indian cricket icon, is the first player to play 200 Test matches, and has scored the most Test and One-Day International runs in his career.

Born on 24 April 1973 in Mumbai, to Ramesh and Rajni Tendulkar, a young Sachin fancied playing tennis in his younger days. His elder brother, Ajit, introduced him to cricket and put him under the tutelage of Ramakant Achrekar at Shivaji Park.

Sachin's cricket career started with the Kanga League. He had also applied for a place at the MRF academy to learn fast bowling from Dennis Lillee but was rejected by Lillee himself who told him to concentrate on his batting. He followed his advice and in 1988, he scored centuries in all the matches he played for his school. Among them was a partnership of 664 with his friend Vinod Kambli, who also went on to play for India. In December that year, he made his first-class debut for Bombay (now Mumbai) and scored a century. He was soon selected for the Indian team and in 1989 at the age of 16 years; he made his debut against the likes of Imran Khan, Wasim Akram and Waqar Younis. A series to New Zealand followed where he scored 88 in a Test innings. Then followed the tour to England, where he became the second youngest batsman ever to score a Test century. A tour to Australia followed where he scored two more centuries, one of which was at the fiery fast pitch at Perth.

In 1994, Sachin Tendulkar opened the innings in an One-Day international, for the first time, in New Zealand and grabbed it with both hands. Henceforth he became India's premier opener in the shorter form of the game. At the 1996 Cricket World Cup, he was the highest scorer with two centuries, though the team lost in the semi-finals. During the 1999 Cricket World Cup, his father passed away, but he resumed playing immediately after performing the last rites.

In 1996, Sachin took over as the captain of the Indian cricket team. But his record as captain did not match up with his record as batsman, as the Indian team performed quite poorly under his captaincy. He stood down as the captain, after India lost 9 Test matches in a row. At the 2003 Cricket World Cup, he scored more than 600 runs to take India to the final which they lost to Australia. The next 2003-04 series against Australia saw him scoring a double century at Sydney. Later in the series in Pakistan, Tendulkar again continued his good form with the bat and became part of the first Indian team to win a Test and One-Day series in Pakistan.

Cricket was taking its toll on his body and 'tennis elbow' forced him to rest for a considerable period of time. Even though he was on and off the cricket field, he surpassed Sunil Gavaskar's record of 34 Test centuries in 2005. The next few months he was either injured, or not scoring big, which by then was his natural standard. The decline in form continued in 2007, when the Indian team made an early exit from the World Cup and there were calls for his retirement. But after the World Cup, he slowly got back to his groove and continued scoring like he did before.

Sachin now holds the record for the most runs and the most centuries scored in both forms of the game. He is the first cricketer to score a double century in an ODI. In 2012, he scored his 100th international hundred in a match against Bangladesh, and shortly after that he retired from One-Day Internationals.

He played just one Twenty20 international in his career and in the IPL he always played for his home team Mumbai Indians. After Mumbai Indians managed to win the 2013 IPL, Tendulkar announced his retirement from the IPL too.

GOOD TO KNOW

- To improve his batting, Achrekar would place a one rupee coin every time he went to the nets and the bowler who would get him out would get the coins. If he remained undefeated in the whole session, he would get the coin!
- After passing Sunil Gavaskar's record of 34 Test centuries, Tendulkar acknowledged receiving a pair of cricket pads from the Little Master when he was just 14-years old by regarding that gesture as the greatest source of encouragement for him.
- The Indian government conferred the Bharat Ratna on Sachin Tendulkar immediately after his retirement, making him the youngest person to be named for the presitigious award.

QUIZ

1. Against which team did Sachin Tendulkar play his last ODI?
   a) Pakistan
   b) Australia
   c) New Zealand

   Answer: Pakistan

2. Which former great cricketer once said that Tendulkar reminded him of himself?
   a) Dennis Lillee
   b) Sunil Gavaskar
   c) Don Bradman

   Answer: Don Bradman

3. Against which team did he score the first double century in One-Day Internationals?
   a) West Indies
   b) South Africa
   c) New Zealand

Answer: South Africa

GLOSSARY

- MRF Academy: is a premier cricket academy in Chennai for learning the intricacies of pace bowling. Dennis Lillee was the first chief coach of the institution.
- Kanga League: Named after Dr HD Kanga, it is a local league which commenced in 1948 for club teams from Mumbai.
- Tennis elbow: or simply lateral elbow pain, is a condition where the outer part of the elbow becomes sore and tender. Since the pathogenesis of this condition is still unknown, there is no single agreed name.

SAINA NEHWAL

Saina Nehwal is a badminton player, and the first Indian to win a medal in badminton at the Olympic Games.

Saina was born on 17 March 1990 in Hisar, Haryana. Both her parents, Dr Harvir Singh and Usha Nehwal, were former badminton players of the state of Haryana.

Dr Singh was an agricultural scientist and at the time of her birth, he was associated with the Chaudhury Charan Singh Agricultural University in Hisar. Later, he changed his job and joined the N.G. Ranga University in Hyderabad.

Saina's career took a major turn when she came under the tutelage of Pullela Gopichand in Hyderabad. Saina burst into the global scene in 2006, when she won the the Philippines' Open after beating players who were ranked much higher than her. In 2008, she won the World Junior Badminton Championship held at Pune by beating Sayake Sato in two games. At the 2008 Beijing Olympic Games, she reached the quarter-finals but lost the match to Maria Kristin Yulianti. Later that year, she won the Chinese Taipei Open beating Li Ya Lydia Cheah of Malayasia in the finals. In 2009, she became the first Indian woman to win a BWF Super Series title when she won the Indonesian Open And she also reached the quarter finals of the World Championship.

Saina Nehwal and Pullela Gopichand were awarded the Arjuna Award and Dhronacharya Award respectively in 2009. The Olympic Gold Quest Foundation signed her on in 2009, to train her for the ultimate glory of an Olympic medal. In 2010, she won the Singapore Open Super Series and in the Commonwealth Games at New Delhi, she defeated Wong Mew Choo of Malaysia to win the gold medal. In December 2010, she won the Hong Kong Super Series. Her achievements earned her the 2010 Rajiv Gandhi Khel Ratna award. In 2012 she won the Thailand Open Grand Prix and the Indonesian Super Series.

Then came the high point in her career when she went on to win the bronze medal at the 2012 London Olympic Games when the Chinese player, Wang Xin, pulled out of the match after an injury. Later that year, she won the Denmark Open.

The first edition of the Indian Badminton League (IBL) was held in 2013. After a bidding war between between the teams, Saina Nehwal was finally bought by Hyderabad Hotshots. In a tournament with top seeded players competing against each other, Saina excelled, leading Hyderabad Hotshots to lift the IBL title.

GOOD TO KNOW

- Saina Nehwal's biography, *An Inspirational Story,* was written by former journalist T.S. Sudhir.
- Her native state's primary school books have a chapter on her life and achievements.
- In 2012, Saina Nehwal became the highest-paid non-cricket sports person in India due to her endorsements.

QUIZ

1. In 2006, in which multi-sport games did Saina win a Bronze medal in the Mixed Events category?
   a) Commonwealth Games
   b) Olympic Games
   c) Asian Games

Answer: Commonwealth Games

2. After her exploits in the 2012 London Olympics, who presented her the keys of a luxury car sponsored by her home state government?
   a) Sania Mirza
   b) Mohammad Azharuddin
   c) Sachin Tendulkar

Answer: Sachin Tendulkar

3. In 2012, which university conferred Saina Nehwal with an honourary degree?
   a) Kolkata University
   b) Benras Hindu University
   c) Mangalayatan University

Answer: Mangalayatan University

GLOSSARY

- BWF: or Badminton World Federation, is the international governing body for the sport of badminton.
- Dronacharya Award: is an award presented by the Government of India for excellence in sports coaching. The award comprises of a bronze statuette of Dronacharya, a scroll of honour, and a cash component of ₹500,000. The award was instituted in 1985.
- Arjuna Awards: was instituted in 1961 by the government of India to recognize outstanding achievement in National sports.

SANIA MIRZA

Sania Mirza is the highest ranked women's tennis player from India and the first to win a WTA tour title.

Born on 15 November 1986 in Mumbai, Maharashtra, Sania grew up in Hyderabad, and was introduced to tennis by her father at the age of six. Mahesh Bhupathi's father C.K. Bhupathi mentored her during the early days of her career. At the junior level, Mirza won more than twenty titles in both singles and doubles tournaments. In 2003, Sania won the junior doubles event at Wimbledon. That year, she also reached the doubles semi-finals and quarter-finals at the French Open and US Open respectively.

In 2002, Sania partnered Leander Paes to win the bronze medal in the mixed doubles event of the 2002 Busan Asian Games. In 2003, she played in her first WTA tournament, held in Hyderabad, but lost in the final round. At the 2003 Hyderabad Afro-Asian Games, she won four gold medals. In 2004, she won her first WTA title, when she partnered Liezel Huber to win the doubles title at the Hyderabad Open. In 2005, she qualified for the Australian Open where she reached the third round only to be beaten by Serena Williams. But later that year, she won her first WTA singles title at Hyderabad when she defeated Alona Bondarenko in the finals. In Dubai Open that year, she defeated the reigning US Open champion Svetlana Kuznetsova. In 2006, Mirza posted big wins against the likes of Svetlana Kuznetsova, Nadia Petrova and Martina Hingis, and won three medals at the 2006 Doha Asian Games.

In 2007, Sania was ranked No. 27 in the world, which was the highest rank achieved by an Indian player. At the 2008 Beijing Olympic Games, she suffered a wrist injury, and eventually bowed out of the competition. In 2009, she partnered Mahesh Bhupathi to win her first Grand Slam title, the Australian Open. The duo also went on to win the 2012 French Open title. At the 2010 Delhi Commonwealth Games, she won a silver medal in the singles event and a bronze medal in the women's doubles event. In 2011, she reached finals of the French Open Women's doubles with Elena Vesnina where they lost to Andrea Hlavackova and Lucie Hradecka. In the 2012 London Olympic Games she partnered Leander Paes but the duo lost in the quarter-finals to a team from Belarus.

Sania Mirza married the Pakistani cricketer, Shoaib Malik, in 2010.

GOOD TO KNOW:

- When Sania Mirza is not playing in tournaments, she trains for 5-6 hours daily.
- In women's doubles Sania Mirza was once ranked 7th in the world. This has been her highest career ranking.
- Mirza is the first Indian woman tennis player to earn over a million dollars in tennis.

QUIZ

1. In 2004, Sania Mirza received which award from the Indian government?
   a) Arjuna Award
   b) Bharat Ratna
   c) Padma Bhushan

Answer: Arjuna Award

2. In which city did Sania Mirza win her first Grand Slam tournament?
   a) Paris
   b) Melbourne
   c) London

Answer: Melbourne

3. Which of these teams, appointed Sania Mirza as their brand ambassador in the 2013 Indian Badminton League?
   a) Banga Beats
   b) Hyderabad HotShots
   c) Delhi Smashers

Answer: Delhi Smashers

GLOSSARY

- WTA: or The Women's Tennis Association, founded in 1973 by Billie Jean King, is the principal organizing body of women's professional tennis.

SOURAV GANGULY

Sourav Ganguly is a former Indian cricketer, who retired as India's most successful Test captain of his time. He was a left-handed batsman, who bowled right-handed when required.

Born on 8 July 1972, Sourav was introduced to cricket by his elder brother Snehasish. He was initially attracted to football, but when his brother established himself as a first-class cricketer, he started taking cricket seriously. His father supported his goal, and provided for indoor cricket nets and a multi-gym for the brothers inside their house. He rose gradually through the ranks of age-group cricket and school cricket. By 1989, he was in contention for a place in the Bengal team. He was selected to play in the final Ranji Trophy match of the 1989-90 season in the place of his brother. He scored twenty-two runs.

Sourav performed well in the 1990-91 first-class season. He was a part of the Indian team that toured Australia in 1991-92. In Australia however, he got a chance to play in only one One-Day International (ODI) against the West Indies. He scored just 3 runs. He was dropped and issues were raised about his temperament to play at the highest level. He got back into domestic cricket, and started grinding it out at every level he played. With time, his scores improved in both limited-overs and the longer format of the game. Following an innings of a hundred and seventy-one runs in the 1995–96 Duleep Trophy, he was recalled by the national team for a tour of England in 1996, in the middle of intense media scrutiny. He played only a single ODI, in Old Trafford, Manchester, where he scored forty-six runs, but was omitted from the team for the first Test. Ganguly made his debut in the second Test at Lord's, becoming the third debutant in the history of cricket to score a century on that ground. In the next Test match at Trent Bridge, he made a hundred and thirty-six runs, becoming only the third batsman to make a century in each of his first two innings (after Lawrence Rowe and Alvin Kallicharran). By 1996, he graduated to batting for opening with Sachin Tendulkar in ODIs, and thus started one of the greatest cricketing partnerships of all time. They hold the world record for the highest overall partnership runs scored by a pair in ODIs (8,227 runs).

In 1998, in the final match of the Independence Cup in Dhaka, against Pakistan, Ganguly scored a century as India successfully chased down a target of three hundred and fifteen runs. Later, in March 1998, he was part of the team which won a Test series against Australia where he contributed with the ball. By then he was a regular member of the Indian cricket team, and played in the 1999 Cricket World Cup. However, the Indian team did not do too well in the competition, and was ousted before the semi-finals. In the 1999-2000 season, India lost a series of Tests to both Australia and South Africa. This involved a combined total of five Tests. Ganguly struggled, scoring two hundred and twenty-four runs at an average of 22.40; however, his ODI form was impressive, with five centuries over the season taking him to the top of the ratings for batsmen. Sourav Ganguly was then chosen to lead India in the five-match ODI series against South Africa. India emerged victorious, but the series also brought out betting scandals involving international players. Ganguly took charge of a young team and slowly the results started improving.

In the 2000 ICC Knock Out Trophy, India lost to New

Zealand in the final, despite him scoring a century. The all-conquering Australians arrived in India in 2001, after recording sixteen consecutive Test victories. They thrashed the Indian team in the first Test, but Ganguly rallied his players, who in turn produced superhuman efforts to turn the tide by winning the remaining two Test matches. Rahul Dravid and VVS Laxman's famous partnership, and Harbhajan Singh's bowling efforts remain the highlights of that Test series.

In the final match of the 2002 NatWest Trophy against England, India pulled off a spectacular win by the efforts of Mohammad Kaif and Yuvraj Singh. In 2003, the Cricket World Cup was held in South Africa. Under Ganguly's captaincy, India reached the finals for the first time since 1983. Hopes were high, but India lost the final to Australia. For Ganguly personally, the tournament was a batting success as he scored three centuries. Later in the 2003-04 series in Australia, Ganguly again led from the front, bringing out creditable performances from his team-mates to draw the series. In 2004, he led India to victory, in both the Test and the ODI series in Pakistan, becoming the first Indian captain to achieve the feat. But by the end of 2005, his form dwindled. He was dropped from the Indian team, and his deputy Rahul Dravid took his place. He was briefly drafted into the team for the series against Pakistan, but his poor form continued. Finally in 2006, he made a comeback in the series against South Africa becoming the top Indian scorer. India won their first-ever Test match on South African soil by virtue of his batting efforts. In the 2007 Cricket World Cup, despite him playing well, India failed to advance from the group stage. On 12 December 2007, Ganguly scored his maiden double century while playing against Pakistan. He scored two hundred and thirty-nine runs in the first innings of the third and final Test match of the series. Ganguly remained prolific in both Test and

ODI cricket in the year 2007. He scored eleven hundred and six Test runs at an average of 61.44 (with three centuries and four fifties, becoming the second highest run-scorer in Test matches for that year. Ganguly played his last test match in October 2008 against Australia. In the same year, he was named the icon player of the Indian Premier League (IPL) team, Kolkata Knight Riders, and led the team for two seasons without much success. He was later picked by Pune Warriors, and led the team in one of the two seasons that he played.

GOOD TO KNOW

- Despite being a natural right-hander, Ganguly started batting left-handed so that he could use his elder brother's cricket kit.
- Sourav Ganguly retired from One-Day Internationals after taking exactly hundred wickets and hundred catches.
- After retiring from all forms of cricket, Ganguly became a commentator. He was lauded for his job which provided a former captain's insight into the modern game.

QUIZ

1. In how many matches did Sourav Ganguly captain India?
   a) 49
   b) 50
   c) 51

Answer: 49

2. Against which team did Sourav Ganguly win the most matches as captain?
   a) Australia
   b) South Africa
   c) Zimbabwe

Answer: Zimbabwe

3. Which nickname did Sourav Ganguly get from his Indian team-mates?
   a) Boss
   b) Sir
   c) Dada

Answer: Dada

GLOSSARY

- Lord's: Lord's Cricket Ground, generally known as Lord's, is a cricket venue in St John's Wood, London. It is considered to be one of the most hallowed cricket grounds in the world.
- NatWest Trophy: or the NatWest Series, were international cricket tournaments staged in England between 2000 and 2005, played between three international teams.
- ICC Knock Out Trophy: the ICC Champions Trophy was inaugurated as the ICC Knock Out Tournament in 1998, and has been played approximately every two years ever since. Its name was changed to the Champions Trophy in 2002.

SUNIL GAVASKAR

Sunil Gavaskar is a former Indian cricketer, who is considered as one of the finest opening batsmen of all time. He set world records for the most Test runs and the most Test centuries by any batsman. He was a part of the team that won the cricket World Cup in 1983. He was the first Test player to cross the 10,000-run mark. He is also the first cricketer to have scored centuries in each innings of a Test, thrice.

Sunil Gavaskar was born on 10 July 1949 in Mumbai (then Bombay). He studied at St Xavier's High School, and continued to attend St Xavier's College. A talented cricketer in school, Gavaskar made his first-class debut in the 1966-67 season but was not successful initially.

When he finally got to play his first game, he scored a duck. A century in the final and big scores later helped him get selected to the national team for the 1970–71 series in West Indies. Gavaskar made his debut for India in the second Test at Port-of-Spain. He scored over 60 runs in both innings and remained not out in the second to earn India their first win at West Indies. In each of the next three Test matches, he went on to score hundreds with two in the final match at Trinidad (124 and 220) to register India's first ever series win in West Indies. His tally of 774 runs in his debut series is still one of the very best performances on debutant cricketer.

With his splendid debut series, expectations from Sunil Gavaskar became very high, but in his subsequent forays he failed to live up to them. He next scored a Test century against England in the 1974 series and was elected as the stand-in captain in New Zealand in 1975-76. He led India to a win in his debut Test as captain. In the 1976 West Indies series he was back to his old form and became the first Indian batsman to score more than 1,000 Test runs in a calendar year.

In 1978-79, Gavaskar was again appointed as the captain of the Indian Test team. He led his team to a 1-0 win in his first series as captain against West Indies. In the 1983-84 series against West Indies, he scored his 29th and 30th Test centuries to surpass Sir Don Bradman's record. In his last foray as India's captain, he led the team to win the 1984-85 Benson Hedges World Championship of Cricket limited over's tournament. In his last Test innings in 1987, he scored 96 against Pakistan.

Sunil Gavaskar was always remembered for his opening batting in Test matches while his One-Day performances were quite mediocre by his standards. He scored his only ODI century in the 1987 Cricket World Cup against New Zealand.

He has received numerous awards including the Padma Bhushan and the Col CK Nayudu Lifetime Achievement Award for Cricket in India.

He has written many books on cricket including *Sunny Days* (autobiography), *Idols* and *One Day Wonders*. Gavaskar also dabbled with acting in films. He played the lead role in the Marathi film *Savli Premachi*. He also made a guest appearance in a Hindi film titled *Maalamal*.

After retirement, he has been a popular commentator, both on TV and in print.

GOOD TO KNOW

- After he scored a record number of runs as a debutant in the 1971 series in West Indies, the famous calypso singer

Lord Relator composed a song on him that describes how he batted like a wall.

- When Sunil Gavaskar was a new born baby, he was accidentally exchanged with another infant, the son of a fisherman, in the hospital. But Madhav Mantri, his uncle and an ex-Test cricketer, noticed that the baby did not have the small hole in the left earlobe that he had seen the previous day and helped prevent the possible mix-up.
- The Border-Gavaskar Trophy has been instituted in honour of Sunil Gavaskar and Allan Border.

QUIZ

1. Who was the captain of the team for which Sunil Gavaskar made his first-class debut?
   a) Kapil Dev
   b) Mansur Ali Khan Pataudi
   c) Chandu Borde

   Answer: Mansur Ali Khan Pataudi

2. In 1987, where did Gavaskar score a hundred, his only three figure score at the venue, in his farewell match?
   a) Lord's
   b) Eden
   c) MCG

   Answer: Lord's

3. In 1994, which honourary post did Gavaskar adorn for Mumbai?
   a) Governor
   b) Mayor
   c) Sheriff

   Answer: Sheriff

GLOSSARY

- Away series: in cricket, Test matches are generally played in home and away cycles. So after any home series against a particular team, the host team visits its opponent to play an away series within 1-2 years time.
- Benson Hedges World Championship of Cricket: was a limited overs tournament held to commemorate the 150th anniversary of European settlement in Australia.

SUSHIL KUMAR

Sushil Kumar is a world champion wrestler and the first Indian to win back-to-back individual Olympic medals.

Sushil Kumar was born on 26 May 1983 in a village called Baprola, Delhi. His father, a former wrestler, and his cousin who was training to become one, inspired him to take up the sport.

At the age of fourteen, Sushil began his traditional training at the akhada that was a part of the Chhatrasal Stadium. He was initially trained by local trainers, and later by the former Asian Games gold medallist Satpal Singh. Having endured tough training conditions, his hard work paid off when he started winning both national and international titles.

Sushil made a mark at the junior level when he won gold medals in the 1998 World Cadet Games and the 2000 Asian Junior Wrestling Championship.

As a senior, he won the bronze medal in the 2003 Asian Wrestling Championships, the gold medal in the 2003 Commonwealth Wrestling Championships and finished fourth in the 2003 World Wrestling Championships.

Sushil performed poorly at the 2004 Athens Olympic Games, where he finished fourteenth in the 60kg category, but he fared well in the competitions that followed. He won gold medals in both the 2005 and 2007 editions of the Commonwealth Wrestling Championships and finished seventh in the 2007 World Wrestling Championships. At the 2008 Beijing Olympic Games, he competed in the 66kg freestyle category. Though he lost the first-round to the eventual finalist Andriy Stadnik of Ukraine, he won all three of his repechage rounds to win the bronze medal for India. Later, he revealed that he had no masseur during the bronze medal match, and that the team manager Kartar Singh, a former Asian Games medallist himself, was kind enough to step in as an acting masseur.

Sushil became the first Indian to win a World Championship medal, when he beat the Russian wrestler Alan Gogaev in the 66kg freestyle category, in the final of the FILA 2010 World Wrestling Championships held at Moscow, and clinched the gold medal. He kept up his good form at the 2010 Delhi Commonwealth Games, and won the gold medal after he beat the South African wrestler Heinrich Barnes in the final.

Sushil was India's flag bearer in the opening ceremony of the 2012 London Olympic Games. At the games, he reached the final of the 66kg freestyle category, but lost to Japan's Tatsuhiro Yonemitsu and claimed the silver medal, becoming the first Indian to win two individual Olympic medals.

Sushil Kumar is the recipient of the Arjuna Award (2005) and the Rajiv Gandhi Khel Ratna award (2008).

GOOD TO KNOW

- When training, Sushil consumes almost 3,600 calories a day, but as he approaches a competition his intake is cut down to 1,600 calories.
- Sushil Kumar was the final baton bearer who handed the Queen's Baton to Prince Charles in the queen's Baton Relay for the 2010 Commonwealth Games Opening ceremony.

QUIZ

1. What was awarded to Sushil Kumar in 2008 by the Indian government?
   a) Arjuna Award
   b) Padma Bhushan
   c) Rajiv Gandhi Khel Ratna Award

Answer: Rajiv Gandhi Khel Ratna Award

2. Sushil Kumar's training ground, Chhatrasal Stadium, was renovated for which event?
   a) 1982 Asian Games
   b) 2007 Nehru Cup Trophy
   c) 2010 Commonwealth Games

Answer: 2010 Commonwealth Games

3. Sushil Kumar was offered a piece of land to start a wrestling academy by the government of which of the following states?
   a) Uttar Pradesh
   b) Punjab
   c) Haryana

Answer: Haryana

GLOSSARY

- FILA: is The International Federation of Associated Wrestling Styles, also known in French as *Fīdīration Internationale des Luttes Associīes* (FILA).
- Akhada: is the traditional enclosed space for the practice of wrestling in India. Normally in Akhadas, the wrestlers compete with each other in a clay-topped court.

VIJENDER SINGH

Vijender Singh is a boxer who won the first boxing Olympic medal for India at the 2008 Beijing Olympic Games.

Vijender was born on 29 October 1985 in Bhiwani, Haryana. He was inspired by Raj Kumar Sangwan's exploits at the international level, which earned the latter the Arjuna Award. He was supported by his brother, Manoj, who was also a successful boxer.

Vijender was trained by Jagdish Singh, a former national-level boxer. He won the silver medal at the sub-junior nationals and the gold medal at the senior nationals in 1997 and 2000 respectively.

Despite being a newcomer, Vijender won the silver medal at the 2003 Hyderabad Afro-Asian Games. At the 2004 Athens Olympic Games, in the welterweight division, he lost to Mustafa Karagollu of Turkey. At the 2006 Melbourne Commonwealth Games, he lost to South Africa's Bongani Mwelase in the final to claim the silver medal. After these exploits, he moved up in the weight divisions, and at the 2006 Doha Asian Games, he won the bronze medal in the middleweight division.

This led to his strong participation at the 2008 Beijing Olympic Games, but there was doubt whether he could overcome his back injury. But he recovered quickly and qualified for the 2008 Olympic Games. After that he spent a considerable time training in European countries and boxing with much fancied opponents.

Vijendar Singh qualified for the 2008 Olympics by winning a qualifying event in Kazakhstan despite having a back injury. Then he trained in Germany where he also did well in the President's Cup which he regarded as the 'dress rehearsal' for the Olympic Games. After that he came back to India and joined the special training camp that was organised for the Indian boxers who qualified for the 2008 Olympic Games. Here, they were extensively trained with video footage of their opponents to prepare themselves better.

At the 2008 Beijing Olympic Games, though Vijender lost the semi-final match to Cuba's Emilio Correa, he was guaranteed the bronze medal by virtue of his win over the Ecuadorian southpaw, Carlos Gongora, in the quarter-final.

Vijender won the bronze medal at the 2009 World Championships. That year, he was also voted as the top-ranked boxer in the middleweight (75 kg) category list by the International Boxing Association. At the 2010 New Delhi Commonwealth Games, he won the bronze medal after he lost a controversial semi-final match to Anthony Ogogo of England. At the 2010 Guanzhou Asian Games, he defeated the two-time Uzbek world champion, Abbos Atoev, in the final to win the gold medal.

Vijender was a strong contender for a medal at the 2012 London Olympic Games, but he lost to Abbos Atoev of Uzbekistan, 13–17 in the quarter-final.

GOOD TO KNOW

- Vijender appeared on Bollywood actor Salman Khan's game show *10 Ka Dum*.
- In his own words, he took part in modelling after his Olympic success to bring the spotlight back to the sport of boxing.

QUIZ

1. In 2009, who along with Vijender Singh and Sushil Kumar jointly received the Rajiv Gandhi Khel Ratna Award?
   a) M.C. Mary Kom
   b) Gagan Narang
   c) Saina Nehwal

Answer: M.C. Mary Kom

2. The 2008 Olympic Games, who along with Jitender Kumar, lost in the quarter-finals?
   a) Sushil Kumar
   b) Akhil Kumar
   c) Abhinav Bindra

Answer: Akhil Kumar

3. In 2010, with which award did the Indian government honour Vijender Singh?
   a) Padma Bhushan
   b) Padma Shri
   c) Padma Vibhushan

Answer: Padma Shri

GLOSSARY

- Welterweight: in amateur boxing, competitors with body weight between 64-69 kg compete for the welterweight division.
- Middleweight: in amateur boxing, competitors with body weight between 69-75 kg compete for the middleweight division.
- South Paw: is a term given to a left-handed person.

VISWANATHAN ANAND

Viswanathan Anand is the first Indian chess Grandmaster and former World Champion. He won his fifth World Chess Championship in 2012.

Viswanathan Anand was born on 11 December 1969 in Mayiladuthurai, Tamil Nadu.

As a young child, Anand had his first chess lessons from his mother when they moved to the Philippines. His mother would write down chess problems from a television programme and after Anand came back from school; the mother-son duo would solve the problems together. The prizes in this programme were books and they managed to win so many that at one point of time the authorities are said to have commented, "Take all the books you want, but don't send in any more solutions."

The national sub-junior champion in 1983 was followed by the title of International Master in 1984. In 1987, he became the World Junior Chess Champion and followed it up the next year with the Grandmaster norm at the age of eighteen.

By 1991, he had won top-level international tournaments leaving behind competitors like Anatoly Karpov and Garry Kasparov. In 1995, Anand beat Gata Kamsky in the Candidates final of the PCA World Chess Championship and played against Garry Kaspoarov in the final. In 1998, he won the FIDE Candidates final beating Michael Adams, and again played Karpov. Although physically exhausted, he ended the regular match with a 3-3 score but Karpov won the rapid play-off round to clinch the World Championship.

Anand won his first World Chess Championship in 2000. He failed to defend the title in 2002, when he lost to Vassily Ivanchuk in the final. In 2005 he could not cross the last few stages and finished 1.5 points behind the eventual winner Veselin Topalov. In 2007, Anand won the FIDE World Championship in Mexico City, after he finished ahead of Boris Gelfand and Boris Kramnik. In 2008, he went to Bonn to defend his title against Kramnik. Of the 12-game challenge, Anand needed only 11 to register his victory. In 2010, Anand defeated Topalov in the final. In 2012, Moscow hosted the match for World Chess Champion and Anand's opponent was Boris Gelfand. The match was a tie, and after regular rounds, he won the rapid tie-break rounds to be the champion again for the fifth time. In 2013, he was defeated by Magnus Carlsen.

Viswanathan Anand is married to Aruna Anand, who also acts as his manager-cum-secretary. They have a son named Akhil.

GOOD TO KNOW

- Anand has won the Chess Oscar in 1997, 1998, 2003, 2004, 2006 and 2007. The Chess Oscar is awarded to the year's best player based on a poll conducted by the Russian chess magazine, *64*.
- Till 2012, Anand was one of six players in history to crack the 2800 mark.
- In 1991-92, Anand became the first recipient of the Rajiv Gandhi Khel Ratna award, the most prestigious sports award in India.

QUIZ

1. What is the title of Vishwanathan Anand's autobiography published in 1988?

a) *Sunny Days*
b) *My Best Games of Chess*
c) *A Shot at History*

Answer: ***My Best Games of Chess***

2. Where were Viswanathan Anand and his family members living when his mother copied chess problems from television?
   a) Peru
   b) Sydney
   c) Philippines

   Answer: Philippines

3. In 2010, what did Anand donate in an auction arranged by the NGO 'The Foundation' that works for underprivileged kids?
   a) His 2010 World Championship Gold medal
   b) His chess set
   c) His Grandmaster title

   Answer: His 2010 World Championship Gold medal

GLOSSARY

- FIDE: or The World Chess Federation is an international organization that connects the various national chess federations around the world and acts as the governing body of international chess competitions.
- PCA: or Professional Chess Association was a body floated mainly by Garry Kasparov in the early 1990s as a counter to FIDE.
- Norm: in chess is a high level of performance in a tournament. Several norms are one of the requirements to receive a title such as Grandmaster from the world chess governing body.

GENERAL

AMARTYA SEN

Amartya Sen is an economist who was awarded the Nobel Prize in Economics in 1998 for his work in welfare economics.

Amartya Sen was born on 3 November 1933 on the campus of Rabindranath Tagore's Visva-Bharati in Shantiniketan, West Bengal. His father, Ashutosh Sen, taught chemistry at Dhaka University. He spent much of his childhood in Dhaka, and attended St Gregory's School. However, he soon moved to Shantiniketan, after which he studied at Presidency College in Calcutta, and then at Trinity College in Cambridge. He earned a bachelor's degree from Trinity College in 1955, a master's degree in 1959 and his PhD the same year.

Amartya Sen taught at Jadavpur University in Calcutta from 1956, and then taught at the University of Delhi, the London School of Economics, the University of London, and the University of Oxford. He then went to Harvard University in 1988, where he was professor of economics and philosophy. After ten years at Harvard, in 1998 he was appointed master of Trinity College, Cambridge, a position he held until 2004, after which he returned to Harvard as Lamont University Professor.

Amartya Sen worked on welfare economics, which evaluates economic policies and their effects on the well-being of the community. His methods of measuring poverty provided information for the betterment of the economic conditions of the poor. His interest in famine and poverty came from the personal experience of the Bengal famine (1943), in which thirty lakh people died.

Many countries and international organizations dealing with food crises, have been influenced by Amartya Sen's work. His views and theories have led policy makers to find ways to replace the lost income of the poor.

With a part of the Nobel Prize award money, Amartya Sen founded the Pratichi Trust in 1999. It works in the areas of education, child nutrition, healthcare, and gender equality. He was awarded the Bharat Ratna in 1999.

Amartya Sen has written many books, including *Poverty and Famines, On Ethics and Economics, Commodities and Capabilities, Hunger and Public Action,* and *The Argumentative Indian.*

GOOD TO KNOW

- Amartya Sen, who worked in the field of welfare economics, is also called the 'conscience of his profession.'
- His work *Collective Choice and Social Welfare* addresses problems such as individual rights, majority rule and the availability of information about individual conditions, inspired researchers to turn their attention to issues of basic welfare.

QUIZ

1. Who is the co-author with Amartya Sen of the book, *An Uncertail Glory: India and its Contradictions*?
   a) Jean Drèze
   b) Susan Athey
   c) Robert Aumann

Answer: Jean Drèze

2. Which of these Nobel laureates is said to have named him 'Amartya'?

a) C.V. Raman
b) Mother Teresa
c) Rabindranath Tagore

Answer: Rabindranath Tagore

3. Which of these actresses is Amartya Sen's daughter?
    a) Nandana Sen
    b) Raima Sen
    c) Riya Sen

Answer: Nandana Sen

GLOSSARY

- Economics: is the branch of knowledge concerned with the production, consumption and transfer of wealth.
- Famine: is a severe and prolonged hunger due to scarcity of food, affecting a large number of people.

MANKOMBU SAMBASIVAN SWAMINATHAN

Mankombu Sambasivan Swaminathan or M.S. Swaminathan, is an agriculture scientist and an international administrator. He is also referred to as the 'Father of the Green Revolution' in India.

Swaminathan was born on 7 August 1925 in Kumbakonam, Tamil Nadu. His father, Dr M.K. Sambasivan, was a surgeon, a staunch follower of Gandhian principles and a reformer of sorts. As a result, the notion of service towards people was ingrained in him from a very early age.

Swaminathan completed his BSc in zoology from Travancore University in 1944. After earning his PhD from the University of Cambridge, he became a research associate in Genetics at the University of Wisconsin, USA.

Swaminathan was trained in Cytogenetics, a branch of genetics that studies inheritance in relation to the structure and function of chromosomes. Using this knowledge, he bred more productive and better quality plant types at the Pusa Institute. He worked closely with associates in his research on essential food crops like wheat, rice, potatoes, sorghum, maize, millet, pulses, vegetables oils, cotton and jute in India.

Swaminathan brought the Mexican semi-dwarf wheat plants, developed by the American agriculturalist Norman Borlaug, to India. After cross-breeding them with the local species, he created a type of wheat plant that yielded much more grain than the existing type.

But the task of convincing the farmers, steeped in traditional agricultural methods, to grow the new wheat, appeared much tougher than anticipated. To demonstrate its benefits, he set up 2,000 model farms in villages outside New Delhi; a step that led to the Green Revolution in India.

Swaminathan held a number of research and administrative positions. Some of them were: teacher, researcher and research administrator at the Central Rice Research Institute and at the Indian Agricultural Research Institute Director General of the Indian Council of Agricultural Research and the International Rice Research Institute; President of the International Union for the Conservation of Nature and Natural Resources President of the World Wide Fund for Nature (India) and Chairman of the Auroville Foundation. He is a Fellow of the Royal Society of London, the US National Academy of Sciences and many other scientific academies in both India and abroad. Currently, he holds the UNESCO Chair in ecotechnology at the M.S. Swaminathan Research Foundation in Chennai.

His role in the field of sustainable food security which envisages food for all, not depending on imports and promoting home-grown food, is unparalleled. He has therefore rightly been called 'the Father of Economic Ecology' by the United Nations Environment Programme (UNEP).

Swaminathan has also won several awards including the Ramon Magsaysay Award for Community Leadership in 1971, the Albert Einstein World Science Award in 1986, the first World Food Prize in 1987 and the Association for Women's Rights in Development (AWID) international award for his contribution to promoting the knowledge, skill and technological empowerment of women in agriculture.

He was nominated to the Rajya Sabha in 2007.

Swaminathan's major books include *Science and the Conquest of Hunger* (1983) and *Agriculture Cannot Wait* (2006).

GOOD TO KNOW

- According to M.S. Swaminathan, India needs an 'Evergreen Revolution' to increase productivity without harming the environment. Evergreen Revolution focuses on increasing productivity that can be sustained forever, without causing any harm to the environment and without using any chemicals.
- M.S. Swaminathan has been acclaimed by *TIME* magazine as one of the twenty most influential Asians of the twentieth century.
- M.S. Swaminathan would have become a police officer, had he not received a fellowship to study genetics in the Netherlands.

QUIZ

1. In 1968, Indira Gandhi released a stamp, to bring to the attention of the public, the beginning of a science-based farm revolution. What was it titled as?
   a) Green Revolution
   b) The Wheat Revolution
   c) The Field Revolution

   Answer: The Wheat Revolution

2. In 1963, who came to India and travelled extensively with M.S. Swaminathan in the wheat-growing areas of North India?
   a) Dr Norman Borlaug
   b) Francis Crick
   c) Peter Mansfield

   Answer: Dr Norman Borlaug

3. The efforts of Dr Swaminathan led the Planning Commission to lay stress on ecological problems of the ________ in the Sixth Five Year Plan.
   a) Ganges
   b) Himalayas
   c) Deccan Plateau

Answer: Himalayas

GLOSSARY

- Cross-breeding: It is the mating of animals or plants from two different breeds or varieties which have superior traits, to enhance the economic value of the offspring.
- Cytogenetics: The study of inheritance in relation to the structure and function of chromosomes.
- Green Revolution: is a general term that is applied to successful agricultural experiments in many developing countries. India is one of the countries where it was most successful.

MOTHER TERESA

Mother Teresa, also known as the Blessed Mother Teresa of Calcutta, was the founder of the Order of the Missionaries of Charity, a Roman Catholic congregation of women to help the homeless and poor in India. She was honoured with the Nobel Peace Prize in 1979.

Mother Teresa was born as Agnes Gonxha Bojaxhiu on 26 August 1910 in Skopje, Macedonia, to Albanian immigrants, Nikola and Drana Bojaxhiu. She was raised by her mother after her father passed away when she was eight years old.

At the age of eighteen, Agnes decided to become a missionary. She travelled to Ireland in 1929 and joined the Institute of the Blessed Virgin Mary, also known as the Sisters of Loreto, where she received the name Sister Mary Teresa. The same year, she sailed to Calcutta as a teacher.

In 1931, Sister Mary Teresa made her First Profession of Vows, and was assigned the Loreto Entally community. She joined St Mary's School for girls as a teacher, and retained the position for seventeen years. After her Final Profession of Vows in 1937, she became Mother Teresa. In 1944, she became the principal of St Mary's School.

In 1946, on her way to Darjeeling from Calcutta she received, what she called, 'call within a call' that inspired her to help the sick and poor. It took her nearly two years to receive permission and on 17 August 1948, she left the convent in a white, blue-bordered sari to begin her long journey of serving the poor.

Mother Teresa worked in the slums of Calcutta, after completing a short course with the Medical Mission Sisters in Patna. Though she had started alone, many of her former students joined her in the mission to serve those who were unwanted, unloved and uncared for.

In 1950, the Holy See recognized Mother Teresa's Missionaries of Charity. The congregation expanded overseas in the 1960s to places like Venezuela, Rome and Tanzania, and eventually to every continent, to provide help to the poor and undertake relief work in events of natural calamities like floods, epidemics and famine.

Mother Teresa founded the Missionaries of Charity Brothers in 1963, the contemplative branch of the Sisters in 1976, the Contemplative Brothers in 1979 and the Missionaries of Charity Fathers in 1984 with the aim of dealing with the spiritual and physical needs of the poor.

She has received numerous national and international awards, including the Padma Shri in 1962 and the Bharat Ratna in 1980.

Mother Teresa passed away on 5 September 1997 in Kolkata, leaving behind a large number of organizations that continue to serve the poor. Though she was ill in the last few years of her life, she remained devoted to the cause. At the time of her death, there were nearly four thousand members of Mother Teresa's Sisters and they were established in nearly 610 foundations in more than 120 countries.

GOOD TO KNOW

- Within two years of Mother Teresa's death, the process to declare her a saint was begun, and she was beatified on 19 October 2003.
- Mother Teresa reached the ranks of the blessed in the

shortest time in the history of the church.

- The logo of the Missionaries of Charity, a rosary-encircled globe with a cross in the centre, was reputedly designed by Mother Teresa herself.

QUIZ

1. What is the name of the exhibition train launched by the Indian Railways to commemorate the 100th birthday of Mother Teresa in 2010?
   a) Peace Express
   b) Charity Express
   c) Mother Express

Answer: Mother Express

2. What is the title of the book on Mother Teresa written by Malcolm Muggeridge?
   a) *Something Beautiful for God*
   b) *In the Service of the Poor*
   c) *Mother and God*

Answer: *Something Beautiful for God*

3. In 2008, Mother Teresa became the fourth honorary citizen of which of these countries?
   a) USA
   b) Germany
   c) France

Answer: USA

GLOSSARY

- Order: is a society of monks, nuns or friars living under the same religious, moral and social regulations and discipline.
- Nun: is a member of a religious community of women, typically one living under vows of poverty, chastity and obedience.

SALIM ALI

Dr Salim Ali was an ornithologist, and the first Indian to conduct systematic bird surveys across India. He was also known as the 'Birdman of India'.

Salim Ali was born on 12 November 1896, in Bombay (now Mumbai). He lost his parents at an early age and was brought up by his maternal uncle, who guided and inspired him to appreciate nature.

He was gifted an air gun when he was a child, and he spent his time shooting sparrows. He noticed that one of the sparrows he had killed had a yellow throat. He was curious and asked his uncle, who took him to the Bombay Natural History Society (BNHS), hoping to find an answer to the question. There, W.S. Milliard, the honorary secretary, told him that the bird was a yellow throated sparrow and elaborated on the various species of sparrows. This conversation affected him deeply and he decided to find out everything about birds that was worth knowing.

In those days, there were few jobs for ornithologists and so he faced years of unemployment and hardship. In 1919, Salim Ali went to Myanmar to run the family mining and timber business. It gave him an opportunity to explore the forests. After returning to India, he applied for a job as an ornithologist with the Zoological Survey of India, but was rejected since he did not have a master's degree in science or a doctorate.

In 1926, after he was appointed as guide lecturer at the natural history section in the Prince of Wales Museum in

Mumbai, he decided to go for further studies. He went on, study leave in 1928 to Germany and researched under a famous ornithologist. But when he came back to India, he still experienced a lack of opportunities in his profession.

Salim Ali offered to conduct regional ornithological surveys for Bombay Natural History Society, since the princely states wanted a record of birds in their region.

While working on this project, he went to different states of the country to record the variety of bird life in India.

After independence, Salim Ali became the society's Honorary Secretary, and later served as its president. He requested the then prime minister, Jawaharlal Nehru, for funds, which helped save the two hundred-year old institution from closing down.

Many organizations and institutions are named after him. Salim Ali Centre for Ornithology and Natural History was established in Coimbatore, Tamil Nadu, in 1990. Pondicherry University established the Salim Ali School of Ecology and Environmental Sciences, the government of Goa set up the Salim Ali Bird Sanctuary and the Thattakad Bird Sanctuary near Vembanad in Kerala is also named after him.

Salim Ali received numerous awards, including the Golden Ark of the International Union for Conservation of Nature, the Golden Medal of the British Ornithology Union, the Padma Bhushan in 1958 and the Padma Vibhushan in 1976. He was also nominated to the Rajya Sabha in 1985.

Some of his books include *The Book of Indian Birds*, *The Birds of Kutch* and *The Indian Hill Birds.*

Salim Ali passed away on 27 July 1987 in Mumbai, at the age of ninety.

GOOD TO KNOW

- Salim Ali was born as Salim Moizuddin Abdul Ali.

- On his return to India from Germany, Salim Ali was unable to find a job, and along with his wife, he moved to Kihim in Maharashtra, where he began to make his first observations of the Baya or the weaver bird.
- Salim Ali's influence helped save the Bharatpur Bird Sanctuary in Rajasthan and the Silent Valley National Park in Kerala.

QUIZ

1. In which state is the Salim Ali Bird Sanctuary located?
   a) Jammu and Kashmir
   b) Goa
   c) Arunachal Pradesh

   Answer: Goa

2. Fill in the blank to complete the name of his autobiography: The Fall of a _________.
   a) *Crow*
   b) *Pigeon*
   c) *Sparrow*

   Answer: ***Sparrow***

3. The bird named after Salim Ali, *Latidens salimalii*, is also known as 'Salim Ali's ______'. Fill in the blank.
   a) Sparrow
   b) Gentoo penguin
   c) Fruit bat

   Answer: Fruit bat

GLOSSARY

- Ornithology: is the branch of zoology dealing with the study of birds.
- Survey: is the examination and record of an area and features of an area of land, so as to construct a map, plan or description.

VERGHESE KURIEN

Dr Verghese Kurien is most famous for his contribution towards building a cooperative movement that made India self-reliant in milk production, while bettering the lives of many villagers. He is also known as the 'Father of White Revolution'.

Born on 26 November 1921 in Kozhikode, Kerala, Verghese Kurien obtained both, his BSc degree in 1940 and mechanical engineering degree in 1943, from Madras University. He completed his Master of Science and Mechanical Engineering degree from Michigan State University in 1948.

He returned to India and was posted in Anand (in Gujarat) at a government creamery, as a part of the bond he had signed with the Government. After the term was over, the then Chairman of Kaira District Co-operative Milk Producers Union, Shri Tribhuvandas Patel, asked him to stay on and help him with his co-operative society.

In 1973, Dr Kurien helped set up Gujarat Cooperative Milk Marketing Federation (GCMMF) which markets the Amul brand. Impressed with his work, Lal Bahadur Shastri appointed him as the founding chairman of National Dairy Development Board (NDDB) to replicate this model in different parts of the country.

In early 1970s, Dr Kurien was asked to head Operation Flood, a government-led project to make India the largest producer of milk in the world. Under this project, a network of milk sheds and village cooperatives were established across the country. It sold milk powder donated from European nations as part of the world food programme, and used the fund for the project. They also developed a process to turn buffalo milk into dry powder.

Dr Kurien received several awards for his work. He received the Padma Shri in 1965, the Padma Bhushan in 1966 and the Padma Vibhushan in 1999. He was awarded the Ramon Magsaysay Award in 1963, the Wateler Peace Prize Award of the Carnegie Foundation for the year 1986, the World Food Prize award for the year 1989, the 'International Person of the year' by the World Dairy Expo, Wisconsin, US in 1993, the 'Ordre du Merite Agricole' by the Government of France in 1997 and the Regional Award 2000 from the Asian Productivity Organization, Japan.

Dr Kurien played a major role in turning India into the largest producer of milk in the world. He also played an important part in empowering rural women by involving them in the cooperative movement.

Dr Kurien passed away on 9 September 2012 in Nadiad, Gujarat.

GOOD TO KNOW

- Dr Kurien refrained from accepting salary from any of the institutions after he turned sixty years old.
- Dr Kurien said that he never drank a drop of milk himself.
- The word 'Amul' is derived from the Sanskrit word 'Amulya' which means 'priceless' or 'precious'. In the subsequent years Amul made cheese and baby food on a large commercial scale, processing buffalo milk again creating by history in the world.

QUIZ

1. What is the name of Verghese Kurien's memoirs?
   a) *I Too Had a Dream*
   b) *How I Landed Up in Anand*
   c) *White Life*

Answer: ***I Too Had a Dream***

2. For making which 1976 film did Dr Kurien suggest that he would make half a million milk farmers of Gujarat give two rupees each?
   a) *Manthan*
   b) *Mirch Masala*
   c) *Rudaali*

Answer: ***Manthan***

3. In 1963, in which category did Dr Kurien receive the Magsaysay Award?
   a) Community Leadership
   b) Public Service
   c) Government Service

Answer: Community Leadership

GLOSSARY

- Creamery: is the term given to a factory that produces butter and cheese.
- Cooperative: A farm business or other organization which is owned and run jointly by its members, who share the profits or benefits. It is an organization owned by and operated for the benefit of those using its services.
- The Amul Model of dairy development: is a three-tiered structure with the dairy cooperative societies at the village level, federated under a milk union at the district level and a federation of member unions at the state level.

www.ingramcontent.com/pod-product-compliance
Lightning Source LLC
LaVergne TN
LVHW010637110826
845149LV00014B/2857

* 9 7 8 8 1 2 9 1 2 9 3 8 3 *